HF5415.33.U6 M67 2007
0134110661409
Moschis, George P.,

Baby boomers and their
 parents : surprising
     c2007

Baby Boomers
and Their Parents

MARKETING BOOKS FROM PMP

MARKET RESEARCH

The 4Cs of Truth in Communication: *How to Identify, Discuss, Evaluate and Present Stand-out, Effective Communication*

Consumer Insights 2.0: *How Smart Companies Apply Customer Knowledge to the Bottom Line*

Dominators, Cynics, and Wallflowers: *Practical Strategies for Moderating Meaningful Focus Groups*

Moderating to the Max! *A Full-Tilt Guide to Creative, Insightful Focus Groups and Depth Interviews*

The Mirrored Window: *Focus Groups from a Moderator's Point of View*

Religion in a Free Market: *Religious and Non-Religious Americans—Who, What, Why, Where*

Why People Buy Things They Don't Need

MATURE MARKET/ BABY BOOMERS

After Fifty: *How the Baby Boom Will Redefine the Mature Market*

After Sixty: *Marketing to Baby Boomers Reaching Their Big Transition Years*

Advertising to Baby Boomers

Marketing to Leading-Edge Baby Boomers

The Boomer Heartbeat: *Capturing the Heartbeat of the Baby Boomers Now and in the Future*

MULTICULTURAL

Beyond Bodegas: *Developing a Retail Relationship with Hispanic Customers*

Hispanic Marketing Grows Up: *Exploring Perceptions and Facing Realities*

Marketing to American Latinos: *A Guide to the In-Culture Approach, Part I*

Marketing to American Latinos: *A Guide to the In-Culture Approach, Part II*

The Whole Enchilada: *Hispanic Marketing 101*

What's Black About It? *Insights to Increase Your Share of a Changing African-American Market*

YOUTH MARKETS

The Kids Market: *Myths & Realities*

Marketing to the New Super Consumer: Mom & Kid

The Great Tween Buying Machine: *Marketing to Today's Tweens*

MARKETING MANAGEMENT

A Clear Eye for Branding: *Straight Talk on Today's Most Powerful Business Concept*

A Knight's Code of Business: *How to Achieve Character and Competence in the Corporate World*

Beyond the Mission Statement: *Why Cause-Based Communications Lead to True Success*

India Business: *Finding Opportunities in this Big Emerging Market*

Marketing Insights to Help Your Business Grow

Baby Boomers and Their Parents

Surprising Findings about Their Lifestyles, Mindsets, and Well-Being

George P. Moschis, Ph.D.
Anil Mathur, Ph.D.

Library Commons
Georgian College
One Georgian Drive
Barrie, ON
L4M 3X9

PMP

Paramount Market Publishing, Inc.

Paramount Market Publishing, Inc.
950 Danby Road, Suite 136
Ithaca, NY 14850
www.paramountbooks.com
Telephone: 607-275-8100; 888-787-8100   Facsimile: 607-275-8101

Publisher: James Madden
Editorial Director: Doris Walsh

Copyright © 2007 George P. Moschis, Ph.D. and Anil Mathur, Ph.D.

All rights reserved. No part of this book may be reproduced, stored in a retrieval system, or transmitted in any form or by any means, electronic, mechanical, photocopying, recording, or otherwise, without the prior written permission of the publisher. Further information may be obtained from Paramount Market Publishing, Inc., 950 Danby Rd., Suite 136, Ithaca, NY 14850.

This publication is designed to provide accurate and authoritative information in regard to the subject matter covered. It is sold with the understanding that the publisher is not engaged in rendering legal, accounting, or other professional services. If legal advice or other expert assistance is required, the services of a competent professional should be sought.

ISBN-13: 978-0-9786602-4-6

Contents

Foreword	vii
Acknowledgments	ix
Chapter 1. An Overview: Two Generations	1
The Aging of the Population	2
Why We Should Be Concerned	4
About Our Studies of Baby Boomers and Their Parents	6
Some Surprising Findings	6
Chapter 2. What's On Their Minds as They Age	23
Feeling, Thinking, and Acting Younger	23
Defying Aging	27
Concerns and Desires	32
Chapter 3. Physical and Emotional Well-Being	53
Physical Health	54
Emotional Health	70
It Matters What and How We Think	78
Chapter 4. Lifestyles	81
Living Arrangements	81
Work After Retirement	84
Lifelong Learning	88
Leisure	92
Volunteering	99
Religiosity	100
Caregiving	101
Preparing for Old Age	104

Chapter 5. Financial Affairs — 108
- Spending Habits — 108
- Saving Habits — 111
- Financing Retirement — 115
- The Affluent — 117

Chapter 6. What They Have, What They Use — 129
- What They Own — 129
- Who Is More Materialistic? — 138
- What Kinds of Services They Prefer — 139

Chapter 7. Buying Habits — 145
- Reasons for Patronage — 146
- Buying Products — 154
- Information Sources — 157
- The Internet as a Source of Information or a Purchasing Channel — 167
- Loyal Customers — 175
- Dis/Satisfaction and Complaints — 182
- Excessive Buying — 184

Chapter 8. Planning for Longevity — 186
- Determinants of Longevity and Life Satisfaction — 186
- Strategies for Longevity and Well-Being — 195
- Improving Quality of Life — 202

Chapter 9. How Businesses Can Profit by Making Their Mature Customers Happier — 206
- Understanding the Needs of Your Mature Customers — 206
- Profitable Business Strategies That Can Enhance Well-Being — 217
- Strategy-Effectiveness Testing, Implementation, and Feedback — 224

Index — 225

About the Authors — 231

Foreword

MANY WORDS have been written about the baby-boom generation, most of them cliches. *Baby Boomers and Their Parents* is different. You hold in your hand a unique work about boomers based not on stereotypes and punditry, but upon original research by Dr. George P. Moschis, professor of marketing and director of the Center for Mature Consumer Studies at Georgia State University, and Dr. Anil Mather, associate dean and professor of marketing at Hofstra University.

Baby Boomers and Their Parents sheds light on the aging of the population by examining how two generations are going about it—boomers and their parents—and dissecting their similarities and differences using empirical studies of health and well-being, emotional and financial status, buying habits, and lifestyles.

The United States is in the midst of fundamental demographic change. The aging of the baby-boom generation is rapidly transforming our culture from one dominated by the middle-aged to a new domination by the old. The shift from a middle-aged mindset to an elder perspective has both pros and cons, and *Baby Boomers and Their Parents* will tell you both sides of the story in its examination of boomers in middle age and their parents in old age. Most important, it will tell you how boomers are likely to differ from their parents as they reach old age.

As someone who has tracked the baby-boom generation for more than 25 years, and railed at the media for misleading characterizations of boomers, I was gratified to find within these pages research that tells it like it is. The blunt facts: Boomers are not as financially well off as their parents. Boomers are in worse health than previous generations were at the same age. Boomers are the generation most terrified of aging.

But aging they are, and in these pages you will find out how gracefully (or not) they are going about it. This is a must read for researchers in the field of aging, businesses preparing for the growing dominance of older consumers, organizations positioning themselves for the new demographic realities, and aging boomers themselves.

CHERYL RUSSELL
Editorial Director
New Strategist Publications

Acknowledgements

THIS BOOK would not have been made possible without the assistance and support of several individuals and organizations. First, we thank those organizations and agencies that supported financially the research efforts of the Center for Mature Consumer Studies (CMCS), including the American Association of Retired Persons (AARP) Andrus Foundation, United States Department of Agriculture, International Council of Shopping Centers Educational Foundation, Direct Marketing Foundation, MedicAlert, and Whirlpool Corporation.

Also, we thank the hundreds of organizations in the U.S. and other countries that purchased CMCS reports, providing funds that enabled us to conduct numerous large-scale studies over the past twenty years. We are also indebted to several organizations that gave us the opportunity to learn more about the different generations by allowing us to use data from their surveys, including the AARP, Metropolitan Atlanta Chapter of American Red Cross, and the National Association of Home Builders. We also appreciate the opportunity to collaborate with Unitron Corporation on research that has produced useful insights into the lifestyles of baby boomers and their parents.

We acknowledge the support of our research efforts by the departments of our respective universities, especially the encouragement and support provided by Georgia State University's Provost, Dr. Ron Henry, for enhancing the activities of CMCS. We express our appreciation to our former students and colleagues who helped us in different ways over the years, including Dr. Euhun Lee, Dr. Karen Gibler, and Dr. Gerry Mills for allowing us to use their dissertation survey data; Dr. Roy Moore, Dr. Pradeep Korkaonkar, Dr. Harash Sachdev, Dr. James Lumpkin, and Dr. Ruth Smith for their input into several of our studies; and our many graduate assistants and doctoral students who helped us with our surveys.

We thank several other individuals who contributed to the development of this book, including Sharon Sullivan and Carolyn Barbour for preparing drafts of the manuscript, and Milton Smith for allowing us to use his insights and life experiences. Our book editor, Doris Walsh, made invaluable suggestions for revising and expanding the materials in this book and contributed to its final format. We thank her for all her contributions and for working with us so diligently.

The writing and preparation of materials for this book took much time away from other activities we like to do with our families. We thank all the members of our families for allowing us to spend time away from them while working on this project. Last, but not least, we thank the thousands of individuals who participated in our studies and gave us their valuable time by answering questions in our surveys. We dedicate this book to them.

CHAPTER ONE

An Overview: Two Generations

THIS BOOK IS ABOUT two of the most resilient generations in American history: the baby boomers—those born between 1946 and 1964—and their parents. Our research shows that these two generations are resilient for different reasons. Baby boomers refuse to grow old. They defy aging more than any other generation in human history. Such resilience is shown in their efforts to stay young and in their state of mind about old age and aging. In their efforts to fight aging, baby boomers have extended middle age indefinitely. They tell us old age does not start till a person reaches the age of 80, even though individuals in this age group also admit that, for their parents, old age started at 50.

The older generation, on the other hand, is resilient because it has experienced the greatest increase in life expectancy and longevity in human history. When most of these older folks were born, they were not expected to ever reach retirement because life expectancy was lower than the predicted retirement age of 65. During the lifetime of those born in the early part of the twentieth century, life expectancy increased by 30 years, a greater increase than was attained in the previous 5,000 years! As a result, an increasingly large number of people from this generation are spending more years in retirement than they spent in the labor force. But the parents of baby boomers also are believed to be resilient for their continuous accomplishments. Many who are living to old age continue to make contributions to society as workers, volunteers, grand-

An increasingly large number of people from the senior generation are spending more years in retirement than they spent in the labor force.

parents, and even caregivers. In his book, *The Greatest Generation*, Tom Brokow discusses the various accomplishments of this group of people, most of whom are also the parents of baby boomers.

However, our primary interest in these two generations is not for their resilience but because they are helping to redefine the age distribution of the population and how we think about aging and the aged. The aging of the population today is without parallel in the history of humanity and is the most important demographic shift to ever occur. Increases in the proportions of older persons (aged 60 or older) are accompanied by declines in the proportions of the young (under 15 years of age). By 2050, the number of older persons worldwide will actually exceed the number of young for the first time. This reversal has already begun in the more developed regions of the world.

> By 2050, the number of older persons worldwide will exceed the number of young for the first time—a reversal that has already begun in the developed world.

The Aging of the Population

The number of people over age 60 will quadruple in the next 50 years. One in five (or 2 billion) people will be over age 60, up from one in ten (or 600 million) in 2002. While this approximate increase in the percentage of older people represents a global average, developing countries are expected to experience even more dramatic changes in age composition. The older population in developing nations is expected to increase by 200 to 300 percent over the next 35 years. In China, for example, the older population will double to nearly 400 million in about 27 years. For some developing countries like Malaysia and Kenya, the rate of increase in the older population is expected to be seven to eight times higher than in industrialized countries like the United Kingdom and Sweden. In the United States, the number of people aged 60 and older is expected to double by 2030.

Two major factors are responsible for the rapid aging of the earth's population: the high birth rates in the Post-World War II years and the dramatic increase in life expectancy. Most nations of the world, especially the industrialized countries, experienced unprecedented high birth rates after World War II. In the United States, for example, birth rates during this period nearly doubled. Ninety-two percent of GIs who came back from the war got married, and 84 percent of them had children, many children—thus the reason for the moniker, "the baby boom generation." The second force responsible for the aging of the population has been the rapid increase in life expectancy. This is due mainly to better public health, including immunizations, sanitation, nutrition, and medical advances.

The aging of the population has already begun to affect every man, woman, and child in the world; and it will affect you, your children, and your children's children in the years to come. This effect could be felt at the workplace, within the family, or indirectly through government actions and economic impacts. For example, the number of people becoming caregivers to older relatives has increased in recent years. According to a recent study co-sponsored by the American Association of Retired Persons (AARP), one in four people in the United States provides care to older relatives, a figure that shows an increase of 250 percent from the 1990s alone. This new role, for which there is usually little preparation, has adverse economic and emotional consequences on caregivers. Job performance suffers due to the strain of caregiving responsibilities, and increased stress has negative consequences on the caregiver's emotional well-being and quality of life.

Today, there are approximately 50 million people (or someone in 23 percent of U.S. households) are involved in caregiving for someone aged 50 or older. Of these caregivers, 26 million are also employed full or part-time elsewhere. According to MetLife Vice President James Weil, the nation's total losses from elder care responsibilities by far exceed the combined earnings of America's eight largest corporations. Furthermore, at the corporate level, organizations must decide whether to keep or hire older workers as opposed to incurring the higher costs of hiring, training and keeping younger workers who

> *Today, approximately 50 million people are involved in caregiving for someone aged 50 or older.*

are becoming increasingly scarce. All nations have begun to feel the impact of this aging population as the increasing numbers of older adults put pressure on their pension and healthcare systems.

Why We Should Be Concerned

What this means for you the reader is that you are likely to spend a major portion of your life at a stage known today as "old age" or "retirement." If you are an employer or a product or service provider, you are likely to be dealing with more workers or customers who are in this stage of life. Many people, both young and old, are not prepared to accept or experience this change. While most of us expect to reach old age, we probably have incorrect perceptions of late life and older people, even as we approach the transition from middle to old age ourselves. Very little is known about the older person's needs, challenges, and views, probably because we have not experienced old age or because we have uninformed opinions about the aged because we have not been told or taught about late life.

While most of us expect to reach old age, we probably have incorrect perceptions of late life and older people.

Of course, you may ask: "Why is it important to understand older people and late life?" If you are a marketer or a person in charge of product development, the more you understand the effects of later life on your customers and how they think, the better you will be able to do your job. But life isn't all about work.

If you are a younger person, such knowledge will help you enhance the quality of your own life when you reach old age. Many older people say how happy they would have been if only they had done some things differently. Understanding the factors that contribute to the older person's well-being can help establish a happier and more fulfilling late life. This knowledge will also help you perform your role as a caregiver, should you need to become one.

While most people are prepared for roles they assume at different stages in life, such as the role of a "worker," "spouse," and "parent," few people receive preparation for the role of a "caregiver" to an older relative. However, unless you lost your parents at a relatively young age, chances are that you are going to be a caregiver to an elderly person, most likely your parents, your in-laws, or your spouse. The average person in the United States spends approximately 17.5 years caring for his or her child(ren), but also spends approximately 18.5 years caring for an older relative. Caregivers often assume this role unexpectedly and are totally unprepared for the responsibilities that come with it. A lack of understanding of the elderly individual's needs and views often leads to poor performance on the part of the caregiver, lower satisfaction with life for the care receiver, and increased stress for both parties.

The average person in the United States spends approximately 17.5 years caring for his or her child(ren), but also spends approximately 18.5 years caring for an older relative.

Knowledge about living in late life is not only important for younger people but for older persons as well. As people age and experience new circumstances, they need to compare their views and experiences such as health problems with others who have experienced similar situations. Knowing how most other people at similar stages in life think and feel about the same things you are experiencing helps validate your own views and develop a more accurate picture of the world and the circumstances you face. Furthermore, because not every older person experiences aging and old age the same way, you can learn about the habits and lifestyles in late life that are likely to promote successful aging, longevity, and well-being.

This book was written to help readers better understand life in the middle years and beyond, especially the factors that affect longevity and quality of life. In order to gain better insight into the lives of people at these stages, we present the life circumstances of the middle-aged (baby boomers) and older adults. By comparing the needs, views, and actions of individuals in these age groups, we believe that we can learn how a person's life may change due to aging, and how life satisfaction can be enhanced later in life. While some of the differences between the generations of baby boomers and their parents may be because they were brought up in different times, the observations can still be useful in that they provide insights into how older persons of tomorrow may differ from today's older people.

About Our Studies of Baby Boomers and Their Parents

Over the past two decades, we have surveyed thousands of people of different ages from different walks of life. The scope of our surveys has varied over the years, and each survey was aimed at helping us learn something new. We present some of the findings of these more than two-dozen studies here. Most of these studies are based on large-scale national surveys. We also present the findings from select studies by other researchers.

For the purpose of this presentation, we have relied only on studies that focused on issues concerning people in middle and later life. We have addressed questions concerning these individuals' physical, emotional, and financial well-being.

Some Surprising Findings

In the next few sections, we will present some of the highlights of our studies, and we will discuss these findings in greater detail in the chapters that follow. When we present findings from our studies as well as other studies, the reader should keep in mind that the reported generational differences cannot necessarily be interpreted as changes people experience as they age. Differences among age groups of people within a generation and between generations in particular, can be due to three main factors or a combination of them: aging, cohort, and period.

Aging effects can be physical changes that affect the performances of our bodily systems, such as the onset of chronic conditions that force people to alter their lifestyles; the result of psychological aging, such as increasingly thinking of oneself as an older person; or social aging into roles that are socially recognized as appropriate for older persons.

Differences also can reflect *cohort effects*. Cohorts refer to groups of individuals who experience the same event within the same time interval—we can think of our two generations as two main cohorts, although the older generation can be further broken down into subcohorts such as War Babies, Great Depression, and GIs, as examples.

Differences can also be due to *period effects*, which refer to the differential impact on age groups of the social milieu and events of the time as, for example, the effect of college education on different generations due to changes in the things that people learn in college over the years. More than one of these factors can also come into play. For example, in comparison with the older generation, all baby boomers grew up with television and by the time they reach age 65 they will have spent an average of 11 years in front of the TV— much more than their parents at that age.

In this book, the terms "seniors," "elderly," "parents," and "older" are used invariably to refer to the generation aged 60+, while "younger" refers to the baby boomer generation. We use the term "mature" to refer to people in both generations.

Physical and emotional well-being

Baby boomers are in worse health today than previous generations at the same age. Despite the increasing preoccupation with health and efforts to diet and exercise, the average baby boomer's health is worse today, compared with adults of the same age 20 years ago. In general, the number of adults who are overweight and obese is on the rise.

Stress is taking its toll on the health of baby boomers and their parents. Increasing stress and poor eating habits due to greater time pressure are the main factors responsible for the declining health of the middle-aged population. These factors stem, in part, from the increasing emphasis people have put on their careers and social progress, as well as the added responsibilities of being caregivers to their older relatives.

Americans in general, and baby boomers in particular, are under extreme time pressure. A little over 90 percent of baby boomers and three-fourths of their parents, most of whom are retired, experience time pressure in their daily living. Time pressure is a major source of stress that is taking its toll on Americans' health. Seven in ten baby boomers experience on-going stress, compared with only four in ten of their parents. Both age groups experience significant, acute types of stress due to unexpected events such as major conflicts with family members or accidents. During such events, at least four in five middle-aged and older folks experience elevated levels of stress.

Time pressure is a major source of stress that is taking its toll on Americans' health.

The pursuit of a successful career is not good for one's health. Pursuing a successful career and competing for recognition and job promotion seem to have adverse effects on our health. The most successful people are the least healthy. They tend to experience a larger number of health problems earlier in life, and use a larger number of prescription drugs than their less successful counterparts.

What and how we think has a direct effect on our health. Achieving or maintaining good health in later stages of life requires not only taking care of your body by exercising and eating healthy foods, but also having the right attitude. We found three important psychological factors affecting a person's health: how one reacts to stressful circumstances, how a person feels about himself or herself, and how optimistic a person is about the future.

If you want to be healthy, learn to manage stress. Stress is perhaps the single most important psychological factor that affects our health and shortens our lives. Learning to avoid, manage and reduce stress can add years to your life. With age, people learn to manage stress better, especially if they have experienced similar stressful circumstances in the past. We seem to have learned how to exercise and eat well, but we are less skillful at managing our emotions.

Not every way of managing stress is good for your health. When people experience stress-inducing circumstances in their lives, they tend to react to them using two types of coping mechanisms. They either try to face the problem that affects them, deal with it, resolve it and put it to rest; or they choose to avoid confronting the problem that affects them. People who try to avoid the problem often choose to "medicate" their feelings, and some of these responses may have severe consequences on the person's physical health in the long run. Facing and dealing with problems, rather than avoiding them, is far better on our health.

People who have higher self-esteem are healthier. Our *self-worth*, or how much we think of ourselves, can affect our physical health. We believe that those who think more of themselves also think they have greater control over their lives, and as a result, can better handle life's challenges that may adversely affect our health by creating emotional problems.

Compared with those who feel more positive about themselves, people who experience lower levels of self esteem tend to have a larger number of chronic health problems and constantly worry about health problems they may have. These are the people who are most likely to use prescription drugs and dietary products due to health problems. Those who have a low opinion of themselves tend to engage in behaviors like shopping, gambling, and using alcohol, tranquilizers, antidepressants or sleeping pills in order to feel better. In addition, middle-aged and older people who do not think positively about themselves are less likely to have stable social relationships. Many of them are single, divorced, and live alone. People with the lowest self-esteem tend to be the least educated, have fewer assets, and are mostly women.

Depression is another psychological outcome of life's negative experiences that affects our health. Like stress, depression psychologically drains us and weakens our immune system, making us more susceptible to disease. People with high self-esteem are four times less likely to be depressed than those with low self-esteem. This difference is significant given the high percentages of people who experience depression on a long-term basis. For example, nine in ten baby boomers and their parents who lose their spouse are likely to experience depression. Eighty-one percent of people will become depressed over the loss or death of a pet or the loss of a parent or a close family member (64 percent). Women are almost twice as likely as men to experience the blues.

Optimists are healthier and happier. Clearly, a person's outlook on life appears to affect his or her emotional and physical well-being. Pessimists worry about what the future might bring, such as not being able to retire in comfort, falling below the present standard of living, or not being physically fit to do the required daily chores. In comparison with optimists, pessimists are more concerned with having chronic health problems such as poor vision and hearing, diabetes and heart conditions, in part because they are likely to have such chronic problems. On the other hand, optimists are much happier with the way they look and are less likely to be affected by age-related changes to their body and appearance. Specifically, optimists are less likely than pessimists to be concerned with changes in the shape of their bodies, hair and skin, and make less effort to look younger than they actually are.

Back problems are common among baby boomers, and arthritis is the most common problem among their parents. When it comes to specific health problems experienced by the two generations, back or spine problems are the most frequently mentioned health conditions for baby boomers, whereas for the older generation arthritis and high blood pressure are somewhat more common.

You may not inherit your parents' health problems if you think positively about yourself. Generally speaking, if your parents have or had a chronic condition, you have about a 50-50 chance of developing the same health problem before you die. But your attitude and lifestyle affect the odds of inheritance of these ailments. We found that the higher your self-esteem, the lower the chances that you will inherit your parents' chronic health problems. Also, your level of education and income are associated with your likelihood of developing a chronic health condition in middle years and later life. Having more resources apparently enables a person to engage in preventive health care or attend to chronic problems more effectively once they appear.

Health problems tend to appear in a sequential and, therefore, predictive way. We studied patterns of disease development and found that there is a definite pattern or sequence of development of various forms of disease. That is, if you have already experienced one specific health problem you are at a higher risk of experiencing other types of disease. Such knowledge can help you proactively address the onset of these health conditions by taking actions that would stop, deter, or delay their development by, for example, exercising and eating a proper diet.

Baby boomers are the most health-conscious group of people. Baby boomers try to exercise and diet more than any previous generation. Nine in ten baby boomers have changed their lifestyles in order to improve their health. Such changes usually involve more exercise and eating healthier foods. Yet most people do not follow these changes for an extended period. Although boomers are more knowledgeable today about nutrition, they are less likely than their parents to sacrifice good taste for good nutrition. The older generation is also more health-conscious than any previous group of older adults. The majority exercise regularly and eat healthy foods. However, the two generations differ in the main reason for their health-consciousness: Baby boomers exercise and diet primarily because they want to look good and appear youthful, whereas their parents do so in order to feel good and stay healthy.

How they feel about old age and aging

Baby boomers are the generation most terrified of aging and old age. Baby boomers, especially older baby boomers, are the group most preoccupied with the way age affects their physical appearance. They will do anything they can to keep their youthful looks. In general, baby boomers are not as happy as their parents are with the way they look. Ask any plastic surgeon and he or she will tell you the age range of the person who comes in for plastic surgery or botox shots. As the older baby boomers reached their late 40s and early 50s, the number of cosmetic procedures skyrocketed. For example, in the late 1990s, the five-year increase of botox procedures was an astonishing 2,300 percent! Female baby boomers are by far the most preoccupied with the way aging affects their bodies, and as a result they are twice as likely as men to diet regularly.

Good health is the major source of happiness in later life. When the parents of baby boomers passed their 50s, most of them resigned to the idea of being old or even looking old and became more interested in staying healthy. With age, good health increasingly becomes the major source of happiness in later life, as people experience the assault of chronic health problems that threaten their lives and lifestyles. People become more satisfied with their lives after they change their lifestyles to improve their health, especially after they start an exercise or diet program and begin to have frequent check-ups. And yet the vast majority of baby boomers, in contrast to their parents, do not have regular physicals even though the majority has a regular doctor.

People grow physically old but stay mentally young. Just because people come to terms with the changing shape of their bodies does not mean that they also grow older psychologically. Beginning in their mid 30s, the person's subjective age, that is, how old one feels and thinks he or she is, increasingly lags behind one's chronological age. When you ask the parents of baby boomers to tell you how old they feel, whether they feel or act their age, they will tell you that they think, feel, act and even look an average of 15 years younger than their chronological age.

Financial well-being

Baby boomers do not have much. When it comes to money matters, the ageless and resilient baby boomer generation becomes the most handicapped generation. The older generation has ten times as much wealth as their children's generation. Boomers are not as well-off financially as their parents because they have enjoyed spending their money more than saving it. And many of them spend more than what they can afford, putting themselves in debt. Nine in ten baby boomers are under serious financial strain trying to keep their current standard of living, and more than 80 percent have difficulty paying their bills on a timely basis. Even among those baby boomers who have annual household incomes greater than the average American family, two-thirds of them are concerned with keeping up with bills. Those living in southern states have saved the least, while westerners have saved the most. Thus, unexpected caregiving responsibilities not only have adverse consequences on the baby boomers' emotional well-being, but also on their financial well-being.

> Boomers are not as well-off financially as their parents because they have enjoyed spending their money more than saving it.

Baby boomers will buy things they cannot afford, while their parents will buy only if they can afford to. Parents of baby boomers normally do not spend money on things they cannot afford, while their children simply use plastic if they cannot afford to buy something. Baby boomers use a large number of credit cards to increase debt and finance a higher standard of living. Three times as many of them as their parents use American Express, and twice as many use Discover. People with less education and income are also more likely to seek immediate gratification and do not want to save for something as long as they can charge it.

Baby boomers count on their children. At retirement, the average baby boomer is likely to have one-third of their present income or half of the income that they will need to keep their present standard of living. More baby boomers than their parents count on their children for financial support during their retirement years. Three times as many of them as their parents plan on receiving help from their children. Baby boomers have saved little for their retirement years, and they are aware that they will have to work, at least part-time, after they "retire." Twice as many baby boomers without children as those with children plan to go back to work after they retire.

Millionaires are not what you think

When we look at the other side of the coin, those people in their middle and later years of life who are financially well-off, we see some interesting generational differences.

Most affluent older adults are wealthy because they have earned most of their wealth, whereas most affluent baby boomers have inherited their wealth. Our findings about financially well-off people seem to dispel some commonly held stereotypes and myths about affluent individuals. Contrary to conventional wisdom, the average millionaire is a salaried employee who does not let others manage his or her money, borrows more, and takes greater risks in investing. Millionaires are driven by the desire to make or leave a legacy for their children and to help others. Among those who are affluent, the older generation appears to be a far more sophisticated group than their baby boomer children when it comes to managing assets.

Self-made millionaires are less charitable. We also found some interesting generational differences between self-made millionaires and those who inherited their wealth. Self-made millionaires, who told us that they wanted to build wealth so that they can pass it on to others, actually keep their money for themselves. Once they make it, they have a difficult time giving it to others. Self-interest actually dominates their decision on how to spend their money. Self-made millionaires want to keep their money so they can retire earlier than most people, and they are less motivated to leave a legacy than those millionaires who inherited their wealth. Although millionaires tend to be more charitable than non-millionaires, self-made millionaires give less to charities than those who inherited their fortunes.

Self-made millionaires are less motivated to leave a legacy than millionaires who have inherited wealth.

Affluent baby boomers want to work less, make more, and spend most of it. We found that the financial goals of affluent baby boomers are different from those of their parents. The younger generation wants to make money fast, retire early, enjoy life, and pass some of their wealth to others. On the other hand, their parents' main preoccupation is with the preservation of their wealth. To the extent they can, baby boomers are interested in leaving an inheritance for their children, while their parents are interested in giving equally to their families and charities. Those most concerned with leaving an inheritance to their children or relatives are those with the fewest assets.

Lifestyles

Everyone wants to travel, but few can afford it. Surveys suggest that baby boomers approaching retirement years are looking forward to having fun, more so than any preceding generation. Fun has been in short supply in the lives of baby boomers who have been struggling with the crises of their middle years. They are looking forward to experiencing the good times they presently miss.

Travel is the most preferred leisure activity for persons of any age. There is almost no middle-aged or older person who would not like to travel. Unfortunately, those who want to indulge the most are those who have the least free time and money. Health determines whether or not a person can travel, whereas income determines how far and for how long a person travels. But many present and future retirees will never take their dream vacations because of the constraints of work and limited financial resources. Travel for many will be little more than weekends of driving short distances from their homes and staying at budget hotels. Only a small percentage of them, those who are physically fit and financially well-off such that they will not have to work during retirement, will get to travel to exotic destinations, take cruises, and go on safaris.

Travel is the most preferred leisure activity for persons of any age.

Work after "retirement" will be the norm in the beginning of the twenty-first century. A significant percentage (36 percent) of people aged 65 and over is in the labor force. Many of these individuals have retired and gone back to work, while others have decided to delay retirement. We can expect increasing numbers of people to be working in late life. Between two-thirds and 80 percent of the pre-retirees do not plan to fully retire. But unlike their parents, many of whom work to stay active, challenged, and stimulated, an increasing number of retirees, most of whom are baby boomers, will have to work for monetary reasons.

In preparation for post-retirement work, many middle-aged and older adults go back to school. The majority of them, especially those in pre-retirement years (aged 55 to 64), take courses that will help them sharpen their job-related skills and keep up with rapid technological changes. Many find a wide variety of courses stimulating and self-enhancing, while enjoying the added benefits of social interaction. For instance, people who unexpectedly find themselves in new roles for which they were not adequately prepared, such as the role of a widow or caregiver, value learning the skills they need in order to more effectively perform that role, such as learning to better manage their money.

In preparation for post-retirement work, many middle-aged and older adults go back to school.

Baby boomers are most preoccupied with their careers, less with family and retirement. For most baby boomers, retirement is an ambiguous stage in life. Most of the younger generation are not quite sure when they want to retire, if they should retire, where they are going to be and what they will be doing after they retire. In one of our studies we found that only one in ten baby boomers had made the decision to spend most of their retirement years at a particular place or location. The vast majority of people in the younger generation want a comfortable retirement, but they have not been planning for it. They are more preoccupied with their careers and less with retirement. For many baby boomers, family life also takes a backseat to their careers. The average baby boomer is likely to have changed jobs or employers four times more than his or her parents.

Caregiving is becoming an integral part of the average American's lifestyle. As mentioned earlier, the number of middle-aged and older adults who are becoming caregivers has been increasing dramatically, and the trend is going to continue as the baby boomers age and life expectancy increases. An increasing number of people in America provide care and assistance of all sorts, not only to their aging parents but also to their adult children, hence the label for baby boomers as the "sandwich generation." They could also be called the "club sandwich generation" because an increasing number of them provide care to their grandparents and grandchildren as well.

Television viewing and reading are favorite pastime activities of people in both generations. People in the older generation watch more TV than their children, but they also read more newspapers and books. The percentage of older people who read the daily papers is double that of their children. Three-fourths of baby boomers and nearly all of their parents watch the news on a daily basis. More than half of the people in both generations watch comedy and drama shows for entertainment. Older folks with lower levels of income and education as well as those who live alone in southern and north-central states are most likely to watch comedy shows. Older women who have lower levels of education and income and live alone are the best audience for dramas.

With age, people want to give back more. Besides watching television and reading the paper, the most popular activities for more than half of the people in both generations are their hobbies. Volunteering is also becoming a preferred way to spend one's free time. It has become the most important part of a retirement plan, second only to travel. Interest in volunteering increases with age until the person starts experiencing health problems, usually after age 75. Two-thirds of the older generation sees volunteering as an important aspect of their lives, especially empty-nest women in their late 60s and early 70s.

The majority of older people garden and/or engage in various types of gambling. Half of people in these generations gamble or play some game of chance. Gardening is the most popular outdoor recreation activity, especially among middle-class retirees and empty nesters. Nearly three-fourths of this group gardens on a regular basis. Pre-retirement and early-retirement years are the time when most people take on new hobbies or recreational activities. The average woman at this stage in life is likely to take on a new hobby every three years, while the average man is likely to do so every five years.

Buying habits

The younger generation is far more obsessed with shopping and buying. In comparison with their parents, baby boomers are far more obsessed with shopping and buying things. Many show signs of compulsive, impulsive and excessive buying. For example, more than twice as many baby boomers as their parents would buy something even though they could not afford it, buy on impulse, go on a shopping spree, take on a major credit card debt, and make only the minimum payment on their credit cards. By contrast, older people who are spendthrifts also tend to have more money to spend. This does not necessarily mean that baby boomers are careless shoppers. On the contrary, baby boomers shop around more than their parents who tend to rely more on their past experience. Those most likely to over-spend on gifts are younger women who have low levels of education and self-esteem.

Older shoppers want "convenience," baby boomers are after "deals." Convenience is the most important reason consumers in both generations say they patronize an establishment. It is of greater importance to older shoppers who are willing to pay higher prices for greater convenience. In contrast, baby boomers are more interested in deals and are more price-conscious than their parents. Older shoppers tend to be more loyal to products and establishments in general, due to the increasing cautiousness and lower willingness to experiment with new things and take risks as we age. Women and east-coasters of both generations are more venturesome in buying new products, as opposed to men and those who live in other parts of the country.

Both generations are unhappy with the marketplace. If you have difficulty opening the packages or containers of some products you buy, you are not alone. Two in three people in the older generation and one in three baby boomers find packages and containers difficult to open. Similarly, nearly every shopper is likely to report frustration with the small size of lettering on products, but the older shoppers are those who are the most frustrated.

Baby boomers complain more. Baby boomers are generally unhappier with the marketplace, and they complain more than their parents. People in both generations who live in eastern states are the most frequent complainers when they are not happy with the products they buy. Baby boomers and their parents are most satisfied with grocery stores and least satisfied with their doctors. Healthcare professionals and insurance companies are by far the service providers who are seen as taking advantage of their customers. Eight in ten baby boomers make it a point to let others know of products or services with which they are not content.

Many people in both generations pay attention to advertising, especially older people who spend more time watching television and buy products because they like the ads. But many of those who tell you that ads have influenced their decision to buy a product will also tell you that they have avoided buying products whose ads they found offensive or irritating.

Older consumers use plastic as often as baby boomers. Although the majority of people in both generations prefer paying cash for most things they buy, many of them use plastic. Contrary to stereotypes, today's older consumers use plastic as often as baby boomers to pay for purchases. Credit card users tend to have more education and income. East-coasters are the heaviest credit card users while southerners are least likely to use credit.

Contrary to stereotypes, today's older consumers use plastic as often as baby boomers to pay for purchases.

What they have, what they want

A home is the younger person's sign of success, the older person's sign of independence. A house is still the most important tangible possession for baby boomers and older people. Men, especially older men, consider ownership of a single-family house to be a symbol of status and success. Having a home is of utmost importance to even the poorest people. With age, people also consider their home to be a symbol of independence. The longer a person lives in a single-family house, the less likely he or she will want to move. Older people, even those who cannot function independently, will tell you that they would rather die than move into a nursing home. Many older people who eventually have to give up their homes do not move into a retirement community or a nursing home. An increasing number of older, frail Americans move in with their relatives, mainly for financial reasons. Those with less than adequate resources count on their relatives to support them financially if their health fails.

Older people, even those who cannot function independently, will tell you that they would rather die than move into a nursing home.

An automobile is the second major possession and often a status symbol. Although baby boomers would frequently like to have a new and expensive car, most of them cannot afford one. Instead, they tend to hold on to the old car for a longer time. In our surveys, we found that those who buy most of the new cars on the market are between the ages of 50 and 75, although baby boomers' main reasons for saving include traveling and buying a new car. On the other hand, their parents, whose main reason for putting money aside is for major home improvements and to cover unexpected medical bills, can also easily afford to buy new cars. Although both baby boomers and their parents are equally aware of the benefits of long-term care insurance, the older generation is more willing to pay for coverage.

Most people are in debt because of their need for immediate gratification. Although baby boomers do not have as much as their parents, a larger percentage of them (28 percent) than their parents (24 percent) use much of the money they earn for personal enjoyment. And the more money baby boomers have, the more they spend on themselves. We found those who admit to spending a lot of their money on themselves also enjoy spending money more than saving it; they have difficulty sticking to a savings plan, and believe that as long as people can immediately buy things on credit there is no sense in trying to save for them. These are the same people who owe so much that they seldom are in a position to pay off the entire balance on the monthly statements of their charge accounts. A reason for overspending among baby boomers is the strongly held attitudes of this group toward material possessions.

A reason for overspending among baby boomers is their strongly held attitudes toward material possessions.

Their five main concerns

Lack of money. Baby boomers experience more anxieties and fears than their parents in every area of life except health. But what keeps the vast majority of baby boomers and their parents awake at night is most likely to be a financial problem rather than a health problem. The vast majority of baby boomers, even those who are relatively well-off financially, are struggling to make ends meet on a daily basis, while their parents are most preoccupied with their future financial well-being.

Loss of independence is the greatest fear about the future. Deterioration of physical health and financial burdens are among the scariest thoughts about one's future. People fear that they might become dependent on others due to failing health and inadequate finances. However, it is mostly the older generation that does not want to be a burden on their younger relatives. Being financially independent deters the fear of being reliant on others, and thus we believe is the main reason most people in the older generation prefer to hold on to their money rather than spend it.

Personal safety has become a main concern. While a majority of people in both generations will tell you that they are concerned with financial and health matters, especially with regard to their future lives, personal safety is another preoccupation of people in both generations. Our surveys suggest that people in these generations think the world is no longer a safe place, whether they are at home or away. Almost nine in ten people in these groups express some fear of being mugged, robbed, or raped. Also, in this information age, we were surprised to find nine in ten baby boomers and eight in ten of their parents have difficulty in getting useful information on a variety of matters that affect them.

The older generation is much happier than their baby boomer children. Contrary to widely held beliefs that older adults are less satisfied with life, all the evidence suggests the opposite. People in the older generation are happier with the way they look; they have fewer concerns and worries; half of them still see the best years of life to be ahead of them; and they do not feel as socially isolated as their baby boomer children. Sources of unhappiness for the younger generation include lack of money to finance their desired lifestyle, dissatisfaction with their looks, unsatisfactory jobs or career progress, and added care-giving responsibilities.

Many baby boomers and their parents hold inaccurate perceptions of the aged, and most of them are not prepared for late life. We found substantial percentages of people in the two generations who are not aware of the needs of older adults. We uncovered overwhelming evidence showing that people are not adequately prepared to enjoy late stages of life. Nearly every person wants to live a long life, but there is little concern about the quality of life they are likely to experience by living several years or even decades in the "old age" stage of life.

Nearly every person wants to live a long life, but there is little concern about the quality of life they are likely to experience.

In chapters two through seven, we discuss in greater detail the findings presented in this chapter. We also present additional information from our research studies. In chapter eight we draw some implications from our findings for creating strategies for later life that could ultimately lead to a longer and happier life. The last chapter suggests ways businesses can profit by enhancing the well-being of their customers in the two generations.

CHAPTER TWO

What's on Their Minds as They Age

IN THIS CHAPTER we will present some of the similarities and differences between baby boomers and their parents. We will explore their attitudes about their own aging as well as their main concerns, fears, and desires. We will also discuss the characteristics of people in the two generations who have specific mindsets.

How do people feel about getting older when they reach later stages in life? We found that it depends a lot on their life stage. During mid-life people are generally horrified at the idea of aging and approaching death, but later in life they are likely to come to terms with their own mortality and feel less concerned about their old age. In our studies, we specifically tried to find out how they see themselves, their main concerns as they age, and their reactions to their own aging.

Feeling, Thinking, and Acting Younger

We asked people how old they see themselves. In line with other studies, we found that with age, people see themselves increasingly younger than their actual chronological age. The older they are, the larger the difference between their actual age and the age they think they look and feel. Let's take the baby boomers, for example. A little over two in five of both younger and older boomers think that they look younger than their chronological age. However, about half of their parents think they look younger. About half of those aged 55 to 64 think they look younger than their chronological ages, and two-thirds of those aged 75 are of the same opinion.

The older a person gets the younger he or she feels in comparison with his or her age. Among younger baby boomers, only one in three feels younger than his or her chronological age, but nearly half of older baby boomers and 60 percent of their parents report feeling younger than their chronological age, according to one of our nation-wide surveys that we conducted at the Center for Mature Consumer Studies. Regardless of age, women report feeling somewhat younger than their chronological age compared with men.

A number of factors may explain the increasing discrepancy between actual and perceived age. For one thing, the aging person is not likely to feel any different with age. Of course, the onset of chronic conditions and disease increases as one ages, but people tend not to feel the difference. This is because the human body has a remarkable capacity to adapt to its frailties. So, when we look at surveys that ask people how they feel, the vast majority says "very good," regardless of age. Another reason for the discrepancy between actual age and chronological age is that the person's psychological makeup changes little in middle and late life. People's personality or character is shaped by their mid-thirties, and they do not see themselves changing as they age. Even well into old age, people still keep many of the feelings and emotions they had earlier in life, such as their sense of humor and need for romance.

People in mid-life are far more preoccupied than their senior counterparts with the way age affects their appearance. This is not to say that older people do not care, but the older one gets, the less the concern. In one of our studies, we asked baby boomers and their parents if they were concerned with changes they may notice in the shape of their body. About six in ten of these adults told us they are affected by the changes in the shape of their body, but we found these concerns to be of greater importance to the baby boomers that we interviewed. This is not to say that older folks are happy with the way they look. Older people, particularly older women, are not satisfied with their bodies, but they are less preoc-

> People in mid-life are far more preoccupied than their senior counterparts with the way age affects their appearance.

cupied with the way they look than their baby boomer children.

We wondered if these differences in importance of appearance across age groups were the natural result of a person's adaptation to the new look of their bodies and redefinition of their self as "older," and coming to terms with the inevitability of aging. We also wondered if these differences were due to the recent emphasis on health and fitness, a trend more likely to be ingrained in the lifestyles of baby boomers than those of their parents. To find answers, we went back to the same people we surveyed five years earlier and asked the same questions. We found that about one in five baby boomers and their parents who were initially concerned with the changes in the shape of their bodies had stopped worrying about them. These findings led us to believe that regardless of age, people at different stages of life who become preoccupied with their physical appearance will eventually come to terms with it and stop worrying. However, we did find that women are more sensitive to these changes and have greater difficulty accepting them, especially older women and older people who live alone.

In contrast, we also found many of those baby boomers who were not initially concerned became affected by changes in their body's appearance five years later. Specifically, about half of baby boomers, but only one in five of their parents, became *more* concerned with the changes in the shape of their bodies over a five-year period. The vast majority of the older folks were as concerned as they were before, with one in five becoming less preoccupied with their body shape. Thus, not only are older people less concerned about the way they look, but such concerns change relatively little with age. These findings led us to believe that the two age groups are experiencing aging rather differently, with the baby boomers becoming increasingly concerned about the way their bodies look and their parents maintaining a status quo.

The two age groups are experiencing aging differently: baby boomers are more concerned about the way their bodies look while their parents maintain a status quo.

While body changes may be noticed only by the aging person and be concealed with appropriate clothing, we were interested in learning how people in middle and later life respond to changes in their appearance that are noticeable to others. We asked more than 3,000 Americans over age 35 how concerned they are with changes in their hair and skin, and found that about two-thirds of baby boomers and their parents are affected by such concerns. Women, especially older women from lower classes, are far more concerned than men about these physical changes. When we went back to the same people five years later and asked the same question, twice as many baby boomers as their parents (26 percent vs. 13 percent) expressed a greater concern with the appearance of their hair and skin. Preoccupation with these types of physical changes increased more among older baby boomers than among their younger counterparts, with half of the older baby boomers (compared with just 6 percent of younger baby boomers) expressing increased preoccupation with their skin and hair appearance over a five-year period. On the other hand, 28 percent of the older generation surveyed became less concerned, compared with 12 percent who became more concerned. The remaining 60 percent remained just as concerned with the changes in their skin and hair as they were five years earlier.

The way people think about their aging has a lot to do with their opinion of themselves or their *self-worth*. People who have a low opinion of themselves, compared with those who feel good about themselves, tend to be more concerned with changes in their physical appearance; they are not only preoccupied but also worried about them. Furthermore, those with lower self-esteem try to look a lot younger than their age. By contrast, those with a positive attitude about themselves tend to worry less about changes that happen to their face and body and are also more than twice as likely to look forward to later years in life.

The way people think about their aging has a lot to do with their opinion of themselves or their self-worth.

While many people in later stages of life resign themselves to the idea of losing control over their looks, most of them see little connection between appearance and well-being. They still see a lot of good years ahead of them, in part because they do not see themselves as old. In one of our surveys, we asked people across the country if they are preoccupied with feelings and thoughts that their prime years of life may be behind them. We found that only three in ten baby boomers and only half of their parents think they have lived the best years of their lives. Baby boomers who think that they are over the hill tend to be less educated, have deceased parents, and live with others. The death of one's parents can affect how old that person feels. Those in the older generation who do not see much life ahead of them tend to be of lower social classes and have limited resources. Generally speaking, people with higher education find new meaning in life as they age, and see the later stages in life equally as fulfilling as earlier stages. The older folks who think that their prime years in life are ahead tend to hold on to this thought. Only one in five of those we surveyed over a period of five years indicated increasing concern that the prime years of life may be behind them.

Defying Aging

We also wanted to know how baby boomers and their parents react to aging. Specifically, we wanted to know if those who feel younger than their age and are concerned with their appearance are likely to do something about it. We asked people if they were trying to look younger than their actual age. While a little over one-third of baby boomers and their parents are "somewhat" preoccupied with trying to look younger than their age, twice as many baby boomers as their parents (26 percent vs. 13 percent) are "very" preoccupied with activities that make them look younger. As they age, women try much harder than men to look younger, up until about age 75. Those who try the hardest have few economic resources, live alone, and tend to be unmarried.

During mid-life, people find all kinds of ways to fight aging. It is the time when most people consider having anti-aging procedures, and an increasing number of them are going under the knife. Nearly 11.5 million cosmetic surgery procedures were performed in the U.S. in 2005, according to the American Society for Aesthetic Plastic

Surgery. Numbers gathered by the American Society of Plastic Surgeons (ASPS) show that 44 percent more women and 42 percent more men had cosmetic surgery in 2005 than in 2000. Botox injections led the increase with 3.8 million, representing a nearly fourfold increase during the same time frame. More and more baby boomers are having plastic surgery, and many people have started having these procedures at younger ages, according to research recently reported by *ABC Morning News*. Yet about three-fourths of them would not consider having a tummy tuck, plastic surgery, liposuction, Botox, or a hair transplant to enhance their looks, according to a 2004 survey by Del Webb, the nation's leading builder of homes for retirees. However, two-thirds of women and one-third of men (mostly in mid-life) admitted they would consider cosmetic surgery if they knew it was completely free and safe, according to the survey reported by ABC. These findings, as well as those of our surveys, show that baby boomers are not as happy with the way they look as their parents presently are or probably were in their mid-life years; and they suggest possible cohort effects, implying that baby boomers' preoccupation with their body image may persist into older age and be of greater importance than it presently is for their parents. The aging Americans' love affair with plastic surgery is likely to continue as new techniques and technology help reduce the adverse effects of these procedures, such as scarring and recovery time, and become more affordable and socially acceptable.

Other people seek the fountain of youth in chemical substances like growth hormones. Despite a lack of scientific evidence on the effectiveness of such products, thousands of baby boomers and their parents believe that growth hormones make them leaner and more muscular, give them more energy and improve their sex lives. And while the product's effectiveness is based on testimonials of satisfied users, scientific evidence suggests that growth hormones do not improve functional performance, according to Dr. George Merriam, professor of medicine at the University of Washington, Seattle. Highly charged debates on the effectiveness of the potent substance have done little to deter the growth in the product's demand, as reflected in annual growth-hormone sales for Genentech, the original producer of synthetic growth hormones.

Exercise and diet are the most common, lowest risk and most cost-effective methods of fighting aging for people of any age in midlife and beyond. In several of our surveys, we found that about nine in ten baby boomers and eight in ten of their parents were making some effort to improve or maintain their health through exercise and diet. However, while the majority of baby boomers are exercising and dieting to improve their appearance, their parents are more likely to exercise and diet for health reasons. Many people in the latter group must watch what they eat and make sure to exercise because they have some type of a chronic condition such as high blood pressure or arthritis. This is not to say that people in late-life are not trying to look good, but the older person's preoccupation with his or her appearance diminishes with age. We asked people aged 55 and older if they were trying to do things in order to look a lot younger than they actually are. We found that over a period of five years nearly three in ten were still as concerned with trying to look younger than their age, just as many actually intensified their efforts to fight aging, but almost four in ten were no longer concerned with trying to look younger.

While the majority of baby boomers are exercising and dieting to improve their appearance, their parents are more likely to exercise and diet for health reasons.

What we have learned from these and other studies is that middle age is a period of crisis for many. Aging is not simply a matter of getting wrinkles and gaining a few extra pounds. It is also a social and psychological process where people approaching late-life stages are being reminded that they are getting old. For example, the arrival of certain birthdays such as 50 and 65 signify the eligibility for benefits such as membership in associations like the AARP and government entitlement programs such as Medicare. Most people learn early in life that these benefits are for those who are "old." People generally think that chronic conditions such as arthritis or diabetes are diseases experienced by old people. Furthermore, mid-life is the time where people start to experience such life events as grandparenthood and retirement that serve as markers of transition into new roles usually reserved for older people.

In previous years, people came to terms with aging and considered themselves "old" at a much earlier age. After all, life expectancy was 47 years just a century ago, and only one to two percent of people lived past the age of 65 in this country. Today baby boomers have redefined old age in their minds, and think that old age will not begin for them until they reach their eighties. Despite a change in the mandatory retirement age for some occupations to 70, baby boomers still think they will retire before they are old because most of them think that age 65 or 70 is not "old age." Perhaps this is why several surveys found that almost four in five baby boomers plan to work at least part-time after retirement.

Physical changes, the onset of chronic health conditions, and socially-shared norms constantly remind baby boomers and their parents of the arrival of old age. Yet despite these reminders, including somewhat drastic changes in appearance, an increasing number of middle-age people are holding on to their youthful image. As life expectancy increases, we tend to redefine in our minds the boundaries of "youth," "middle age," and "old age." A Lou Harris poll in the mid-1970s found that most people thought "youth" years were between the ages of 18 and 24. A similar poll 20 years later found that people thought "youth" years were between the ages of 18 and 40. Today's baby boomers think and feel they are still young, and they wish to have the appearance of a younger person more so than any previous middle-aged generation. And while an increasing number of middle-aged and older people are far from thinking that they are "over the hill" and will try to hold on to their "youthful" image, many people in both generations are likely to eventually come to terms with aging, resign themselves to accepting age-related changes, and will try to enjoy life in different ways.

No other cohort in history has tried to work on its physical condition and appearance as hard as the baby boomer generation. Yet after spending thousands of hours exercising and watching what they eat, many baby boomers do not see the desired results. Consequently, many refuse to give up some of life's little pleasures. For example, when we asked baby boomers to tell us whether they now sacrifice good taste for good nutrition in comparison with 15 to 20 years ago, only a third of them said they do. By contrast, nearly half of their parents report a preference for healthy foods over tasty meals compared with their previous eating habits.

The older generation's relatively more frequent sacrifice of good taste for good nutrition is primarily due to a desire to stay healthy and prevent or control disease. Baby boomers desire healthy food because they want to maintain or improve their appearance. As people age, they become more comfortable with their appearance and the extra pounds many of them carry. They do not care as much about losing weight. For instance, one survey asked older people if they wanted to lose 20 or more pounds. They found that 41 percent of people aged 55 to 64, 37 percent of people aged 65 to 74, and only 22 percent of people aged 77 and older expressed a desire to lose that amount of weight.

Rather than changing one's physical appearance in order to combat aging, a safer and relatively effortless way to preserve one's youthful image is to not act one's age. People do not make many changes to their lifestyles just because they grow older. Rather, they keep on doing what they have enjoyed and feel comfortable doing. As a result, when they are asked if they act their age, they tend to believe that they act much younger. The older the respondents, the more they are likely to say they do not act their age. In one of our surveys, 43 percent of baby boomers, compared with 71 percent of their parents, said they do not act their age. Nearly half of older baby boomers, compared with 37 percent of their younger counterparts, admit to not acting their age. Only one in three of those aged 55 to 64 and only one in four of those aged 75 and over admit that they act their age. Similarly, the same study found that although people age, their needs, interests, and lifestyles do not change much. Only one in three parents told us that their interests were similar to those of people their age, compared with 71 percent of baby boomers who admitted the same.

Concerns and Desires

Baby boomers tend to experience more anxieties and fears than their parents in nearly every area of life except health. In general, among people in middle and later years of life, health is among the greatest concerns, along with personal safety and financial concerns. In several of our surveys we asked people of both generations to tell us how concerned they were with experiencing a variety of life circumstances. We have summarized the results of these surveys and have presented them in Table 2-1. The table shows the average percentage of people in each group who report they are concerned "a lot" or "somewhat" with experiencing each item shown, and whether or not the percentages of the groups are statistically different.

Health, personal safety, and finances are among the greatest concerns for people in their middle and later years.

TABLE 2-1

Main Concerns of Baby Boomers and Their Parents
percent "concerned a lot/somewhat"

	Baby Boomers	Parents	Significant Difference
Health			
High blood pressure	62	69	Yes
Arthritis	57	74	Yes
Poor heart condition	58	68	Yes
Visual or hearing problems	66	76	Yes
Diabetes	50	55	Yes
Visual problems	58	67	Yes
Hearing problems	58	69	Yes
Kidney or bladder problems	45	68	Yes
Gum disease or dentures	55	57	No
Remembering to do things	44	54	Yes
Money			
Having a hard time sticking to a savings plan	37	24	Yes
Seldom paying off entire balance of monthly charge card statements	30	17	Yes
Losing money (cash or savings)	72	67	No
Being able to keep up with bills and weekly expenses	83	61	Yes
Being financially independent	86	74	Yes
Being able to maintain your current standard of living	92	82	Yes
Appearance/Looks			
Noticing changes in the appearance of your hair or skin	64	67	No
Looking a lot younger than you actually are	34	35	No
Noticing changes in the shape of your body	63	58	No

	Baby Boomers	Parents	Significant Difference
Age & Aging			
Becoming immobile due to physical impairment	64	75	Yes
Not being able to take care of yourself when you get older	81	88	Yes
Being physically fit to do the required daily chores	79	84	Yes
Thinking the prime years of life may be behind you	31	52	Yes
Maintaining the respect of others in late life	60	72	Yes
Activities of daily living			
Finding someone to do home or appliance repairs	53	65	Yes
Getting good financial, tax or legal advice	84	72	Yes
Getting useful information on things that affect you	91	83	Yes
Being able to do your shopping and run errands	60	52	Yes
Being able to fix your meals	51	42	Yes
Finding time to do all the things you want to do	92	74	Yes
Knowing where to call for assistance on what to do or how to do certain things	61	57	No
Having to depend on others for routine daily tasks	50	67	Yes
Work & Retirement			
Keeping your job or going back to work	78	32	Yes
Not being able to work, at least part-time, after retirement	46	43	No
Choosing a satisfying retirement lifestyle	77	66	Yes
Social			
Losing touch with friends and relatives	79	64	Yes
Having someone to talk to	65	47	Yes
Feeling that no one cares for you	48	36	Yes
Being unable to participate in community and social activities	53	57	No
Dealing with the loss of a loved one	83	80	No
Safety & Security			
Being mugged, raped or robbed	86	85	No
Having your home/apartment burned or burglarized	74	78	No
Being able to contact someone in case of emergency	72	60	Yes
Becoming increasingly vulnerable to crime and fraud	74	76	No
Leisure			
Finding ways to enjoy yourself (such as travel and entertainment)	79	60	Yes
Making time to enjoy simple pleasures (i.e., a beautiful sunset, etc.)	83	68	Yes
Being able to attend special events and activities	59	43	Yes
Self-improvement			
Improving or maintaining your health through exercise and diet	90	79	Yes
Learning to do new things	79	63	Yes
Caring for others			
Having to take care of your aging parents	67	27	Yes
Being able to help others through volunteerism	68	64	No
Leaving an inheritance/legacy for your children or relatives	59	62	No
Being able to make significant contributions to charities	51	59	Yes

Health

Health is the most important ingredient in a person's happiness and well-being. Concerns with health intensify in later life as people experience an increasing number of ailments associated with aging. Health usually becomes the number one concern in people's lives after they experience a life-threatening event such as a stroke. Both baby boomers and their parents are almost equally concerned with having *high blood pressure*, with roughly two-thirds of them expressing at least some concern. In both groups, the least educated are those most preoccupied with their level of blood pressure. Older adults who live with others, especially those living with a spouse, are more concerned than those who live alone.

Although *arthritis* is an "old man's disease," more than half (57 percent) of baby boomers are concerned with either having or getting arthritis, compared with three-fourths of their parents. Interestingly, only one in five of those baby boomers who are concerned actually have experienced this chronic condition. By contrast, those among the older generation who say they are concerned with arthritis tend to be only those who have experienced the ailment. Regardless of whether or not people have arthritis, those most preoccupied with the disease tend to be of lower socioeconomic backgrounds. Among baby boomers, those who report preoccupation with this malady tend to live in rural rather than urban areas. In general, women are more concerned than men about the disease. Although the odds of having arthritis increase with age, preoccupation with this health problem levels off around age 65. In fact, we found that over time, the older generation's concern about the ailment tends to lessen.

Although arthritis is an "old man's disease," more than half (57 percent) of baby boomers are concerned with either having or getting arthritis.

Most baby boomers (58 percent) and their parents (68 percent) either have experienced or are concerned they might experience a *poor heart condition*. People from lower socioeconomic backgrounds tend to be the most concerned, while those in urban areas downplay the risk of heart problems in comparison with those who live in rural areas. Surprisingly, nine in ten baby boomers who are concerned with this health problem have not even been diagnosed as having a heart problem. By contrast, a little over half (57 percent) of their parents who are concerned have not experienced this problem.

Nearly as many baby boomers (50 percent) as their parents (55 percent) are concerned about having or getting *diabetes*, in spite of the fact that fewer in the younger group have had the disease. Of those baby boomers who are concerned about this chronic condition, only 18 percent were diagnosed as diabetic, with the remaining 82 percent being concerned even though they do not have this health problem. In general, people in both generations from lower social classes are more concerned with having the disease. As people age, they become less concerned about diabetes, even though they become increasingly vulnerable to this chronic health condition. Among people in the older generation, those most concerned tend to live in southern states, rural areas, and with others.

Nearly as many baby boomers as their parents are concerned about having or getting diabetes.

Visual problems are of concern to the majority of baby boomers and their parents. Fifty-eight percent of baby boomers and two-thirds of their parents are concerned with their present or future ability to see clearly. Although most adults adapt well to their failing vision, men tend to be more preoccupied with their vision than women as they get older. The baby boomers most concerned with visual problems tend to be unmarried, live in rural areas, and belong to lower socioeconomic classes. Parents who are most concerned are those in older age groups, live in western rather than eastern states, and belong to lower socioeconomic classes as well. A similar share of baby boomers and their parents are concerned with their *hearing*. Men are concerned the most, and so are those adults who are in lower social classes and those who live with others. Concern with hearing problems increases with age. It is interesting to note that a larger share of baby boomers than their parents are concerned with visual and hearing problems even though they have not been diagnosed with such health conditions. It appears that baby boomers' concerns in these areas reflect greater health consciousness and need for preventive health care, and in the case of hearing these concerns may be linked to their recognition that loud music may have damaged their hearing.

Problems related to *kidney and bladder* are on the minds of nearly half (45 percent) of baby boomers and two-thirds of their parents. Concerns with these physical ailments also increase with age as the body becomes vulnerable to kidney and bladder disease, and lower-class adults express greater concerns with the dysfunction of these bodily systems than adults from upper social classes. Regardless of age, the majority of middle-aged and older people are concerned with *gum disease* and having to wear dentures. Women and the poor are worried the most about the health of their mouths.

Money

Another area of major preoccupation of both groups is *finance*. Generally, baby boomers are under more financial strain than their parents. A larger percentage of the younger group (92 percent) than the older generation (82 percent) are trying to make ends meet, expressing concern with their ability to keep their *current standard of living*. Those older adults who do not have enough are more concerned with keeping what little they have, whereas those who are financially better off are not as concerned. The desire for maintaining one's current standard of living is lower among those in the older generation who live in western states than among those living in other parts of the country. It is also most important to those older folks who live with others.

> Baby boomers are under more financial strain then their parents.

Being *financially independent* is a major goal of both generations, although a larger percentage of baby boomers (86 percent) than their parents (74 percent) are concerned with it. Being financially independent is of less concern to people as they grow older. As expected, people with fewer economic resources strive to achieve this goal more than those facing better financial circumstances. Women, in general, have a greater desire for financial independence than men. Among baby boomers, unmarried people strive for financial independence the most, while among the older generation those most concerned tend to be women, as well as those who are still employed and live with their children. Continuing to work even after retirement is the only way these groups believe they can maintain their economic independence in the future.

While the majority of people in mid- and later life are concerned with paying their bills, baby boomers have the greatest difficulty *keeping up with bills and weekly expenses*. A little over four in five (83 percent) of baby boomers, compared with two-thirds of their parents, are concerned with bill payments. Although nearly all baby boomers with incomes less than $20,000 have difficulty paying their bills, a full two-thirds of those who earn more than $50,000 a year are concerned with keeping up with bills as well. Parents of baby boomers are increasingly less concerned with keeping up with bills and weekly expenses with age, while older women report a greater difficulty in paying their bills than older men. Older women from lower social classes, and those who live with others have the greatest difficulty paying their bills.

One of the major financial concerns expressed by both generations is their *fear of losing money*. This concern is the same among people in both generations, with about seven out of ten people expressing such a fear. Regardless of age, people from lower social classes are those most concerned, and baby boomer women are more concerned than their male counterparts.

One of the major financial concerns expressed by both generations is their fear of losing money.

Old age

People in both generations are terrified of old age. They are primarily concerned with their inability to keep their independence and becoming a burden on younger relatives, according to our research as well as results of other studies, such as those reported by the Pew Research Center in 2006. Our surveys at the Center for Mature Consumer Studies have revealed that about eight in ten baby boomers and nine in ten of their parents have some fear about not *being able to care for themselves* when they get older. Older baby boomers are more concerned than younger baby boomers, and women in the older generation with fewer economic resources are those most concerned.

The fear of *not being physically fit* to do day-to-day activities in later life scares most people in both generations. About eight in ten people in both groups express some fear about such a possibility. Baby boomers who live in western parts of the country are those least concerned, while those living in eastern and southern states are most fearful. Generally speaking, people with fewer economic resources worry the most about keeping fit enough for doing daily chores in late life. It appears that people with adequate financial resources think that they will be able to pay others for performing daily chores on their behalf, in the event their physical condition deteriorates.

> People with fewer economic resources worry the most about keeping fit enough for doing daily chores in late life.

The thought of possible deterioration of health in later life reminds people in both generations, especially those with inadequate financial resources, that they might become a burden on others. When we asked people in both generations across the country if they were preoccupied with the possibility that they *might have to depend on others* for routine daily tasks, half of baby boomers and three-fourths of their parents indicated some concern. Baby boomers with children, and older women with limited financial resources in particular, are those most concerned about having to depend on others for routine daily tasks. Again, having adequate resources seem to make people feel more secure that they will not become very dependent on others. While the majority of baby boomers and their parents are afraid that they might *become immobile due to physical impairment*, the older folks worry the most. In one of our national surveys, we found 62 percent of baby boomers and three-fourths of their parents worry to some extent about a devastating physical impairment. People in mid- and later life who are concerned the most tend to be in lower social classes. Among older people, those most likely to be concerned about becoming immobile due to physical impairment are unmarried, unemployed, and live alone. The fear of becoming impaired increases with age.

Day-to-day living

As people try to live normal lives they are faced with a number of challenges and circumstances. We were surprised to find the *extreme time pressure* people are under, especially baby boomers. A little over nine in ten boomers and a surprising 74 percent of their parents, most of whom are retired, experience time pressure in their daily living. We found that whether people were employed or retired had little to do with their need for time to do everything they want to do. Surprisingly, baby boomers who are unmarried and those without children feel the time crunch the most. Among the parents of baby boomers, those who experience time pressure the most are the youngest, particularly women.

The most frustrating thing in the lives of many mature adults is *getting helpful information* on a variety of things. Approximately nine in ten baby boomers and slightly more than eight in ten (83 percent) of the older generation are concerned with getting useful information on matters that affect them. This frustration is partly due to their lack of knowledge about sources of information and partly due to perceived credibility of the sources of information. Both baby boomers and their parents are equally concerned with identifying sources of reliable and useful information, with about two-thirds of people in the two generations expressing concern with finding places to call for assistance. Those most concerned are people in lower social classes, and baby boomer women in particular. Furthermore, a lack of ability to obtain useful information does not appear to be a matter of availability or accessibility to sources. Those people in both groups who are the most concerned are more likely to live in urban rather than rural areas.

Similarly, *getting good financial, tax, or legal advice* is of greater concern to baby boomers than their parents, with 84 percent and 72 percent of the people in these two groups expressing concern, respectively. This problem is of special concern to women in both generations, and it becomes less important with age. Baby boomers with lower education and income as well as those who are not married have the hardest time getting helpful information on finances, taxes, and legal matters. Among the older generation, in contrast, those most concerned are younger, female, and from lower social classes.

Older people feel more dependent on others for routine daily tasks than their middle-aged children. Among baby boomers, those with children feel more dependent on others compared with those without children. Among people in the older generation women with limited financial resources are the most concerned. However, the older person's dependency on others does not seem to be in the areas of fixing one's meals, shopping or running errands. *Being able to fix meals* at home is of greater concern to baby boomers than to their parents. Half of the middle-aged people are concerned with meal preparation, compared with 42 percent of their parents. Women are the most concerned as well as those from lower social classes. Among the older generation, meal preparation is a bigger deal for those who live in the South than those living in the West. Similarly, baby boomers express a greater concern with doing their daily *shopping and running errands* than their parents. Six in ten adults in the younger group and a little over half of their parents are concerned with being able to shop and run errands. Among baby boomers, those expressing the greatest concern with their ability to shop and run errands tend to be unmarried women from lower social classes who live alone. Among the aged, those who are not married are most concerned.

The majority of both baby boomers and their parents have difficulty *finding a good repairman* to fix problems around the house. This problem is of greatest concern to women and generally to older people living in the South.

As expected, people in the older generation tend to be more forgetful than their middle-aged children. Baby boomers without children are more concerned with being forgetful than their counterparts with children. This concern increases with age in later life. Among those in the older generation, those most preoccupied with their ability to remember tend to be in lower social classes and live in rural areas.

Work and retirement

Over the last several decades, the trend has been toward early retirement, but we are beginning to see signs of a reversal in the retirement age. Our recent research found one-third of people aged 65 to 74 are still fully employed, but only a small percentage of the 75-and-over group (3.3 percent) is in the work force. Many of those who are working have officially retired at some earlier time and re-entered the labor force. Specifically, 36 percent of those aged 65 and over have *gone back to work after retirement*, either part-time or full-time. One in six of those aged 75 and over who presently work has decided to continue working after retirement. As of 2005, more than half (60 percent) of the 60-year-olds were employed, according to the Bureau of Labor Statistics. Both generations are equally interested in working at or after retirement, but half of the people in each cohort express *concerns that they might not be able to work*, even part-time, during their retirement years. Those concerned the most tend to have fewer financial resources, are likely to be married, and live in southern rather than western states. Among baby boomers, those who want to work during retirement are likely to be single and live alone, while among those in the older generation it is by far people who live with their children who hope to have a job in later life. Twice as many in this group, in comparison to older empty nesters (56 percent vs. 26 percent), express fear they might not be able to be or stay employed during retirement years.

> One in six of those aged 75 and over who presently work has decided to continue working after retirement.

How long people stay employed depends on their life circumstances. Retirement is most common among people who are well off. For example, we found that one-third of people age 55 and over with assets worth more than $75,000 are retired, compared with only 6 percent of those who had assets valued at less than $75,000. Obviously, many people prefer to keep working because of monetary reasons. A little over one-third of the retirees who stay at home have annual incomes of more than $40,000. By contrast, nearly two-thirds of those who are still employed earn more than $50,000 annually, in comparison with half as many of those "stay-at-home" retirees who report the same amount of income.

Money is not the only reason present and future retirees want to work. Employment has several non-monetary benefits that make people feel good about themselves and enhance their feelings of self-worth. To the extent that their work is not physically demanding, many people who qualify to receive retirement benefits prefer to stay in the labor force. Perhaps this is the reason why one of our surveys found that of people aged 55 and older, a larger percentage of those with a college education were still employed.

Today more than ever before, people approaching retirement are concerned with quality of life. In one of our surveys we found that three-fourths of baby boomers and two-thirds of their parents expressed concern with the kind of life they have, or are going to have, in retirement years. People in pre-retirement years, ages 55 to 64, expressed the greatest concern, with 83 percent of them being preoccupied with their quality of life during retirement, compared with 58 percent of those aged 75 years and older.

Although most people want to have a *comfortable retirement lifestyle*, few of them have planned so that they can have it. Generally people do not like to think about their financial situation during retirement years, despite the fact that many of them are likely to spend more years in retirement than working. Most baby boomers have not been saving enough for a comfortable retirement, and they probably will have to work well into later years in life, as long as they are physically fit and have the opportunity to do so. Surveys of pre-retirees aged 50 to 65 years and baby boomers show that between two-thirds and four in five of them plan to work at least part-time after retirement. The younger pre-retirees feel that they would have to work for monetary reasons.

However, many baby boomers' plans for working during retirement years are likely to be spoiled because of illness and lack of work. About 47 percent of current retirees who retired earlier than planned were forced to stop work because of health problems, especially those with jobs requiring physical labor, according to a 2006 study by the consulting firm McKinsey & Company. The percentage of those who retire earlier than planned is likely to increase because of baby boomers' poorer health in comparison with previous generations. Another 42 percent of the present retirees who retired earlier than planned blamed job loss or downsizing, the McKinsey study found. Age bias is a main barrier in the older person's ability to keep his or her present job or find a new one. Age discrimination charges have skyrocketed recently, according to the Equal Employment Opportunity Commission. According to a 2005 survey by ExecuNet, a job search and recruiting network, nearly 90 percent of executives worry they may soon be discriminated against because of their age, and more than 60 percent believe that age discrimination has become more widespread in the past five years. Many of the baby boomers who manage to keep their jobs and plan to retire at a certain age most likely will postpone retirement. A Korn/Ferry International survey of nearly 2,000 executives in 2005 found 62 percent of executives plan to retire later in life than they thought they would in 2003; 72 percent said they planned to retire after age 60.

Retirement is an ambiguous and uncertain stage in life for those people approaching it. Many of them do not know where they will be or what they will be doing at this stage of life. For example, among baby boomers, only one in ten have actually made a decision on where they would like to retire, while about a third of them have only thought about it. For the majority of baby boomers (55 percent), the thought of where to settle down after retirement has not yet crossed their minds perhaps because so many of them do not plan on retiring. Even among those aged 55 to 64, less than half (47 percent) have thought about a desirable retirement location, and only one in five (18 percent) have made a decision on a retirement place.

Retirement is an ambiguous and uncertain stage in life for those people approaching it.

However, these numbers do not suggest that people don't care about their lifestyle in later life. Seventy-seven percent of baby boomers think about having a relaxed retirement, although they do little to prepare for it. Even their parents, most of whom are retired, make an effort to improve their life during their retirement years, with two-thirds of them considering different ways of improving their quality of life at this life stage. People in the younger generation who are the most preoccupied with life after retirement have less money invested, live with their spouse or children, and still work. Among baby boomers, those most concerned are more likely to be in the higher social classes.

Many baby boomers are more preoccupied with work than with retirement and their present jobs and careers are of utmost importance. In comparison with their parents, they are constantly exploring new career opportunities and greater job mobility is far more common. According to a recent survey of 1,000 Americans ages 45 and older by Euro RSCG, a worldwide marketing communications company, 62 percent of baby boomers surveyed saw a total career change as a viable option, a 2006 issue of the *Journal of Active Aging* reports. In our research, we found that baby boomers are four times more likely than their parents to have changed jobs. Specifically, about one in five baby boomers reported changing employers or jobs, compared with only one in 20 of their parents. The career "success syndrome" is much more a way of life today among working baby boomers than it was among their parents. Job or career change leads to greater monetary rewards and it is often the result of preparation for, and success in, one's occupation. Therefore, we were not surprised to find that those who told us they had experienced success in their work or personal life also had higher income and education, and a larger percentage of them (50 percent) were men rather than women (41 percent). Interestingly, the highest concentration of people who felt successful live in the western states (60 percent), while the fewest live in the eastern states (40 percent), and 44 and 43 percent occupy the north-central or southern regions, respectively. We also found that the most prosperous people have high levels of self-esteem.

But success comes with a price. The pursuit of a successful career and competition for recognition and job promotion seem to take their toll on our physical well-being. We found that among those adults who said that they had experienced significant success at work

> The career "success syndrome" is much more a way of life today among working baby boomers than it was among their parents.

or in their personal lives, almost half (48 percent) have used prescription drugs for chronic ailments, compared with only 38 percent of their less successful counterparts. While we did not have direct evidence that declining health was the result of success at work and in one's personal life, it is highly unlikely that people succeed because of their poor health.

Relationships

The need for social interaction is very strong in people of both generations. Two-thirds of baby boomers and half of their parents have *a need for someone to talk to*. According to one of our studies, baby boomers who are unmarried and without children, and older adults who are retired or unemployed have the greatest need for socialization. Contrary to the conventional belief that the elderly tend to be socially isolated, we found no evidence to support this view. While nearly half (48 percent) of baby boomers have the feeling that no one cares for them, only a little over one in three (36 percent) of their parents share that feeling. Among people in the younger generation, the feeling of isolation is stronger among women and those who are not married and have no children. In general, people from lower social classes tend to experience social isolation more than those of higher social classes.

The loss of a loved one, especially a spouse, is the most traumatic event a person is likely to experience in life. *Dealing with the loss of a loved one* is as difficult for younger people as it is for older people, with eight in ten adults of both generations expressing grief over such a loss. Loss of a close family member is harder on baby boomer women than it is on their male counterparts. Among the older generation, those in middle-income classes are affected the most.

People approaching late stages in life become increasingly preoccupied with *how others react to them because of their age*. Many are worried about letting other people's judgments and perceptions affect their own sense of self-worth. When we asked several thousand middle-aged and older people if they are presently concerned with whether others would respect them in late life, six in ten baby boomers and seven in ten of their parents said that they are indeed concerned. Those with fewer resources who have children are the most concerned, as are the parents of baby boomers who live in eastern states.

Personal safety

Personal safety is a major concern among people in both generations. In one of our studies, we found that about 85 percent of baby boomers and their parents have some fear of *being mugged, robbed, or raped*. Women in both generations are more concerned than men with the possibility that they might experience such crimes. Among people in the older generation, those most concerned are likely to belong to lower social classes and live in urban areas. In the same survey, three-fourths of the people in both generations told us that they were increasingly concerned with their vulnerability. Women in the younger group feel most *vulnerable to crime and fraud*, while those in the older generation who feel most vulnerable tend to be retirees who live alone and are in lower social classes.

The fear of *a fire or burglary in their home* is experienced widely among baby boomers and their parents. Three-fourths of people in both groups are concerned with burglaries or a possible fire in their homes. Women in the younger generation are more concerned than their male counterparts, while among the older generation those most afraid are the less educated living in larger cities, who are unmarried and live alone. Baby boomer women tend to feel more helpless in emergencies, especially those women who come from lower social classes and are not married. Although people in the older generation are not as concerned as their baby boomer children, those who worry the most about *who to call in emergencies* are less educated, unmarried, and live alone.

Having fun

The lifestyles of people in mid-life and beyond include a heavy dose of leisure time and activities. While baby boomers have less free time than their parents, a lot more of them are looking for ways to indulge themselves. About eight in ten in the younger generation, compared with six in ten of their elders, are constantly looking for *ways to entertain themselves*. Preoccupation with self-indulgence declines with age, but regardless of age those most preoccupied are people who have *fewer* economic resources. Among baby boomers, those who are most likely to be looking for self-indulgence tend to be women who have no responsibilities or commitments such as children or a spouse to care for. Of course, having money also helps. On the other hand, those in the older generation looking for fun things to do are more likely to live with others than to live alone, and chances are they are less educated than the average person. The older person's ability to have fun depends on whether his or her spouse is free from work obligations and has no care-giving responsibilities to other relatives.

For most people in middle and later years in life, fun often involves *learning to do new things* like taking on a new hobby or attending a class. We found that eight in ten baby boomers and six in ten of their parents want to learn how to do new things. Among baby boomers, those most interested in developing new hobbies tend to be women without spousal and parenthood responsibilities who live in urban areas. Among the older generation, however, it is people in lower social classes who have the greatest zest for learning new things. The desire to learn is greater among older women than among older men, and those who live alone have a greater need for intellectual stimulation than those who live with others.

For the average middle-aged and older person the most frequent entertainment outside the house involves participation in, or attendance at, special events and social or community activities. About six in ten baby boomers and four in ten of their parents try *to attend special events and activities*. Among baby boomers, a larger percentage of women (70 percent) than men (55 percent) are trying to find ways and time to attend events, especially those baby boomers who are not married and childless, and live alone on a small monthly check. On the other hand, those in the older generation most preoccupied with finding ways to get out of the house tend to be the youngest parents, mainly women who do not work, and those who have low incomes and education. Although a large percentage of people in both generations make an effort to do things outside the house, it is usually those in the older generation who find time more frequently to go out. In one of our 2005 surveys, we found that 27 percent of those in the older group, compared with 22 percent of their baby boomer children, said that they were attending various events (social, cultural, sports, etc.) quite often or very often. Apparently, baby boomers are more burdened with other responsibilities that tend to interfere with their entertainment plans.

Staying healthy

With age, people become more interested in being healthy and less interested in looking good. This is not to say that physical appearance is not important in middle and later life, but people tend to give up their efforts to maintain a youthful body image as many concede to losing the "battle of the bulge" they have fought for years. They begin to come to terms with the inevitability of their aging body and accept their physical changes, shifting their focus to health-related behaviors that maintain or improve their health rather than merely the shape of their bodies. By the time people reach their mid-50s, most have come to terms with their new body shape and are less concerned about it. In one of our surveys, we asked people to tell us if they had gained a lot of weight in the previous 12 months. Baby boomers and their parents were equally likely to report weight gain. But those between the ages of 55 to 64 had the highest percentage of people reporting weight gain in the previous 12 months, with one in six of them reporting excessive weight gain in this time frame. An earlier study found that the desire to lose weight clearly drops with age after the mid-50s, and in one of our 2005 national studies a larger percentage of those in the older generation (75 percent) than baby boomers (68 percent) agreed with the statement, "Feeling good is more important to me than looking good."

> By the time people reach their mid-50s, most have come to terms with their new body shape and are less concerned about it.

The differences in the preoccupation of the two generations with their looks and health in general appear to be driven by biophysical aging, such as change in metabolism and the onset of chronic conditions, over which we have less control as we age. Yet, it is possible that many of today's baby boomers will not "age-out" of their efforts to keep a youthful appearance, or they may not concede to physical aging as much as their elders did in their forties and fifties. This type of cohort effect would expand and redefine the market for anti-aging products and services—from foods to plastic surgery—that either can make people look younger than their chronological age or create hope of maintaining an ageless self.

People who feel good about themselves are also those most likely to take better care of their bodies. In the same study, we found a larger percentage of people with low self-esteem than those with high self-esteem (16 percent vs. 11 percent) said they had gained a lot of weight in the previous 12 months. Of course, we are not sure whether weight gain is the cause or the consequence of low self-esteem, but we suspect it is a two-way street. We did find, however, that people who are happy with their present lifestyles or habits tend to be nonsmokers and those who in the past have tried to *improve their health through exercising and dieting*. Apparently, the ability to control one's body and health habits leads to higher self-esteem and happiness. This perhaps explains why in the same study we found those most satisfied with their current lifestyles tended to be nonsmokers or ex-smokers.

Our research as well as studies reported by the American Dietetic Association (ADA) show that, with age, people become increasingly concerned with their nutrition. For example, studies show that eating nutritious food becomes increasingly important to people as they age, and that older people are heavier users of vitamins and minerals than their younger counterparts, according to a 2000 report on Americans' food and nutrition attitudes and behaviors reported by the ADA.

Findings from these studies suggest that concern with exercising and dieting is driven by different motives in the two generations.

Baby boomers are concerned because they want to look good and defy aging, whereas their parents are primarily concerned with staying healthy and living longer. The differences in the motivations of the two generations are also shown in a 2003 study conducted by the International SPA Association (ISPA) in which spa-goers of all ages were asked the reasons for visiting a spa. The study found that the percentage of people who try to take off pounds in order "to improve appearance" declines with age, while the percentage of those who say "to improve physical health" increases with age. Change in health-related motives and priorities with age is in part due to the increasing awareness of one's vulnerability to disease, as shown by the seniors' greater efforts to stay healthy during high risk periods. For example, the 2005 National Health Interview Survey of the National Center for Health Statistics shows that of all Americans who had flu shots, 61 percent were aged 65 and older and 21 percent were aged 50 to 64, compared with just 16 percent of children (aged 17 and under).

Caring and giving

As people age, they generally want to do more for others. First, they become increasingly more charitable. Half of baby boomers and a larger percentage (59 percent) of their parents would like to make significant contributions to charities. Surprisingly, the older adults most likely to make contributions to charities have less money than those who do not want to help charities financially. One-third of people in the older

> As people age, they generally want to do more for others.

generation who do not have much money feel that the best way to help the needy is by giving monetary donations. Only 13 percent of those with substantial savings feel the same way. However, according to one of our studies, the vast majority of the wealthy (88.4 percent) compared with 60 percent of the poor feel that people should frequently use their skills to help the needy.

Besides money, baby boomers and their parents are interested in *helping others through volunteerism*. Two-thirds of baby boomers and their parents see volunteering as an important aspect of their lives. Among baby boomers, women outnumber men when it comes to expressing interest in doing volunteer work (79 percent vs. 63 percent), and empty nesters are more interested than those with children living at home. More than half (55 percent) of older women, compared with one in four older men, are of the opinion that people should volunteer a lot of their time for the needy. Once people in these age groups start volunteering, they keep on doing it for a relatively long time. Over a five-year period, for example, eight in ten adults kept the same level of interest in volunteering. However, those who have more wealth are less likely to stay interested in helping charities by giving their time, compared with those who do not have as much. And a much larger percentage of women (30 percent) than men (10 percent) in the older generation feel that people should give belongings to charities even if they can still use them. Those who give the most money and time to charities are women aged 65 to 74 and those who have fewer assets.

We also found that the reasons people give to charities vary with age and the type of charity. For example, while two-thirds of people aged 55 to 74 give to feel better about themselves, only four in ten of those aged 75 and older give for this reason. The most important reason people aged 55 to 74 give to religious organizations is because of their desire to control the organization's decisions. Giving enables one to participate in important decision-making processes. Nearly half of the people surveyed in this age group gave this reason for their support of religious organizations, compared with 23 percent of the 75 and older age group. The oldest group's main reason for giving to religious groups is to memorialize a loved one who has died, with nearly four in ten giving for this reason, compared with only one in five of the group aged 55 to 74.

> *The most important reason people aged 55-74 give money to religious organizations is their desire to control the organization's decisions.*

Finally, people in mid- and later life give much of their time and wealth to their relatives. We found half of those aged 55 to 74 and one-fourth of those aged 75 and over feel that people should help their relatives financially, and we were surprised at the level of support provided by older parents to their baby boomer children. We found more than half (55 percent) of those aged 55 to 74 and one-fourth (28 percent) of those aged 75 and over give a fair portion of their income to their families. The more assets the older group has, the larger the portion of their income they give to their families. Besides money, people in the older generation also give material possessions to their families and relatives. One in six adults aged 55 to 74 and 37 percent of those aged 75 and over have given material possessions to their loved ones. They also give a lot of their time. Three-fourths of those aged 55 to 74, compared with 43 percent of those aged 75 and over, give many hours of their time to their families and relatives. Many have thought about *leaving an inheritance or legacy for their children or relatives*. Six in ten baby boomers and about as many of their parents have plans to leave assets to their heirs when they die. Older people most concerned with their ability to leave assets to their children or relatives are more likely to be those who have fewer assets and those who live with their children. In one of our studies, we found that 86 percent of older adults aged 55 and over with savings in excess of $20,000 have included relatives in their wills, and 21 percent have included religious organizations. Among those with less than $20,000, only six in ten have included relatives in their wills, and virtually none of them included religious organizations. The decision to leave assets to their children is not necessarily irreversible. Over a period of five years, we found that one in four of those initially contemplating leaving an inheritance were having second thoughts and were not interested in the idea. But about half of those who had no initial interest did indeed develop interest in leaving an inheritance. People in the older generation whose parents are still alive are those most likely to change their minds. Over a period of five years, two-thirds of those with a living parent, compared with just one in three of older adults with deceased parents, changed their minds as to whether they should leave an inheritance to their children or relatives. And while baby boomers are more interested in giving to relatives than to charities, their parents are equally interested in giving to their family as they are in giving to charities.

CHAPTER THREE

Physical and Emotional Well-Being

HOW HEALTHY ARE PEOPLE in the two generations? The answer depends on how one assesses health. When asked about their health, the vast majority of people say that their health is either "good" or "excellent." Government surveys show that people's subjective assessment and reporting of their health status changes very little into old age. That is, for example, a 50-year-old and an 80-year-old are likely to tell you that they are in good health. But we know that people experience a larger number of health problems with increasing age.

Then why do people assess their health as "good" regardless of age? We believe there are three reasons. First, the human body has a remarkable ability to adapt to its own frailties, so those who experience pain or discomfort get used to it and feel almost as good as they felt before their ailment. Second, we believe people think of their health in relative terms and usually use the health of other people in their own age group as a frame of reference in evaluating their own health. Finally, many people do not want to admit to themselves or to others that their health is not good, because admitting one's own frailties or poor health is threatening to an individual's self-esteem. It is as if they are accepting the idea that they are approaching the end of their lives. People struggle to preserve the disease-free, healthy self-concept they held earlier in life. And while an increasing number of people will admit to having a number of health problems, they will still say that they are in good overall health. This problem with self-reporting on one's own health status means that people's health, particularly their physical health, is best assessed by examining the number and types of chronic health problems they have experienced, rather than their own subjective evaluation of their present health status.

Physical Health

Good health does not just mean living free of disease, but also includes a sound state of mind. An increasing number of health professionals consider mental status as part of a person's state of health, and recent scientific discoveries in the medical field point to a strong connection between mind and body. Therefore, it is important to look at both physical and emotional aspects of health. This chapter addresses the physical health of baby boomers and their parents by examining various chronic conditions that appear in later life, and explores the emotional health of these two generations.

Chronic conditions

Chronic conditions are physical ailments that people are likely to experience for a long period of time. The onset of many chronic conditions occurs in the later stages of life, and once they appear many of them afflict the individual the rest of his or her life. Physiological changes in a person's bodily systems, such as the urinary system and the cardiovascular system, are responsible for many of the chronic conditions a person experiences, although environmental and lifestyle factors facilitate or deter their development. In several of our studies, we examined the onset of the most frequently reported chronic conditions. We also studied their prevalence across diverse groups of baby boomers and older adults.

Table 3-1 shows the percentage of adults in specific age brackets that report that they have experienced chronic conditions most likely to occur to people in the middle and later years of life. Table 3-2 gives us another look at the health conditions of the two generations, in lower and higher income brackets, by showing the number of prescription drugs they use as well as the average number of chronic conditions for which they have received help or treatment. As expected, the onset of chronic health problems increases with age, but income level also affects a person's health, regardless of age. We have found that the higher the income, the healthier the person.

TABLE 3-1

Recipients of Help or Treatment for Select Chronic Health Problems

percent of baby boomers and their parents

	BABY BOOMERS		PARENTS	
Condition	Younger	Older	Younger	Older
Chronic orthopedic, back or spine problems	28	28	33	33
Stroke	0	1	1	3
Heart or circulatory disorder	2	6	12	26
High blood pressure	9	15	28	38
Vision problem (not glasses)	6	7	15	23
Kidney or bladder disease	5	5	11	6
Nervous system disorder	4	4	4	9
Diabetes	3	2	6	8
Respiratory disorder	7	7	13	15
Arthritis or rheumatism	10	13	25	26
Hearing problem	3	8	15	26

TABLE 3-2

Prescription Drug Use and Chronic Health Problems

averages for baby boomers and their parents in two income classes

	BABY BOOMERS		PARENTS	
	Higher	Lower	Higher	Lower
Number of prescription drugs presently used	1.0	.7	2.1	1.5
Number of chronic health problems	1.1	.9	2.4	1.5

Orthopedic problems, a back or spine injury, are the most frequent health problems that people experience before old age. To our surprise, we found that *back problems* are equally common among the young and the old. About three in ten people in both generations report a back or spine problem. This problem does become more common, however, after a person reaches his or her mid-70s.

Back problems are equally common among the young and the old—about three in ten people in both generations report a back or spine problem.

As expected, Table 3-1 shows most chronic problems become

increasingly common with age. *High blood pressure* is a common ailment among older adults. One in three indicated they have high blood pressure, compared with one in eight baby boomers. In another study, we found 35 percent of people age 65 and over received treatment for high blood pressure. However, age is not the only factor that relates to this ailment. Lower-income and lower-educated people, both baby boomers and older adults, report this health problem almost twice as frequently as those in upper-income classes. We suspect that the main reason for the higher incidence of this ailment among the lower social groups is due to differences in lifestyles. The higher social groups are better informed about health and tend to take better care of their bodies.

We also found that one in five parents of baby boomers have been diagnosed with and received treatment for *heart* or *circulatory disorders*. This condition is far less common among baby boomers, with only one in 20 reporting the health problem. Heart-related problems such as stroke are far more common among men than among women, but are more likely to be fatal among those older women who experience them, according to government statistics.

Three in ten adults over age 55 report that they received help or treatment for *arthritis* or *rheumatism*, compared with just 12 percent of baby boomers who reported the same behavior. More than four in ten (42 percent) of those aged 75 and over have sought help because of this condition. Lower levels of income and education are also associated with the incidence of this condition. While we do not have a sound explanation for this, we suspect that certain types of manual work take a physical toll on people's joints earlier in life and increase the likelihood of the onset of arthritis or rheumatism. High obesity rates among the less-educated and lower-income older adults can be an explanation for the greater incidence of this condition among these groups. Knees tend to be most vulnerable to this condition, and the most important modifiable risk factor of knee osteoarthritis is obesity, according to a 2005 article in *Arthritis and Rheumatism*. Drugs available today can ease symptoms of osteoarthritis—the most common type of arthritis—but do not help the underlying destruction of the cartilage, the slippery tissue that cushions the joints. Many of those who experience disabling pain get a knee replacement. In 2006, an estimated 400,000 Americans got an artificial knee, and the number who will need an artificial knee by 2030 is estimated at 3.5 million, according to experts of Exponent Inc., a technology-based consulting firm.

One in five Americans in the older generation has been diagnosed with a *vision problem* that cannot be corrected with glasses. One in four report receiving treatment for eye problems other than glasses or contacts. Only one in 15 baby boomers has a similar problem. Unfortunately, uncorrectable vision problems become increasingly common with age and affect the aging person's independence and quality of life. The National Center for Health Statistics estimates, based on results of its surveys released in 2006, that 92 percent of visual impairments of baby boomers could be corrected with glasses or contact lenses, compared with 60 percent of the eye problems experienced by their parents (age 60-plus). Vision problems are most common among people in lower-income families as well as among the very old (75 and older). We also found that, regardless of age, those who are better educated take better care of their eyes and have more frequent eye exams. People with higher education are more likely to see an eye doctor about a serious visual problem than those who are less educated.

One in five Americans in the older generation has been diagnosed having a vision problem that cannot be corrected with glasses.

As expected, *hearing* is a more common problem among the older population, with one in five older adults experiencing problems, compared with about one in 20 baby boomers. Hearing problems are more common among men than among women in both generations.

One in fourteen people in the older generation we surveyed told us that they had *diabetes*. This condition is much less common among baby boomers, with fewer than three percent reporting that they have received treatment for diabetes. Diabetes is most common among those people who also experience other health problems. For example, among users of a large number of prescription drugs (3 or more), 16 percent have diabetes, compared with just 2 percent of those who use fewer prescription drugs.

The prevalence of a *urinary disorder* increases with age, although it is not exclusively an old-person's disease. In one of our surveys, one in 20 baby boomers and one in eight of their parents reported they had been diagnosed with or received treatment for some type of urinary disorder. This condition is relatively more common among people in both generations who are experiencing other types of chronic conditions. Those having a urinary problem are three times as likely as those without it to take three or more different types of prescription drugs. It is also interesting to note that this problem is twice as common among people who have low self-esteem, compared with their high-esteem counterparts, with 12 percent and 6 percent reporting a urinary disorder, respectively. We do not know precisely why those with lower self-esteem are more likely to develop this problem, but there appears to be a strong possibility that this disease is linked to the person's emotions. For example, we know that people with low self-esteem are more susceptible to stress-induced problems, suggesting a possible link between stress and incontinence. It is also possible that incontinence leads to lower self-esteem.

Twice as many people in the older generation as baby boomers (14 percent vs. 7 percent) have been diagnosed with and received treatment for *respiratory disorders*. This type of disorder is also more common among those who have experienced other types of chronic conditions. For example, people who have experienced three or more other chronic conditions are six times as likely as those who have experienced fewer (less than 3) or no chronic conditions to report this problem. Similarly, a larger percentage of users of three or more prescription drugs (19 percent), compared with those who use fewer or no drugs (6 percent) report respiratory disorders.

Recent health problems

When we look at a person's overall health based on the number of health problems they have experienced, we expect the older person to have experienced a larger number of problems. For one thing, a larger number of health ailments occur in people with increasing age. Furthermore, because chronic health problems occur in people in later stages of life, the older a person is, the more time he or she has been "at risk" of experiencing a health problem. In order to account for this differential exposure experience, we studied the onset of chronic conditions among people in the two generations over a fixed period of time—five years prior to our survey.

Surprisingly, we found baby boomers and their parents to be equally likely to report the onset of a chronic condition, like high blood pressure and arthritis, with one in five of them reporting at least one chronic condition diagnosed in the previous five years. People between their late 50s and early 70s are most likely to report the onset of a chronic disease. Those with a greater number of pre-existing chronic illnesses are more likely to experience another chronic condition in the next five years. Interestingly, within a five-year time span, a larger percentage of people in lower-income brackets (35 percent) than people in upper-income brackets (17 percent) were diagnosed with a chronic condition. This suggests that these differences in health problems might be caused by other factors more common to the lower-income group. We can speculate that upper-class people engage in preventive health care more than lower class people, either because they have more education and are aware of the benefits of preventive health care, or because they have the necessary resources. These differences in health problems may also be due to different lifestyles between the two income groups.

> We found baby boomers and their parents to be equally likely to report the onset of a chronic condition, like high blood pressure and arthritis.

Apparently, the chronic problems experienced by baby boomers are not as severe as those experienced by their parents. Many health-related problems, such as back or spine pain, may be of relatively short duration, albeit chronic. But for problems experienced by the older generation, such as arthritis, there is little that can be done to treat the disease effectively. This is reflected in the results of one of our surveys asking baby boomers and their parents to tell us if they were being treated for chronic illness. Only one in ten baby boomers, but three in ten of their parents, reported receiving treatment. Thus, while both generations report recently experiencing the onset of a chronic condition, three times as many older adults as baby boomers are currently receiving treatment.

The propensity to experience an illness requiring treatment increases with age, and women are twice as likely as men to be treated for illness at any given point in time. In fact, women reported receiving treatment for a larger number of health problems than males. In one of our studies, we analyzed the health problems of 821 women and 411 men who visited a health fair for free check-ups. A larger percentage of women than men reported that they had received treatment for the following diseases:

Disease	Women	Men
Anemia:	26 percent	vs. 2 percent
High blood pressure:	13 percent	vs. 9 percent
Thyroid disease:	6 percent	vs. 0.5 percent
Fibrocystic disease:	5 percent	vs. 0 percent
Weight problem:	16 percent	vs. 5 percent

Women live a longer time with chronic problems in later life than men.

Given that women have a higher life expectancy than men and therefore age later in life, these findings might come as a surprise to many people. It is possible that health problems experienced by women occur more frequently or earlier in life because of their gender. Also, it might be that women are more likely to seek treatment than men. Regardless of explanation, these statistics suggest that women live a longer time with chronic problems in later life than men.

Medications

Our findings that baby boomers experience fewer severe chronic diseases than their parents is also reflected in the number of prescription drugs used by the two generations, as seen in Table 3-3 below. One in five baby boomers and at least twice as many of their parents take some type of medication. Almost six in ten of the older generation take medications. Twenty-two percent of older baby boomers, compared with 14 percent of younger baby boomers, use three or more prescription drugs. After age 55, nearly half of people (45 percent) take at least three prescription drugs regardless of age. Women use twice as many prescription drugs than men. The heaviest users of prescription drugs are people in lower-income groups. More than half of those in the lower-income households use three or more prescription drugs, but only half as many (one-fourth) of those in higher-income households use the same number of prescription drugs. As the population ages, more prescription drugs are expected to fill medicine cabinets, a trend shown in the statistics of two surveys by the National Center for Health Statistics conducted approximately ten years apart—1991 and 2000. The results show that the percentage of Americans taking prescription drugs jumped between survey periods: those who took at least one drug in the previous month—from 39 percent to 44 percent; and those who took three or more drugs in the previous month—from 12 percent to 17 percent. The trend is also shown in retail prescription drug sales, which have doubled since 2000—albeit, price increases—according to estimates based on the 2006 Statistical Abstracts of the United States released by the Census Bureau.

After age 55, nearly half of people take at least three prescription drugs regardless of age.

TABLE 3-3

Health Status of Baby Boomers and Their Parents

percentage of people who used a number of prescription drugs for chronic conditions

	BABY BOOMERS		PARENTS	
	Younger	Older	Younger	Older
One or more	41	41	44	70
Two or more	14	22	42	53
Three or more	7	11	23	31

The role of heredity

If your parents have chronic health problems, you have a 50-50 chance of developing one or more of the same chronic conditions by the time you reach their age (or the age at which they died).

Parent-child commonalities of health problems start appearing relatively early in life. In one of our national surveys, we examined people's experience with 12 commonly reported chronic health problems. We asked respondents of our survey to tell us if they or their parents had experienced each of the health problems. We found a little over one in five (22 percent) of younger baby boomers reported at least one chronic condition similar to that of their parents. Among older baby boomers, nearly three in ten (29 percent) had experienced a health problem similar to that of their parents, while an average of 40 percent of the older generation reported having a health problem experienced by their parents.

Unlike other parent-child similarities in chronic health problems, similarities in back or spine problems do not appear to increase with age. Nearly three in ten baby boomers report such chronic body aches, compared with one-third of their parents. Baby boomers whose parents experienced an orthopedic problem or had arthritis or rheumatism stand a good chance of developing the same problem before they inherit any other chronic disease from their parents. Later in life, one stands a good chance of inheriting the same eye or hearing problems, as well as any mental disorders or urinary problems experienced by aged parents.

Boomers whose parents experienced an orthopedic problem or had arthritis or rheumatism stand a good chance of developing them too.

Attitude seems to play an important role in determining whether you will inherit a health problem experienced by your parents. We found a larger percentage (36 percent) of people with a low opinion of themselves tend to experience at least one health problem that was also experienced by one or both of their parents, as compared with their counterparts with higher self-esteem (28 percent).

Patterns of disease development

Is there a sequence or pattern of development of various forms of disease? If you have already experienced one specific health problem, is there a higher risk of experiencing certain other types of disease? The answer is emphatically, "yes."

In two of our studies, we analyzed a wide variety of health problems reported by baby boomers and their parents. We used sophisticated statistical techniques to uncover patterns of co-existence of health problems and we determined the co-occurrence of certain problems in people. Thus, a person's experience of a given health problem (problem X) was strongly correlated with a previous experience of another problem (problem Y). We can say with relatively high confidence that those experiencing health problem Y have a probability of experiencing problem X at some later stage in life. We will analyze these patterns of co-variation in health-problem occurrences separately among baby boomers and among their parents.

Among baby boomers. If a baby boomer is diagnosed with one of the following four types of disease, he or she is "at risk" of experiencing one or more of the remaining three: kidney, liver, thyroid, and diabetes. Those baby boomers that have high cholesterol are also prone to high levels of triglycerides and polyps or growth in bowels. Excess weight is associated with high blood pressure and thyroid disease. Those with high blood pressure, in turn, are also likely to develop hearing and vision problems. Similarly, glaucoma is associated with fibrocystic disease and vision problems. Heart disease is most common among those who have diabetes, and vice versa. Heart disease is also associated with high blood pressure. Finally, gout and lung disease (including TB) tend to be related.

It was also discovered that the health of baby boomers depends on the following factors: presence or absence of high cholesterol and triglycerides and the health of blood relatives.

Among parents. The presence of health problems appear serially for the older generation as follows:
- Cholesterol and triglycerides go hand-in-hand.
- Thyroid and kidney disease appear to develop serially.
- Eye and ear problems are developed concomitantly, and those with a hearing problem are also likely to have gout and polyps or growth in bowels.
- Those who have been treated for high blood pressure are strong candidates for cancer.

- Those with liver disease do not tend to have a weight problem.
- Anemia and fibrocystic are concomitant.
- High blood pressure, diabetes, heart or circulatory disorders, and stroke are experienced serially.
- Those who experience arthritis or rheumatism are also likely to experience chronic orthopedic, back or spine problems.
- The health of the seniors is adversely affected by cholesterol and triglycerides, age, heart disease, diabetes, blood relative's health, lack of education, and lack of money (low income).

Health-related lifestyles

For the purpose of discussion, we have grouped health-related lifestyles into "healthy" and "unhealthy." The first category includes activities such as regular check-ups, dieting and exercising, while the latter category includes behaviors that may adversely affect one's health, such as smoking and excessive drinking.

Healthy. About nine in ten baby boomers and eight in ten of their parents are preoccupied with improving their health condition through exercise and dieting. Those most concerned are the older adults with higher education and income.

At some point in their lives the majority of people in both generations have tried to control their weight. About three fourths of people up to age 65 have tried exercising or dieting, but less than half (45 percent) of those aged 75 and older have been on a diet or exercise program. Women outdo men when it comes to caring for their physical shape; they are more likely than men to attempt to control their weight by dieting rather than exercising. Regardless of gender, those most concerned about their body's shape have higher education and income, and they are more likely to live in urban rather than rural areas of the country.

The percentage of baby boomers and their parents who exercise varies according to the definition of "exercise." Our surveys found that about half of people in these cohorts exercise regularly. Men and those with higher income and education levels exercise more than their female, lower income and education counterparts. The proportion of people who exercise at home increases with age, according to a 1990 Gallup Organization poll of 801 regular exercisers. The study found a little over 34 percent of those in the 35 to 49 age group, compared with 41 percent of those in the 50 to 64 bracket, and 52 percent of the 65-plus crowd were exercising at home. In one of our studies, we found 40 percent of adults in any age group own and use exercise equipment at home. In another study of ours, we found one in five baby boomers has a health club membership. Those aged 55 to 64 are equally likely to visit health clubs, but membership declines after age 65. However, the 2005 study of sports participation by American Sports Data, Inc. found people aged 55 and older had increased their fitness participation over the previous six years by 33 percent, compared with a growth rate of 13 percent for baby boomers aged 35 to 54. This growth was fueled in part by the availability of less taxing forms of exercise equipment such as Pilates and stationary cycles. Those who can afford exercise equipment and health club memberships are, as expected, those with the most financial resources and the highest levels of education. Apparently, the elderly increasingly engage in more simple and less taxing forms of exercise, such as walking.

Most studies today reveal that nearly nine out of ten Americans are trying to take steps toward a healthier diet, but most of them do not try very hard. Regardless of age, nearly three in ten adults tend to diet frequently or regularly. The oldest baby boomers are the most health conscious, with 40 percent of them dieting regularly. Adults of both generations with the highest levels of education are the ones most likely to go on a diet. Twice as many women as men diet regularly.

Nearly nine out of ten Americans are trying to take steps toward a healthier diet, but most of them do not try very hard.

People learn continuously about nutrition, but younger people learn the most. According to one of our studies, 90 percent of baby boomers report increased knowledge in the area of nutrition over the previous 15 to 20 years, compared with their parents' 83 percent knowledge increase. Even the oldest people report substantial knowledge gain (78 percent) over the same time frame. Women have gained more knowledge about nutrition than men over this time period, with nearly nine in ten women compared with eight in ten men reporting increased knowledge about nutrition. Those with higher income and education levels know the most, while people living in western states have gained more knowledge than those living in north-central states.

Older people are far more likely than their baby boomer children to alter their eating habits. While nearly half (46 percent) of the parents' generation report sacrificing good taste for good nutrition now compared with 15 to 20 years ago, only one-third of the baby boomers report the same change. The oldest parents are those most likely to have made the greatest change in their eating habits. This is in part due to dietary restrictions associated with the onset of various chronic conditions that require special diets. In one of our studies, we found that parents of baby boomers were three times more likely than their children to buy or order dietary meals, with 15 percent and 6 percent, respectively, reporting usage. Dietary meals are ordered and consumed increasingly with age.

Older people are far more likely than their baby boomer children to alter their eating habits.

The vast majority of baby boomers do not see a doctor regularly. Approximately one in four of them do not have regular check-ups, compared with only one in ten of their parents who do not go to the doctor regularly. Generally, the older a person, the more likely he or she is to have a personal doctor or a regular source of medical care. Women are more likely than men to visit their doctor regularly, as are those adults with more money and better education. Two-thirds of unmarried people, compared with half of those married, have a regular source of medical care. Three-fourths of those in higher-income families, compared with half of their lower-income counterparts, have a regular doctor. A long-term relationship with a doctor is more often the result of a need for treatment for illness and medication monitoring than a desire for preventive health care.

The vast majority of baby boomers do not see a doctor regularly.

How does a person's health affect his or her satisfaction with life? When people make a lifestyle change for the purpose of improving their health, they seem to feel better about themselves. Perhaps this is the reason that when people start dieting and exercising regularly, and develop a relationship with a personal doctor, they are more likely to be satisfied with their lifestyles than their counterparts who abstain from these types of health-related behaviors. In one of our studies we found that one in three of both baby boomers and their parents had made a change in their lifestyles to improve their health in the previous 12 months.

Unhealthy. Many baby boomers and their parents have unhealthy habits. About one in twenty adults admit to drinking more than two alcoholic beverages daily. Women, lower-income and older adults drink slightly less than the average person. Baby boomers drink more than their parents. Three in ten boomers report an increase in the consumption of alcoholic beverages in the past 12 months, compared with 17 percent of their parents. Men drink twice as much as women. Those in the work force hit the bottle more frequently than their unemployed or retired counterparts.

Baby boomers drink more than their parents.

Twenty-one percent of all adults smoke, with women being less likely than men to light up (18 percent vs. 24 percent), according to the Centers for Disease Control (CDC) 2006 statistics. The same source reports that a greater share of baby boomers (22 percent) than their parents (9 percent) smoke. Adults from lower-income homes are twice as likely as their upper-income counterparts to smoke. The less educated and those who are married tend to smoke the most. The vast majority of smokers (about 95 percent) in the two oldest generations picked up the habit during their teen years. At least half, and perhaps as many as two-thirds of those who began smoking in their youth, will eventually die from smoking-related illnesses. These statistics are based on a landmark study that began in 1951 and followed nearly 35,000 male doctors

At least half, and perhaps as many as two-thirds of those who began smoking in their youth, will eventually die from smoking-related illnesses.

for 50 years. The study results, which are reported in the June 2004 issue of *British Medical Journal,* show that smokers die about 10 years younger than non-smokers, on average; those who stop smoking at 40 gain nine years of life expectancy, those who quit at 50 gain six years and those who kick the habit at 60 gain three years. According to our studies, half of adults in the older generation have smoked at some point in their lives, with 30 percent of them eventually quitting. Smoking cessation rates vary; they are the lowest for baby boomers, with 18 percent of the ex-smokers already having kicked the habit. People who have stopped smoking, in comparison with those who continue to smoke, tend to live with others, are not in the work force, have low self-esteem, and have a larger number of health-related problems. This last finding suggests that some people may have kicked the habit in response to the onset of an illness, or that health problems are the result of smoking.

People can experience serious accidents and illness at any age, but those between the ages of 55 and 74 are particularly prone to these health problems. More than one in three people in this group report that they have experienced a major injury or illness.

Despite the increasing preoccupation with health among Americans of all ages, including efforts to diet and exercise, growing dissatisfaction with physical appearance and a desire to lose weight, the average adult is not as healthy today as he or she was in previous years, according to government statistics. Health trends in the United States indicate that the percentage of obese people (defined as weighing 30 pounds or more over an average weight of a person of an average height of 5'4") has doubled from 15 percent in the late 1970s to 30 percent in 2005, with an estimated two-thirds of all adults being overweight or obese today, according to the CDC. The proportion of Americans with clinically severe obesity (roughly 100 pounds or more overweight for an average adult man) increased from 1 in 200 adults in 1986 to 1 in 50 adults in 2000, growing twice as fast as the proportion of Americans who are simply obese, according to a study by RAND Corporation reported

Despite the increasing preoccupation with health among Americans of all ages, the average adult is not as healthy today as he or she was in previous years.

in a 2003 article published in *Archives for Internal Medicine*.

Obesity rates are highest among those aged 40 to 69 years. Three-fourths of all overweight individuals fall into the group aged 51 to 69, and people aged 60 through 75 experienced the highest increase in obesity of any age group in the U.S. from 1984 to 2000, according to the CDC. Similarly, the U.S. Administration on Aging reports that obesity is on the rise in older Americans—from 12 percent in 1990 to 19 percent in 2002. The more frequent participation in exercising activities by older adults in recent years may be due to the higher obesity rates among the older age groups. And although an increasing number of older Americans exercise regularly today, most engage in little physical activity or are sedentary. An estimated five in ten adults aged 65 to 75 years are sedentary, and this statistic increases to six in ten for those aged 75 and older.

This epidemic of obesity, combined with the aging of the population, has fueled a dramatic rise in the prevalence of diabetes. In the United States, it is estimated that 17 million people have diabetes, with almost six million cases still undiagnosed, costing the average taxpayer about $175 for obesity-linked illnesses in 2004, according to the CDC. Apparently, the increasing education about the benefits of exercise and good eating habits, and the availability of the increased numbers of healthy foods (e.g., low-fat, low-cholesterol) have done little to help people shed the pounds. Nor has Americans' recent shift in attitude toward health and fitness, which is revealed in a survey conducted by American Sports Data for the International Health, Racquet & Sportsclub Association (IHRSA). Based on the results of this survey, it is estimated that the number of people who exercised regularly in 2002 (did at least one fitness activity 100 or more times per year) was 50.9 million. IHRSA reports that this number is lower than the 51.5 million people who exercised often in 1990. The survey suggests that many people are becoming complacent with their lack of physical health or do not see the relationship between lack of fitness and obesity with its adverse health conditions.

The epidemic of obesity, combined with the aging of the population, has fueled a dramatic rise in the prevalence of diabetes.

Emotional Health

A person's emotional health is an important aspect of one's overall health, since it affects the person's state of mind and sense of well-being, and can cause or contribute to the development of disease. We have researched three important dimensions of a person's emotional health: stress, depression, and self-esteem.

Stress

People experience two types of stress: on-going or chronic stress, and acute stress. The first type of stress is caused by a person's lifestyle and social expectations for that person, as in the case of being a caregiver to an older relative, an employee, a spouse, etc. The second type of stress is often due to unexpected events such as accidents or natural disasters.

Several of our studies revealed that the people most likely to experience stress tend to be younger, employed and female. They also tend to have low self-esteem and are more likely to live in eastern and north-central states than in other parts of the country.

The people most likely to experience stress tend to be younger, employed and female.

Chronic Stress. This type of stress is most common among those in the younger generation. In one of our studies we found more than two-thirds (69 percent) of those under age 55 experience stress on a continual basis, compared with less than half (48 percent) of those older than 55 who experience this type of stress. Those aged 75 and older report the lowest level of chronic stress, with only 43 percent of them reporting on-going anxieties. Forty-four percent of baby boomers and 37 percent of their parents say they are under a lot of stress at home or work. Males experience less chronic stress than females (56 percent vs. 46 percent), and those employed experience more chronic stress than the unemployed (57 percent vs. 44 percent). Also, those with low self-esteem experience on-going stress more than those with high self-esteem (62 percent vs. 39 percent), and as do those with care-giving responsibilities in comparison to those without such obligations (61 percent vs. 47 percent).

Similar findings emerged from another study. We asked people to record the amount of stress they had experienced over a five-year period. The study showed that on-going stress experienced over that time period is most common among people under age 55, with two-thirds of them reporting feeling stressed, compared with 41 percent of those aged 55 and older. The experience of such stress declines with age in later life. It is also more common among females, the employed, caregivers, and those with low self-esteem.

In another study, about half of the adults we questioned agreed with the statement, "stress seems to have been a part of my life," with a surprisingly large percentage of people in the two generations reporting increased feelings of stress in the previous six months. Specifically, two-thirds of the baby boomers and nearly half (47 percent) of their parents reported increased stress during the previous six months. Two-thirds of women, but only half of men reported increased stress in the previous six months. The same study found that people who live in eastern and north-central states experience greater levels of stress than people who live in southern and western states. A significant amount of stress is work-related, with three in five of those in the labor force, compared with two-fifths of those who do not work, reporting increased stress levels. Those with the lowest levels of self-esteem are the most likely to experience the greatest levels of stress as well.

About half of the adults we questioned agreed with the statement, "stress seems to have been a part of my life."

What keeps people awake at night? We examined several of the concerns common to people at middle and later stages in life as possible contributors to their on-going level of stress, and we found a strong association between worries about day-to-day living and levels of stress. Table 3-4 shows the percentage of people who say they are concerned "a lot" about 17 different points and their stress level. This table suggests that the middle-aged and older person's preoccupation with their ability to stay physically fit for doing their daily chores, as well as with their ability to keep their current standard of living, contributes to their stress levels.

TABLE 3-4

Levels of Chronic Stress Experienced by Baby Boomers and Their Parents Who Worry about Life Circumstances

percent concerned "a lot"

	Low Stress	High Stress	Significant Difference
Being able to help others through volunteerism	34	41	Yes
Having poor heart condition	16	21	Yes
Becoming increasingly vulnerable to crime or fraud	20	24	No
Having visual problems that cannot be corrected with glasses	12	18	Yes
Learning to do new things	16	23	Yes
Having arthritis	23	31	Yes
Choosing a satisfying retirement lifestyle	18	23	Yes
Losing touch with friends and relatives	17	22	Yes
Having diabetes	12	16	Yes
Noticing changes in the appearance of your hair or skin	11	20	Yes
Leaving an inheritance/legacy for your children or relatives	16	27	Yes
Looking a lot younger than you actually are	5	8	No
Being able to maintain your current standard of living	26	40	Yes
Being physically fit to do the required daily chores	37	46	Yes
Being unable to participate in community and social activities	11	16	Yes
Thinking that the prime years of life may be behind you	12	19	Yes
Noting changes in the shape of your body	12	20	Yes

Acute Stress. The amount of acute stress a person experiences varies according to the specific stressor. In one of our studies, we asked a large number of adults across the country to tell us if they had recently experienced 25 events that can be potential stressors. Those who indicated they had experienced the specific event in the previous six or 12 months were asked to tell us if they felt stressed when it happened.

Table 3-5 shows the events that many respondents to our survey said they experienced, and the percentage of those who felt "stressed" when they experienced it. Interestingly, major conflict with a family member and worsening financial status were the most stressful events, closely followed by community crisis or disaster, divorce or separation, increased responsibility for aged relative, and chronic illness or condition diagnosed.

There are some interesting differences in the amount of stress experienced. The onset of chronic illness is more stressful to younger mature adults. The same study revealed the vast majority (86 percent) of people aged 55 to 64 experiencing chronic illness tend to experience stress as a result of this, compared with a much smaller percentage of those in the 75 and older age bracket (42 percent).

TABLE 3-5

Adults Who Felt Stressed After Experiencing Each Event

in percent

Major improvement in financial status	13.9
Birth of first grandchild	20.0
Significant success at work or personal life	25.1
Retirement (at own will)	26.1
Last child moved out of household	27.3
Death or loss of a pet (dog or cat)	33.8
Birth or adoption of a child	41.7
Death of a parent or close family member	49.1
Death of spouse	50.0
Reduction in hours of employment or giving up employment (at own will)	53.1
Stopped smoking	58.3
Gained a lot of weight	61.0
Changed jobs, same or different type	61.3
Serious injury, illness or major surgery	65.7
Deterioration of family member's health	66.5
Moved to a different place	67.4
Marriage	72.0
Started work for the first time or after not working for a long time	72.7
Lost job/business or forced to retire	73.3
Chronic illness or condition diagnosed	77.5
More responsibility for aged relative	78.2
Divorce or separation	78.6
Community crisis or disaster (hurricane, crime, fire, flood, earthquake)	80.4
Deterioration in financial status	84.0
Major conflict with family member	86.6

The level of stress people experience as a result of a serious injury, illness, or major surgery also depends on their age. Older adults tend to handle these events a lot better. For example, 79 percent of those aged 55 to 64 said they experience stress due to a major health problem they had not anticipated, compared with 36 percent of those aged 75 and over. The amount of stress a person feels is magnified when he or she must care for another person. Those who must care for others while coping with an injury, illness, or major surgery experience more stress than those with no caregiving responsibilities, with 64 percent and 45 percent, respectively, reporting increased anxiety.

Note some other differences in the level of stress experienced:

- Death of a parent or family member is more stressful among people who live with others compared with those who live alone (56 percent vs. 23 percent).
- Success in work or personal life is twice as stressful among younger adults than among those aged 55 and over (30 percent vs. 15 percent), and among females than males (36 percent vs. 18 percent).
- Major improvement in financial status creates a greater amount of stress among those who live with their spouse (21 percent) than among those who live alone (6 percent).
- Decline in financial resources is more stressful among those with higher-incomes than among lower-income families (91 percent vs. 78 percent). Deteriorating financial status is more stressful among adults who live in western states (85 percent) and north-central states (74 percent) than among those who live in other parts of the country (58 percent).
- Assuming increased responsibility for older relatives creates more stress for lower-class people (91 percent vs. 73 percent).
- Gaining weight is a bigger deal for younger baby boomers (79 percent) than for their older counterparts (56 percent); it is more stressful among those adults who have low self-esteem than those with high self-esteem (70 percent vs. 51 percent).

Depression

Stress and depression go hand-in-hand. A lot of people experiencing stress cannot cope with it and spiral into depression. Stress weakens our immune system, making us more susceptible to diseases. Depression also has its way of affecting health, quality of life, and longevity. Depression is the most prevalent undiagnosed, untreated disease in the world, and probably the most expensive, according to the World Health Organization (WHO). Already the number one cause of disability worldwide, depression is projected to become the second leading cause of premature death by 2020, according to WHO. Depressed people have about twice the death rate of people of the same age who are not depressed, according to cutting edge studies reported in 2005 by researchers of the National Institute of Mental Health. According to these reports, the craving for carbohydrates and the hormone insulin are key players of the biological mischief caused by depression. Many depressed people give in to a craving for carbohydrates because starches subdue anxiety, increasing the body's insulin levels, which, in turn, spur the growth of abdominal fat and inflammation, and increase bad LDL cholesterol, blood pressure and blood clotting.

> *Stress weakens our immune system, making us more susceptible to diseases. Depression also has its way of affecting health, quality of life, and longevity.*

In several of our studies, we looked into the kinds of people who are or may easily become depressed. In one study, we found that women are almost twice as likely as men to report that they are depressed, with 28 percent of them admitting to depression, compared with only 16 percent of men. Lower-income people (those families with household incomes less than the national average) are twice as likely as their higher-income counterparts (28 percent vs. 13 percent) to report that they are easily depressed. People who live alone are more depressed than those who live with others, as well as those who have experienced a larger number of health problems. People with low self-esteem are four times as likely as those with high self-esteem to report that they easily get the blues (34 percent vs. 9 percent). Baby boomers are more likely to experience depression than their parents, as people under the age of 65 are twice as likely as older individuals to become depressed.

> *Women are almost twice as likely as men to report that they are depressed.*

We also studied people's experience of depression within specific time spans, such as 12 months and six months. We found that about four in ten baby boomers reported increased depression levels in the previous 12 months, compared with 28 percent of their parents. Young parents are twice as likely as people aged 75 and older (38 percent vs. 19 percent) to experience higher levels of depression in a six-month time span. Those with low self-esteem are twice as likely as their high self-esteem counterparts to experience the blues, with 47 percent and 22 percent, respectively, reporting an increase in depression in the previous six months. Depression rates among the unemployed are usually lower than among those who work (26 percent vs. 36 percent).

TABLE 3-6

Adults Who Felt Depressed After Experiencing Each Event

in percent

Event	%
Death of spouse	91.7
Death or loss of a pet (dog or cat)	81.3
Lost job/business or forced to retire	68.7
Divorce or separation	67.9
Gained a lot of weight	67.8
Death of a parent or close family member	63.9
Deterioration of financial status	58.2
Deterioration of family member's health	51.1
Major conflict with family member	51.0
Chronic illness or condition diagnosed	42.3
Serious injury, illness or major surgery	41.2
Moved to a different place	34.9
Last child moved out of household	31.8
More responsibility for aged relative	31.0
Reduction in hours of employment or giving up employment (at own will)	24.5
Community crisis or disaster (hurricane, crime, fire, flood, earthquake, etc.)	19.6
Changed jobs, same or different type	13.5
Stopped smoking	12.5
Started work for the first time or after not working for a long time	12.1
Retirement (at own will)	8.7
Birth of first grandchild	5.0
Major improvement in financial status	4.6
Birth or adoption of a child	4.2
Significant success at work or personal life	2.8
Marriage	0.0

Certain events are likely to depress people, especially those events that are stressful. In one of our surveys, we asked people who experienced 25 important events in the previous 12 months to tell us if they felt depressed after they had experienced each of the specific events. Table 3-6 shows the percentage of adults who felt depressed after the occurrence of these events. Nine in ten people whose spouse had died fell into depression, and eight in ten felt depressed after the loss of a pet, which is a surprisingly higher percentage when compared with those depressed due to death of a parent or close family member (64 percent), divorce (68 percent), loss of one's job or business (69 percent), and weight gain (68 percent). None of those who got married in the previous year said they were depressed because they had tied the knot.

> Nine in ten people whose spouse had died fell into depression, \and eight in ten felt depressed after losing a pet.

The extent to which a person is depressed after experiencing a specific stressful event depends a lot on certain characteristics of the person, the most important of which appears to be the person's self-worth or self-esteem. The findings in Table 3-7 give some examples from two of our studies. It shows the percentage of people with low self-esteem becoming depressed after specific life events compared to those with high self-esteem. These findings suggest that, relative to the occurrence of certain events, a person's self-esteem plays an important role in one's experience of depression.

TABLE 3-7

Baby Boomers and Older Adults Who Experience Depression After Select Events by Level of Self-Esteem

in percent

	Low self-esteem	High self-esteem
Relocation	48.1	12.5
Major conflict with a family member	60.5	39.8
Financial status a lot worse than usual	67.9	44.4
More responsibility for aged relative	39.5	19.4
Gained a lot of weight	77.6	53.2
Chronic illness or condition diagnosed	50.0	25.9
Serious injury, illness or major surgery	40.0	20.0

Besides the influence of self-esteem on how depressed people become after specific events, other factors also seem to play a role. Here are some examples.

Serious illness, a major injury or surgery. Compared with their elders, twice as many people under age 55 become depressed (51 percent vs. 26 percent). A larger percentage of caregivers (49 percent) compared with those with no care-giving responsibilities (25 percent), become depressed due to such health problems.

Death of a family member. A larger percentage of those who have several chronic conditions (81 percent), compared with those with few or no chronic conditions (57 percent), experience depression due to this event.

Deterioration of financial status. People who live in urban areas are more likely to become depressed, compared to those who live in rural areas (65 percent vs. 45 percent), when their financial situation worsens.

Gained a lot of weight. A larger percentage (75 percent) of women than men (53 percent) become depressed due to extra body weight.

Chronic illness or condition diagnosed. More than half of people who live in north-central states (56 percent), compared to only 13 percent of those who live in eastern states, become depressed due to the onset of a chronic health problem. A larger percentage of people with care-giving responsibilities (65 percent), compared to those without such responsibilities (27 percent), indicate tendencies towards depression due to this event.

Community crisis or disaster. Nearly half (46 percent) of those in lower classes, compared to just one in ten of upper-class individuals, report depression as a result of community crises or disasters.

It Matters What and How We Think

A person's outlook on life also appears to affect his or her physical and emotional well-being. Pessimism is a state of mind that has a negative impact on the person's well-being. Regardless of age, pessimists are predominantly people in lower-income brackets. For example, we found that six in ten people over age 55 who have annual household incomes less than $35,000, compared with five in ten of those with higher incomes, often think that their prime years of life may be behind them. We also found that, when compared with optimists, pessimists worry more about the following:

- increasingly vulnerability to crime and fraud
- losing touch with friends and relatives
- being unable to participate in community and social activities
- being physically unable to do the required daily chores
- falling below their present standard of living
- being unable to retire in comfort
- being unable to leave an inheritance or legacy

On the other hand, optimists, who have a more positive outlook on life, tend to:

- have fewer health problems or chronic conditions
- be less concerned with having chronic health problems such as poor vision or hearing, diabetes, arthritis, and heart conditions
- be twice less likely to be concerned with changes in the shape of their bodies (32 percent vs. 68 percent)
- be less concerned with learning to do new things
- be much less concerned with changes in their skin and hair
- make less effort to look younger than they actually are

We have learned from our studies that achieving or maintaining good health in later stages of life requires more than taking good care of your body with exercise and healthy eating habits. It is also a matter of attitude. More specifically, good health depends on developing and maintaining a positive opinion of yourself, as well as the ability to deal with negative life circumstances that

Good health depends on developing and maintaining a positive opinion about yourself, as well as the ability to deal with negative life circumstances.

are likely to produce aversive psychological emotions. Such negative emotions and attitudes appear to be associated with poor health, possibly causing or facilitating the development of various physical ailments.

Much emphasis has been placed on achieving good health by means of exercising and eating healthy foods, but little attention has been paid to the psychological dimensions of well-being. We need to better understand how and why emotions and attitudes affect our physical health, and most importantly how desirable psychological orientations develop. Then we might be able to achieve better health by learning to effectively control our emotions.

CHAPTER FOUR

Lifestyles

DIFFERENCES IN THE LIFESTYLES of the baby boomers and their parents become increasingly apparent with age. This is because people, with age, experience an increasing number of life-changing events that alter their lifestyles. Because people live longer today, they have more time for life experiences than previous generations did. For example, life changes such as retirement will see many adults starting a new career, and a divorce between the ages of 40 and 50 may lead to another marriage and the beginning of a new family. We see "retirement" and "empty nest" stages being delayed until age 70 or later. Care-giving responsibilities for aging parents or grandchildren have propelled people into new extended stages of family life cycle and lifestyle. In this chapter, we focus on select aspects of people's lifestyles. Specifically, we will examine the living arrangements of people in middle and later years in life, how they spend their time, and some of the interests and priorities they assign to various discretionary activities. We focus on activities such as travel, work, volunteering, lifelong learning, attendance of religious services, and various events, as well as other hobbies and recreational activities. We have found significant differences in the lifestyles of the people belonging to these two generations, as well as in the lifestyles of individuals within each of these two cohorts.

Living Arrangements

Most people prefer to live in a single-family house. We questioned thousands of Americans about their future housing plans and preferences, and found that most people prefer to stay put, especially those who live in a single-family house. The longer a person lives in a single-family house, the less likely he or she wants to move. However, what a person wants to do in the future and what one actually plans to do are two different things. A 1990 study by the American Association of Retired Persons (AARP) concluded that 32 percent of Americans aged 60 or older expected to move, but only 13 percent preferred to do so, suggesting that one in five people expect to move against their wishes.

The largest majority of older adults have made no housing plans for the future, although they realize that they may have to eventually move to a different type of house. We found that while the largest majority of baby boomers (43 percent) plan to move to or stay in a single-family house, fewer than one in five (18 percent) of the older generation plan to do the same. A greater percentage of the older adults (15 percent) than baby boomers (11 percent) plan to live in an apartment, townhouse, or condominium in the future. A slightly greater percentage of baby boomers (10 percent) than their older counterparts (7 percent) plan to live in a retirement community without healthcare services. However, nearly as many baby boomers (20 percent) as seniors (23 percent) plan to live in a retirement community with healthcare services. Nearly one in twenty (5 percent) baby boomers plan to live in a nursing home at some future time, compared with 7 percent of those aged 65 and over.

Nearly as many baby boomers as seniors plan to live in a retirement community with healthcare services.

One consistent finding that emerges from several studies is that people prefer to move to age-integrated neighborhoods, communities, and buildings. Four in five older Americans prefer living in a neighborhood with people of all ages. Even among people who live in retirement communities, half of them would like to live with people of all ages, according to research done by the AARP.

Why do people want to move from a single-family house into other types of housing? It depends who you ask. There are significant generational differences in the reasons given by people who move from a single-family house into another type of home. In one of our studies, we found that a larger percentage of baby boomers than seniors are of the opinion that people move into an apartment, townhouse, or condominium because of the loss of a spouse (81 percent vs. 65 percent), to have freedom and independence (84 percent vs. 68 percent), to reduce housing costs (75 percent vs. 49 percent), and to be closer to relatives (50 percent). A smaller percentage of them feel they do so to have more social contacts (41 percent vs. 28 percent). Both generations agree that unwillingness or inability to perform house chores is a main reason for such a move (36 percent vs. 34 percent).

Who is likely to live in a townhouse or condominium? People in their 40s and 50s are those least likely to live in a townhouse, with only 10 percent of them preferring this type of housing arrangement. On the other hand, younger baby boomers and people aged 75 and older are those most likely to live in a townhouse, with nearly one-fourth of them declaring a preference for this type of housing.

The older a person gets the less likely he or she is to move from his or her home. We found the vast majority of homeowners do not intend to give up their houses. Within a period of 12 months, twice as many baby boomers as their parents purchased or sold a house (7 percent vs. 3 percent). Those who bought or sold a house had more education and were employed, compared with their less educated and unemployed counterparts. Those most likely to live in the same house tend to be women, live alone, and have less income than their counterparts who plan to move in the future.

The older a person gets the less likely he or she is to move from his or her home.

An increasing number of older people live with their relatives and do so for financial reasons at the expense of losing their independence, particularly in the case of lower-income groups. Slightly fewer than two-thirds of people aged 65 to 74, compared with half (46 percent) of those 75 and over, are of the opinion that many older people want to live with their children. Those who think that older people want to live with their children tend to have lower incomes. A larger percentage of older adults with lower incomes, compared with elderly adults with higher incomes, think they can count on someone to support them financially if their health fails.

Work After Retirement

Several demographic and social changes have been reshaping retirement as a life stage. These changes include the increasing number of women in the labor force, higher life expectancy, and an increasing number of baby boomers entering their pre-retirement years. Perhaps the most important consequence of these changes for the retirement crowd is their return to the labor force. According to a Cornell University study reported in a 2000 issue of *American Demographics* magazine, about 44 percent of people who have retired say they have worked for pay at some point after they retired. Surveys conducted among today's workers reveal new attitudes toward working after retirement, and depending on the age of workers, between two-thirds and 80 percent of those polled said they do not plan to retire fully.

Between two-thirds and 80 percent of those polled said they do not plan to retire fully.

What attracts people to work after retirement? Although the reasons differ slightly between those who are currently employed and those who have already retired, the two most important factors are finances and health. Nine in ten retirees who have worked after retirement said, in two surveys reported in *Business Week* and *American Demographics,* that they did so to "stay active, challenged and stimulated." While a large percentage of those still working plan to work after retirement for these same reasons, a much higher percentage of them than those who are currently retired mentioned a financial need as a main cause for post-retirement employment (43 percent vs. 25 percent). Many of the retirees and most of the baby boomers have not saved enough to finance the ever-increasing number of years that they are likely to spend in retirement.

What keeps retirees and those approaching retirement awake at night is probably concern about inadequate financial resources. Over the past 20 years, our research at the Center for Mature Consumer

Studies has repeatedly shown that a loss of financial independence is the major concern among people over age 55, along with the fear of becoming dependent on others due to deteriorating health. Not having enough money is considered a "very serious problem" among those over age 65, with 41 percent of them admitting to such concerns. When compared with the 32 percent of the over 65 crowd who consider poor health a very serious problem, it becomes clear that financial difficulties are a top concern, according to research done by the National Council on Aging.

What keeps retirees and those approaching retirement awake at night is probably concern about inadequate financial resources.

The financial situation of the pre-retirees, those in their late 40s and 50s, is of even greater concern, although many of them fail to realize the problem or do not want to admit it. For example, according to the 2005 AARP *Aging Indicators Study*, 70 percent of pre-retirees (aged 50 to 64) said they were confident they will have enough money to retire. But the reality is that pre-retirees today, most of whom are baby boomers, have failed to save enough for their retirement. Recent studies show that people who are 10 to 15 years away from retirement have saved an average of $50,000. A comprehensive landmark study by Professors James Moore and Olivia Mitchell of the Wharton School at the University of Pennsylvania, done for the National Institute on Aging in 1997, found that the median value of assets available to an average retiree over the remainder of his life is $325,000 (adjusted for inflation). This figure takes into account retirement savings, pension, Social Security benefits, and home equity. For the average person who, after retirement—at about age 62—is expected to live perhaps another 20 years, $50,000 in the bank account at retirement is substantially less than adequate for a comfortable retirement, especially in light of the growing healthcare costs. Even with coverage from Medicare, Fidelity Investments projects that a 65-year-old couple will need about $200,000 to cover 20 years of health costs, and that does not even include the cost of dental services, over-the-counter drugs, or long-term care—such as nursing home expenses currently estimated at an average of $70,000 annually.

Most retirees who leave their jobs before age 65—the age Medicare kicks in—face even steeper expenses because fewer and fewer workers receive retiree health benefits (13 percent in the private sector), and this trend is expected to continue, according to the Employee Benefit Research Institute. Health insurance premiums for a single person aged 60 to 64 averaged nearly $4,200 in 2004 (family policy premiums averaged $7,250), and these figures did not include deductibles, co-payments, and other out-of-pocket costs. For many workers, this is a good enough reason for delaying retirement. When a 2005 survey by the National Association for Variable Annuities asked pre-retirees, "What is your greatest fear about retirement?" the majority (28 percent) indicated "high health care costs," followed by "running out of money" (24 percent) and "inability to maintain standard of living" (18 percent). And while those nearing retirement are less likely to go without health insurance, an estimated 14 percent of baby boomers do lack coverage.

Additional commercial and academic studies, including several produced by the Pension Research Council at Wharton School in 2006, point to inadequate financial preparation of baby boomers for retirement. Researchers at the University of Pennsylvania found that baby boomer wealth was nearly 15 percent lower than that of people their age 12 years ago. Similarly, the Center for Retirement Research at Boston College found that 43 percent of working households in 2004 were at risk of having too little income to fund retirement, an increase from 31 percent in 1983.

Studies have also tried to uncover the reasons for the less than adequate financial preparation among baby boomers. Based on findings of our own studies and those of other researchers, we have identified three main reasons. The first reason is financial illiteracy that is widespread among older Americans. Surveys of some 22,000 persons, sponsored by the National Institute on Aging along with the Social Security Administration and administered by the University of Michigan bi-annually since 1992, find that the main reason people fail to plan for retirement is due to their lack of knowledge about basic financial

People fail to plan for retirement because they lack of knowledge of basic financial concepts.

concepts such as compounding interest and inflation, a conclusion also reached by Wharton School researchers in 2006.

The second reason for inadequate retirement savings, we believe, can be found in the baby boomers' attitudes toward saving and spending. Our research on baby boomers that started in the mid-1970s when many of them were still teenagers has revealed that baby boomers took for granted and considered necessities things their parents considered luxury products, such as homes, cars and major appliances. This generation of consumers was brought up during prosperous times, in comparison with their parents who had experienced economic hardships during the Great Depression years. Unwilling to do without these "necessities," baby boomers have been inclined to spend, and even go into debt to own them, which does not leave much money in their bank accounts. Emily Kessler of the Society of Actuaries shares this explanation. As she put it in her presentation at the 2006 Wharton Impact conference, "They have not known, as a cohort, what it's like to do without." Their attitudes toward material possessions are translated into actions. For example, in the mid-1980s, a time when the older baby boomers should have already saved for retirement, the research we conducted with Dr. Thomas Stanley, a former colleague and co-author of the best-selling book, *The Millionaire Next Door*, found that the average BMW owner—typically an older boomer—had just $3,000 in savings while the younger owners were in debt.

> *Baby boomers took for granted and considered necessities things their parents considered luxury products, such as homes, cars and major appliances*

The third reason for less than adequate retirement savings is cultural; it relates to people's orientations to relevant time horizons. In comparison with with people in Eastern cultures like Japan's that are long-term oriented, Americans tend to set shorter time-horizons in achieving their goals. They are more impatient in getting or doing the things they desire in life. This point is exemplified in a statement recently made by Brian Perlman of Matthew Greenwald & Associates, who studied investing and spending decisions three to four years from retirement: "If you ask people what they want in retirement they talk about going to Italy for a year. They don't talk about the health consequences until you scratch the surface. They look at health as a long-term expense and enjoying life as a short-term expense."

So what does a lack of adequate financial preparation for retirement mean for retirees and businesses? First, it means people have to work longer and save more, or accept a lower standard of living after retirement. Whatever decision the older person makes, he or she is likely to need the help of a financial advisor as retirement approaches. Asset-management services and a wide variety of financial-planning tools are needed for both working retirees as well as those who think they have saved enough. The increasing number of years spent in retirement increases the need for a wider array of financial strategies that will help retirees stretch their savings over a longer period of time. The emphasis of these financial strategies is likely to shift from asset preservation, which characterized the retirement plans of previous generations, to growth strategies. Increasing life expectancy is also likely to widen the gap of life expectancy between the sexes, contributing to a larger number of widows, many of whom will need assistance in managing finances. Thus, financial institutions are likely to be faced with diverse customer demands and opportunities for providing a wide variety of services to people not only before retirement, but well into the later years of life as well.

The increasing number of years spent in retirement increases the need for a wider array of financial strategies that will help retirees stretch their savings over a longer period of time.

Lifelong Learning

The need and desire to learn new things is a lifelong objective, but it intensifies later in life. Depending on the subject matter, we see different levels of interest among age groups and between the two generations. For example, one of our recent surveys found that general interest in adult education classes is greater among the older generation (older than age 60) than among baby boomers in general (ages 42 to 60), with 26 percent and 16 percent expressing interest, respectively. In particular, those aged 55 to 64 express the greatest interest, with 36 percent, and those in the 75 and older crowd are the least interested, with only 12 percent. Women are twice as interested as men in adult education, with 25 percent and 12 percent, respectively, and a larger percentage of people who live in eastern states (25 percent) than those who live in the South (14 percent) and the West (15 percent) express interest. The people most interested in adult education are those who live alone, are still in the work force, are in higher social classes, and whose parents are still alive. In another study, we found those who like to take short, self-improvement type of courses, such as learning to use the computer, tend to be older, better educated, live in working households, are in relatively good health, and have deceased parents.

Our research also shows that interest in specific adult education classes such as art and crafts, music or other similar subjects, is higher among baby boomers than among their parents, with 27 percent and 11 percent expressing interest in or having participated in such classes, respectively. Once again, we found that women are more interested than men, with 24 percent of women and only 14 percent of men expressing a desire to take adult education classes. Those with higher levels of education and income tend to be more interested than people with less education or financial resources.

It is the younger baby boomer (born between 1956 and 1964) who is most likely to visit the public library. Nearly three-fourths (or 77 percent) of younger baby boomers, compared with 61 percent of older baby boomers, are likely to be frequent library patrons. As they age, people tend to frequent the public library less, but among the older adults, it is those with higher education and income that are the most frequent users of their library card. Women visit the library more often than men, as do those who are employed and live with others.

However, people in the older generation are also becoming enthusiastic students. The number of senior students more than doubled in the 1990s, with one in five adults aged 65 and over reporting some level of participation in learning activities in the pervious 12 months. For those aged 55 to 64, about four in ten report participation in such learning activities, according to the National Center for Education Statistics. The AARP estimates that the number of people back in school is even higher, with 35 percent of the group aged 65 and older and 52 percent of those between the ages of 55 and 64 attending adult education classes of some kind.

The growing interest in adult education is the result of several demographic and social changes. The recent trend of early retirement and the reality of less-than-adequate retirement savings means that most adults in mid-life find that they will need employment income after retirement. According to Annette Buchanan, author of *Lifelong Learning*, 56 percent of the people between the ages of 55 and 64 seek education for specific job skills. But many retirees also see education as an opportunity for personal growth, as many of them are becoming increasingly aware of the joys that learning can bring to one's life. For example, at age 69, Milton Smith, who had retired 10 years earlier from his job as an Eastern Airlines pilot, decided to pursue a graduate degree in business administration. At age 71, he became Georgia Tech's oldest student to receive an MBA. And yet Milton had no plans to use his degree for employment. He was only interested in completing a program of studies that he found stimulating and self-enhancing.

Milton is just one of the thousands of people in the older generation who go back to college to fulfill their dreams of an education that earlier life circumstances did not allow them to pursue. The challenging task of getting a college degree so late in life enhances the older person's self-esteem and overall sense of well-being.

Of course, there are other reasons why older retirees go back to school. Classes allow them to interact with others, make new friends, and stay socially engaged. In a way, school becomes a substitute for social networks such as co-workers or family members that tend to diminish in a person's later years due to retirement, empty-nest syndrome, or perhaps the loss of a spouse. Many older students enjoy the added benefit of learning skills such as financial management that they suddenly find necessary due to unexpected life transitions or roles for which they did not adequately prepare earlier in life. According to the AARP's *Survey of Lifelong Learning* in 2000, adults aged 50 and older are interested in learning so that they can "keep in touch with themselves, their community, and the world. " Furthermore, these adults are most interested in learning about subjects that would "improve the quality of their lives, build upon current skills, or enable them to take better care of their health."

Educational institutions are responding to the growing learning needs of older students. Presently, there are approximately 2,000 schools in the United States offering programs that target older adults. Courses created for older Americans have included such diverse topics as science, arts and crafts, business, music, computer instruction, home management and financial planning. We have already begun to see universities and other nonprofit organizations offering a wide variety of courses, seminars and educational resources on topics such as financial management and caregiving. Many of these courses are free to older adults, and retired volunteers recognized as experts in their fields frequently lead these offerings. As of 2004, older adults could actually live in college- or university-linked senior housing on more than 60 campuses, according to the *Journal of Active Aging*.

The adult education trend is expected to continue and grow at a faster rate as the baby boomers enter retirement and pre-retirement years. The vast majority of them want to work, but many of their skills are likely to become obsolete due to rapid technological changes. Thus, there should be increasing interest in vocational and job training, something we have already begun to witness. The demand for adult education is also likely to become increasingly more diverse, creating opportunities for the development of a wide variety of courses and seminars that could be delivered through many kinds of instructional systems. Several examples of new course diversity can be seen in the University of Delaware's "Academy of Lifelong Learning" where recently 1,400 students aged 55 and over participated in 110 different courses. Programs that

The adult education trend is expected to continue and grow at a faster rate as the baby boomers enter retirement and pre-retirement years.

would have the greatest popularity are most likely to be those that satisfy older adults' independence needs–for example, those that help retirees maintain their health and financial well-being, courses that promote good health habits and methods of disease prevention, driver training, and effective financial management.

Leisure

Travel

Travel is the number one leisure activity for persons of any age, since almost everyone wants to travel. Even those who have limited time and resources find ways to escape from the daily monotony once in a while. We found in our recent surveys that parents are those who pack their suitcase more frequently for all types of trips. One in three of them, compared with one in five of their baby boomer children, said they travel "quite often or very often." But when it comes to traveling for extended periods of time, we have found that people at nearly every stage in life are equally likely to travel, with the exception of those over age 75. Slightly more than 40 percent of all adults under age 75 take long vacations annually, compared with 27 percent of the elderly over age 75. The more money people have, the farther they can travel and the more days they can afford to be on vacation. Married people with fewer chronic conditions and higher levels of self-esteem are the prime candidates for lengthy trips.

Travel-service marketers entice customers to use their services by providing a wide variety of promotional incentives. Travel membership or discount programs such as frequent flier cards are widely used in the travel industry. We found that 36 percent of all adults in the U.S. currently belong to such membership groups. One in four baby boomers and four in 10 of their parents have special travel memberships or discount cards for airlines, hotels, or car rental companies. Not surprisingly, those with higher incomes and education levels, as well as those living with others, are the individuals most likely to use such promotional programs.

When it comes to foreign travel, again there are few differences in behavior and preferences between the two generations and across age brackets. About one in three of all adults in the U.S. has a valid passport. Those with annual household incomes of $35,000 or more are more than twice as likely as those with lower incomes to have a valid passport, 47 percent versus 19 percent, respectively. More than half (or 53 percent) of those with an annual income greater than $50,000 are ready to travel abroad as soon as they have the opportunity. People living in urban areas are twice more likely than their rural counterparts to travel abroad (36 percent vs. 16 percent). And those living in western states are more likely than those living in north-central states to be world travelers, with 42 percent and 26 percent expressing interest in traveling abroad, respectively. We have also found that one in seven adults travels abroad annually, regardless of age.

Travel seems to be the most common and pleasant activity associated with retirement. When people were asked to indicate whether, during retirement, they currently participate or plan to participate in various forms of leisure travel, almost all retirees (96 percent) and those still working (98 percent) indicated their participation in domestic travel. About two in three retirees have a passport, and as many of those who still work plan to travel aboard. In comparison with those who are retired, those who still work plan to take more cruises and bus tours, buy an RV, or do more adventure traveling, according to a survey reported by *Business Week* magazine.

About two in three retirees have a passport, and as many of those who still work plan to travel aboard.

The findings of this and other surveys suggest that most people approaching their retirement years are looking forward to having fun, more so than any preceding generation. Many middle-aged people of this "sandwiched" generation have been living their lives to help others rather than living for themselves. Fun has been in short supply for baby boomers who have been struggling with the crises of their middle years. They are looking forward to experiencing the good times that are currently lacking in their lives. However, given that many present and future retirees are or will be constrained by work and limited financial resources, travel for many may mean weekends of driving short distances from home and staying at budget motels. But for the smaller percentage of people who are financially well off, physically fit, and not working during retirement, travel will include cruises, safaris, and the promise of exotic destinations.

Whichever way current and future retirees choose to entertain themselves, the diverse leisure lifestyles of the 78 million baby boomers are likely to continue creating business opportunities for the global hospitality industry. The demand for travel and leisure services is likely to increase, especially among older women, as the financial situation of this group continues to improve. Because of the increasing likelihood of being alone in late life, the industry will respond with creative programs to entice the single-woman traveler. Some examples we have already seen include Royal Viking Cruise Line's program that employs single, older men who are available to interact socially with older women passengers, and the ElderHostel and Grandtravel tours designed for grandparents and their grandchildren. The recent terrorist activities notwithstanding, the long-term prospects for the travel and leisure industry are favorable. Conflicting factors such as higher life expectancy, increased ability to travel due to better health, but more monetary and time constraints means there will be more diverse travel and leisure demands from retirees. It is likely that it will be increasingly necessary for businesses to create travel opportunities and services for every budget to satisfy the diverse travel needs and take advantage of this booming market. A recent AMEX-AARP venture appears to capitalize on these trends, offering more than 100 packaged travel arrangements for a range of tastes and budgets.

At-home leisure activities

Television viewing is the most popular at-home entertainment activity. Most people spend more time watching television than engaging in any other at-home activity with the exception of sleeping. The older generation watches more TV than their baby boomer children; the average older parent

Television viewing is the most popular at-home entertainment activity.

spends nearly six hours daily watching television whereas baby boomers watch much less.

We found that about half of the adult population watches comedy and drama programs on a daily basis. Viewers of TV comedy shows tend to be older, with lower education and income levels. They tend to live alone and are more likely to live in southern or north-central states than in other parts of the country. Parents of baby boomers watch more TV dramas than their children. Relative to their counterparts in other demographic groups, these shows are watched more by women with less income and education who live alone and are no longer employed.

People stay up-to-date on current events by watching television news programs more than from any other news source, such as newspapers, radio or Internet. In fact, 77 percent of baby boomers and 92 percent of their parents watch the news on a daily basis. Those in the oldest age groups, as well as the unemployed or retired, are most likely to watch the evening news. Preference for television talk shows focusing exclusively on topics of interest to people at various stages in life, such as health, shopping, finances, politics, and housing, is stronger among those in the older generation than among their children, and is especially strong among those aged 65 and older who live with their children.

People stay informed by watching television news programs more than by newspapers, radio or the Internet.

When it comes to watching premium cable television, baby boomers are the most regular viewers. Thirty percent of them, compared with 22 percent of their parents, pay for subscription to cable channels such as HBO and Cinemax. However, the level of subscription to such channels is relatively high among the "young olds," or those aged 55 to 64, but drops sharply among the older age groups. People who have the most education and income are the heaviest users of these entertainment services, as are those who are still in the labor force and live with others.

Use of home entertaining devices which allows one to control their television viewing times, such as a DVD player, is higher among the younger generation, judging from our research on 2005 ownership of these appliances that shows three in 10 baby boomers own a DVD player, in comparison with one-third of the older generation. This finding is consistent with earlier findings of our studies on the leisure-related lifestyles of the two generations involving the use of VCRs, which also showed two-thirds of baby boomers were using VCRs on a daily basis, compared with only 18 percent of their parents. These findings suggest a continuity of the entertainment-related activities, lifestyles and attitudes toward technological innovations among baby boomers; and they make the case that these orientations will persist in later stages of their lives, painting a different picture of tomorrow's retirees in comparison with their more technology averse parents.

We also have found that people in the older generation are avid readers of magazines. One-third of the older group compared with one-fourth of the baby boomers, read three or more magazines on a regular basis. Those with the most money and education read magazines the most, as do those who are out of the work force. Women read more magazines than men, as do those living alone. People living in southern and western states read more than people living in other parts of the country. However, these readership patterns tend to vary across *types* of magazines. For example, readership of science or arts and crafts magazines is twice as high among men as among women, and westerners are twice as likely to read such magazines on a regular basis than people in other parts of the country. People in the higher social classes, compared with those from lower classes, tend to be the more enthusiastic readers of magazines with arts and science contents.

The older generation are avid readers of magazines.

Just about every older person reads the newspaper on a regular basis. Among literate adults, 90 percent of those in the older generation read the paper frequently, compared with two-thirds of baby boomers, according to one of our studies. In another large-scale national study, we found less than half (47 percent) of baby boomers read the newspaper on a daily basis, compared with 85 percent of their parents, and the most affluent tend to read more frequently. On the other hand, baby boomers listen to the radio more than their parents. According to one of our studies, three-fourths of baby boomers listen to the radio daily, compared with a little over half (57 percent) of their parents. Although radio listening declines with age, it is more frequent among the most educated, wealthiest residents of southern and north-central states.

Attendance at events

When it comes to attending special events, baby boomers do not seem to be as interested as their parents in participating. Eighteen percent of the older group compared with just 13 percent of baby boomers, are season ticket holders to theater, ballet, concert series, or sporting events. In two of our surveys we conducted at the Center for Mature Consumer Studies in the past two years, respondents in the older generation indicated a higher frequency of attendance at various events (social, cultural, sports, etc.) than did their baby boomer children. People with higher income and more education are more likely to attend such events. This is not to say that baby boomers are hermits when it comes to having fun. On the contrary, they are likely to go out periodically, but their attendance habits are more sporadic. For example, twice as many baby boomers as their parents attend some type of cultural event annually. But baby boomers tend to change their habits and preferences regarding cultural events, whereas their parents have more stable attendance habits. Males show more stable event-attendance patterns than females. People with higher income and education levels show greater propensity to change their attendance patterns, as do those living alone and still working. Thus, contrary to the widely-held stereotypes of older persons as "isolated," "inactive," and "recluses," our recent findings suggest quite the opposite.

Other leisure activities

While there is a great deal of variability in preferences for other types of leisure activities, the vast majority of baby boomers and their parents report they have a regular hobby or recreational activity. Besides watching TV and reading, a large number of people in both generations (half of baby boomers and 57 percent of their parents) report engagement in some type of "do-it-yourself" hobby or activity. *Gardening* is among the most popular outdoor activities. While baby boomers and their parents are equally likely to garden, people garden the most right after retirement, with 71 percent of the 65-to-74 age bracket reporting that they garden annually. People who are most likely to engage in this and other similar types of "do-it-yourself" activities, like woodworking or knitting, tend to be in middle-income families and are empty nesters living with their spouse.

Nearly half of those aged 55 to 74 engage in some type of *gambling or game of chance*, compared with lower percentage figures for the younger and older age groups. In another study, we found the same age group (55 to 74 years) to be more likely than other age groups to report that they took on a new hobby or recreational activity during the previous 12 months. Women are far more likely than men to take on a new hobby, with 33 percent versus 20 percent of them likely to do so within a 12-month period, respectively. One-third of people living in eastern states, compared with one-fifth of those living in western and north-central states, tend to take on a new hobby or recreational activity every year, and unmarried people are more likely to do so than those who are married.

While nearly all adults *eat out*, those who patronize restaurants at an increasing rate are the baby boomers, not their parents. Four in ten of the former group, compared with three in ten of the latter, increased their visits to restaurants in a year's time, according to one of our most recent surveys. Women are more likely than men to report increased frequency of eating away from home, as were those people still in the workforce. Finally, people with low self-esteem reported that they ate out more often than usual during the previous 12 months, compared to those with high self-esteem (41 percent vs. 33 percent, respectively).

Another favorite pastime is *shopping*, especially among women. Baby boomers are likely to go shopping as often as their parents, our surveys in the last two years show. Women are more likely than men to go shopping to take their minds off things, with 19 percent and 7 percent, respectively, reporting such activity in the previous 12 months. One in five (or 22 percent) of baby boomers, but only one in ten of their parents, admit to shopping as a way to relax or escape from daily stresses.

Volunteering

Volunteering is another activity that is becoming increasingly popular among baby boomers and their parents. While a significant percentage of adults in both generations volunteer, engagement in such activities increases sharply upon retirement. More than five million adults aged 65 and over are estimated to provide services to various charitable organizations, a number that represents an increase of about 50 percent over the 1990s. According to *American Demographics* magazine's analysis of MediaMark Research Inc.'s data in 2000, 20 percent of the group aged 70 to 74 volunteer for various organizations. However, our 2005 surveys found one in five adults in the two generations volunteers often, a finding that translates into larger numbers of baby boomer and older volunteers.

Volunteering provides rich rewards during a person's retirement years. It helps an older person combat social disengagement and maintain his or her social well-being and self-worth. Research indicates that those most likely to volunteer tend to have higher incomes, are college-educated, and participate in religious activities as well, since 70 percent of volunteers attend religious services once a week, according to Susan Chamber, author of *Good Deeds in Old Age*.

Regardless of background characteristics, adults in general make special efforts to help others through volunteerism. When asked about their concern with their ability to perform volunteer work, the number of adults expressing such a concern ranged from two-thirds to nearly ninety percent in three different surveys. However, there is some consistency in the profiles of those most interested in volunteer work. They tend to be women aged 65 to 74, from lower- to middle-class families. People in the older generation volunteer more than baby boomers, while older baby boomers appear to be more charitable than their younger counterparts.

The number of older volunteers is expected to increase in the next 20 to 30 years as baby boomers begin to retire in large numbers and remain unemployed. Several surveys that were conducted in the 1990s and reported by senior author George Moschis in an article published in *Generations* in 2001, show that baby boomers plan to engage in various types of volunteer work after retirement. For example, one study found that 74 percent of executives planned to become actively involved in some type of volunteer work after retirement. Fifty-three percent expected to work with charities, 26 percent expected to work voluntarily for business organizations, and 18 percent expected to work for political organizations. Another study found that half of the 50- to 75-year-olds ranked volunteering or community service as the most important part of their retirement plans, second only to travel (57 percent).

There are over 350 centralized volunteer clearinghouses or volunteer action centers across the country. These are connected with numerous senior programs and operate on national and local levels. Experts say that we will need more and different types of community centers to harness the energies of aging but still healthy baby boomers who have "giving back" high on their late-life "to do" list, but also to effectively put the talents of the retirees to better use. An example of an emerging model is the Life Option Center, which was conceived by Marc Freedman, author of *Prime Time: How Baby Boomers Will Revolutionize Retirement and Transform America*. The center offers personal, financial or career-transition guidance, fitness facilities and spiritual exploration, all at a single location. There are likely to be increasing opportunities for the creation of such centers to better serve the needs of aging volunteers as well as those of communities.

Religiosity

Many people faced with difficult situations in their lives turn to God for assistance and comfort. Religiosity seems to increase with age.

In one of our earlier studies, we found that a larger percentage of people in the older generation (41 percent), compared with the younger generation (31 percent), indicated that they frequently attend religious services, praying for help with daily problems. But one of our more recent studies found larger numbers of churchgoers in each of the two generations, with 48 percent and 37 percent of respondents indicating frequent attendance of religious services, respectively. A larger percentage of women than men in the two groups pray for help and guidance in solving problems. People who turn to religion for the same reason tend to be better educated, live with others, are still employed, and have living parents.

As people age, they tend to become more religious, shown by an increase in attendance of religious services. One of our studies found that 16 percent of the people in the older generation, compared with 9 percent of the younger adults, indicated a change in their attendance of religious services in the previous 12 months. Older baby boomers reported the greatest change, with 21 percent of them (compared with 12 percent of younger baby boomers) indicating increased patronage. Adults in both generations with high levels of education reported the greatest change, 17 percent versus 10 percent of the less educated. A larger percentage of those living in southern states (17 percent), compared with those living in western states (8 percent) and eastern states (11 percent), reported a change in their religious activities in the previous 12 months.

Caregiving

The lifestyles of many people in both generations include a heavy dose of caregiving responsibilities and related activities. *Caregiving* is becoming a major part of everyday life. In 1990, there were an estimated 7 million caregivers in the U.S. At the time of this writing in late 2006, we suspected that this number had increased to nearly 50 million people, a seven-fold increase over the 15-year time span, based on the results of a national telephone survey of 1,000 adults conducted by Opinion Research Corporation for Johnson &

Johnson in late 2005. The study estimated a little over 46 million Americans were providing unpaid care to an adult relative or friend at the time. Our studies have found that there are as many caregivers among baby boomers as there are among their parents. Twenty-six percent of baby boomers provide care to their parents, and slightly more (29 percent) of *their parents* provide care to their own elderly parents. These figures are right on target with those provided by the National Alliance of Caregivers that estimated the caregivers on a household basis at 23 percent in 2004, and those of the more recent Johnson & Johnson survey that estimated caregivers on an *individual* basis at 22 percent of the adult U.S. population. Statistics released by the former organization help us describe the average caregiver better by showing their characteristics in numbers and percentages: females (60 percent), married or living with a partner (66 percent), have children under 18 living at home (41 percent), employed full-time (52 percent), average age (46), median family income ($35,000), caregivers' out-of-pocket monthly expenses ($221), and average age of their care recipient (77).

In addition, our research found that approximately four in ten people in *both* generations provide some type of assistance to other relatives. Specifically, we found that one in six baby boomers and their parents assume the increased burden of responsibilities for their aged relatives annually. But people between ages 55 and 65 are burdened the most. Twenty-three percent of adults in this age group experience added responsibilities, and another 30 percent expect these obligations to increase in the near future. Among women, who are the primary caregivers, one in five, in comparison with one in eight men, assume new or added responsibilities each year, and another 30 percent of them (compared with 21 percent of men) expect to assume additional caregiving responsibilities for aged relatives in the near future. Another distinctive characteristic of caregivers is that they tend to be currently employed, with almost two-thirds of caregivers employed full or part-time. The typical caregiver is also likely to have children at home, with one-third of

About four in ten people in both generations provide some type of assistance to other relatives.

them currently living with their dependent children.

Caregiving is normally provided in the form of assistance with activities of daily living, such as fixing meals and housekeeping, as well as with other tasks and chores, such as shopping or running errands. Both types of activities demand time and can be periodically stressful. In fact, our research reveals that the assumption of added caregiving responsibilities is a major reason for elevated levels of chronic stress. The more concerned people are about their aging parents, the higher the level of stress they experience on a day-to-day basis. About two-thirds of baby boomers and 28 percent of their parents report that they are concerned about their ability to care for their aging parents. Those in higher socioeconomic classes are more concerned about this matter than those in lower socio-economic groups.

Added caregiving responsibilities is a major reason for elevated levels of chronic stress.

The amount and type of assistance care givers provide to their relatives depends on the caregiver's gender and income. Here are some examples of assistance provided by caregivers to their older relatives, keeping in mind that women and those with the least money tend to be the primary caregivers:

- Twice as many women as men caregivers help prepare meals.
- Three times as many women as men help their older relatives with personal grooming.
- Twice as many women as men help their dependent relatives decide what gifts to buy.
- Assistance with running errands is most commonly provided by those in the lower-income brackets.

Caregivers to older people are expected to do everything under the sun, including grocery shopping, home maintenance, purchase and repair of products, and driving the older person to different places. But not every caregiver is competent at performing these various tasks, in part due to different gender roles. For instance, men may not be as competent as women at doing household chores such as cooking and cleaning, while women may not be as competent as men at doing home maintenance and repairs.

Regardless of gender, we know from our previous research that most people are not prepared to become family caregivers, a finding that is reinforced by results of the Johnson & Johnson survey. This survey found 58 percent of the adult respondents were only "somewhat" or "not at all" prepared to handle health insurance matters for an adult family member or friend; 56 percent were unprepared to assist with medications; and nearly two-thirds of them were not comfortable with the idea of selling the home of a loved one and moving that person to another location, or settling a will or trust for that person. For this reason, it is not uncommon for a caregiver to request assistance and for the care recipient to have more than one care provider assisting them in different ways. Interestingly, having several siblings does not seem to relieve the caregiver from his or her responsibilities. And because extra help is not likely to come from within one's family, caregivers must turn to organizations that can help. It is for this reason that major caregiving organizations have stepped up their campaigns recently to assist and support caregivers with information, materials and expert advice, such as those available at the website: *www.strengthforcaring.com*.

The Johnson & Johnson survey found 58 percent of the adult respondents were only "somewhat" or "not at all" prepared to handle health insurance matters for an adult family member or friend.

Preparing for Old Age

How well do people in the two generations understand the needs of older adults? How well prepared are they to enjoy their last stages of life? In order to answer these and other related questions, we first tried to find out how much individuals know about the needs of older people. We developed a list of facts that apply mostly to older people and life during old age, and then asked several hundred people in the two generations to tell us whether each of these facts applies mostly to older people or younger people, or to indicate if they did not know or were not sure. We found some interesting differences in the perceptions of old age and old people among the U.S. adult population, as well as between the two generations.

Awareness of older adults' needs

The adult population is least aware of the older person's experience of stress. Only a little over 60 percent of the adults in this country are aware that the elderly encounter stress in day-to-day living. People's awareness of this fact increases with age, with half of baby boomers, in comparison with nearly two-thirds of their parents, being aware of late -life stresses. Middle-income adults are those most aware of the stress older people in their day-to-day living conditions feel, with two-thirds of them reporting such an awareness, compared with 55 percent of adults in the lower and upper-income groups.

> Only a little over 60 percent of the adults in this country are aware that the elderly encounter stress in day-to-day living.

Two in three adults know that the elderly need to take naps frequently, with a larger percentage of men (69 percent) than women (60 percent) being aware of this need. Seven in ten adults know that older people need to use the bathroom more frequently, but a larger percentage of the older generation than baby boomers are aware of this need, with 75 percent and 57 percent declaring such knowledge, respectively.

Three in four people, especially those with higher incomes, know that the elderly have special dietary needs. About the same number of people are aware of the fact that a person's ability to smell and taste chemical substances, such as food, declines in late life, and about three in four know that older people do not need to eat as much food as younger people.

The highest level of awareness exists with respect to older people's ability to remember recent events and their risk of having a fatal fall at their homes, with nearly nine in ten (or 87 percent) of adults being aware of these facts. But not as many adults know that the elderly find new tasks harder to learn, with only 72 percent of them indicating awareness.

Preparation for old age

Our research has uncovered overwhelming evidence that the average person is not adequately prepared to enjoy the later stages of life. The poor health condition of baby boomers has already been discussed and we will not dwell on it again. The same goes for their financial preparation. But there are additional actions one must plan for or take that could enhance a person's well-being in later life as well as that of his or her relatives. In one of our national studies, we presented more than 1,200 adults with a list of decisions and actions considered wise things to do or have in old age or beforehand. We then asked our study participants if they had done each in preparation for old age.

We found that two in three adults in the older generation in this country have a will, compared with only four in ten baby boomers. The more income people earn, the more likely they are to have a will. Almost one in seven adults has made funeral arrangements, with a smaller percentage (12 percent) of those with greater-than-average income, compared with their lower-income counterparts (19 percent), indicating that they have made funeral plans. A relatively small percentage of the adult population talks to their relatives about leaving a legacy or inheritance to their heirs. Women are more likely to discuss these matters than men, with one in four adult women, compared with 18 percent of adult men, indicating that they have had such discussions with their heirs.

Two in three adults in the older generation in this country have a will, compared with only four in ten baby boomers.

One way baby boomers think they can better prepare for old age is by purchasing additional life insurance. Nearly half (46 percent) of baby boomers, compared with one-third of their parents, have purchased additional life insurance in preparation for older life. Apparently, baby boomers view life insurance as a vehicle for family protection because of the increasing likelihood of their death with age in middle and late life. Moreover, people in both generations save whatever they can for their retirement years. And while eight in ten of the people in the older generation and two-thirds of baby boomers have put money aside for their retirement years, we found that this money does not amount to substantial savings for retirement.

Nearly one in ten baby boomers, in comparison with one in three of their parents, have decided on a place for retirement. Men are more likely than women to make a decision on a location for retirement. It appears that people with limited financial resources are likely to stay put and are not concerned with the decision of finding a place for retirement. We found that those who earn less than $20,000 annually are twice less likely than those with higher incomes to have made alternative housing arrangements.

These findings indicate that neither baby boomers who are approaching retirement years nor their parents are adequately prepared for late life. Old age is a life stage nobody wants to experience, much less prepare for, but some people do a better job than others in preparing for it. We tried to learn why some people are better prepared for old age, and found that being a caregiver to an older relative helps people better understand the older person's needs and the lifestyles of the aged. Specifically, people who have been caregivers, compared with those who had never assumed such responsibilities, are more aware of older adults' needs. In addition, caregivers have done more to prepare for old age, regardless of their age. Having adequate income helps people plan for their desired lifestyles in late life. Based on this study, we concluded that there is little formal preparation for old age, and learning of older people's needs and desired lifestyles tends to be incidental.

CHAPTER FIVE

Financial Affairs

WHEN IT COMES to handling money, baby boomers are far from being carbon copies of their parents. On the contrary, our research found several interesting and surprising generational differences in these people's financial habits and economic choices. We found that people in these age groups differ with respect to their need for *saving* versus *spending* their assets and the reasons for doing so.

Spending Habits

Baby boomers and their elderly parents spend their money in a rather similar way, with one major exception—the older group is more charitable. One in three older individuals, in comparison with 16 percent of baby boomers, give more than five percent of their income to charities. Similarly, the older group gives more to relatives in the form of gifts of cash and securities.

While spending habits do not differ significantly between the two generations, their attitudes toward spending versus saving are rather different. Baby boomers were found to be favorably oriented toward spending, in comparison with their parents' more conservative attitudes. Half of the baby boomers, compared with three in ten of the older generation, admitted that they enjoy spending money more than they enjoy saving it. The result of a positive attitude toward spending is usually larger credit-card debt. When the same people in our study were asked to tell us if they pay the entire balance on their monthly credit-card statements, nearly 30 percent of baby boomers, in comparison with 17 percent of their parents, said they seldom pay off the entire balance. Regardless of generation, those from lower social classes and those living with others have more difficulty paying off credit card debt than their counterparts from higher social classes who live alone.

As expected, those who have more money tend to spend more, regardless of age. Even among retirees, we found evidence that suggests a greater inclination to spend among those with more assets. For example, in one survey we found nearly three-fourths of those aged 65 and over with assets in excess of $100,000 agreed with the statement, "Retirees should enjoy their money by spending all of it," in comparison with 59 percent of those with fewer assets.

Use of credit

As we mentioned earlier, the baby boomers' favorable attitude toward credit is translated into larger credit-card debt. Baby boomers report higher use of credit cards than their parents, and typically those with higher levels of education, more income, living in urban areas with their spouse, and still working report the most credit use. Baby boomers are somewhat more likely than their parents to use a VISA card, 74 percent versus 68 percent, respectively. Twenty-one percent of baby boomers and 16 percent of their parents use American Express cards. The older generation tends to make more use of department store cards, with 74 percent of the older group and 66 percent of baby boomers owning such credit cards. Males tend to use MasterCard and American Express more than females, though it is women who tend to use more department store cards.

One of our studies was designed to address questions concerning the use of credit cards at various stages of life. The study results dispel the conventional belief that older people do not use credit cards because they have negative connotations of credit due to, for example, the Great Depression years. Credit card use does not significantly differ with respect to different age groups. A major finding that emerges from this study is that older people may use credit cards less frequently due to changes in their lifestyles and

Older people may use credit cards less frequently due to changes in their lifestyles and other circumstances associated with age, and not age per se.

other circumstances associated with age, and not age *per se*. Rather, various circumstances may create or suppress opportunities to use credit cards. For example, after people retire they do not have as many occasions that require them to use their credit cards, whereas baby boomers may pay for a variety of work-related purchases and usually use their credit cards. Among those who have equal opportunities to buy things, there is no difference in credit card usage between the two generations. Similarly, the study found that ownership and use of credit cards was fairly similar among younger and older adults with annual incomes over $40,000. We concluded from this and other studies that *baby boomers use credit to finance a higher standard of living, while their parents use credit for convenience.*

> Baby boomers use credit to finance a higher standard of living, while their parents use credit for convenience.

The younger generation is more favorably disposed to using credit and they do not hesitate to put themselves in debt. Baby boomers use a greater number of cards to spread debt and they make use of revolving credit to a greater extent than their parents. In a national study of 695 adults, we found that 37 percent of baby boomers, in comparison with only 12 percent of their parents, had taken on major credit-card debt during the previous 12 months. Another 31 percent of baby boomers, compared with only 8 percent of the older generation, had made the minimum payment on credit cards. In another study of 666 adults, we found that nearly half (46 percent) of baby boomers, in comparison with 17 percent of their parents, experienced a significant increase in charge or credit-card debt during the previous three years.

More baby boomers than adults in the older generations value a personal line of credit or overdraft privilege, with 45 percent versus 36 percent reporting such a preference, respectively. Individuals who appreciate this service tend to be younger, better educated, have higher incomes and more assets, and live in urban areas with their children.

Why the greater inclination to spend among baby boomers? It may be because baby boomers were brought up during more prosperous times than their parents and thus became accustomed to a higher standard of living. This translates into a more liberal attitude toward spending and a general attitude favoring spending money over saving it. In one of our large-scale studies, we found that people who enjoy spending money more than saving it, in comparison with those who prefer saving over spending, were twice as likely to seek immediate gratification and use credit rather than saving for the purchase of products. They are more likely to admit to using much of the money they earn or have for personal enjoyment, and report a greater use of credit cards or charge cards. Furthermore, the baby boomers' greater inclination toward spending may also be the result of life circumstances specific to that stage of life.

Baby boomers tend to experience more life-altering events, creating new needs for products and services. As their needs change, so do their spending habits. For example, according to a national study of 866 adults, three in ten baby boomers, compared with two in ten of their parents, had changed the amount or type of their insurance in the previous 12 months. As new needs develop, the younger generation is looking for ways to finance the new expenditures, and they often resort to using credit. In the same study, we found a larger percentage of those adults who had experienced the increased responsibility of caring for an aged relative had received professional financial or legal advice, compared with those who had no added care-giving responsibilities (32 percent vs. 22 percent). Those with added caregiving responsibilities were also more likely to report changes in the amount or type of insurance they had, compared with those with no added responsibilities (29 percent vs. 21 percent).

Saving Habits

Our research leads us to believe that baby boomers are not as likely as their parents to save. We asked a random sample of nearly 1,200 adults to tell us what they thought about "saving," and we found differences between baby boomers and their parents in saving practices and opinions about saving. For example, 37 percent of baby boomers, compared with 24 percent of the older generation, admitted that they had a hard time sticking to a savings plan. Eighty-two percent of the older group, compared with 73 percent of baby boomers, agreed that it is better to save even if you have to do without a few things. Baby boomers of all ages have equal difficulty saving, but this problem decreases with age. As expected, those with fewer economic resources, as well as those with children still at home, experience this problem to a greater extent than people with adequate financial resources. Twice as many southern as western baby boomers (48 percent vs. 23 percent) report difficulty sticking to a savings plan.

While we do see differences in the savings habits of the two generations, the fact remains that people try to save whatever they can. But we also see differences in the *way* the two generations save. For example, when it comes to investing, younger people are willing to take more risks. In one of our studies, we asked adults to tell us the types of investments they have or prefer to have. Safe investments such as money market funds were preferred by a larger percentage of older adults than by baby boomers, with 57 percent and 42 percent reporting such a preference, respectively. On the other hand, baby boomers were more likely than their parents to express a preference for moderately risky investments, such as balanced mutual funds or Ginnie Maes—mortgage-backed securities—with 35 percent of baby boomers, compared with 16 percent of older adults, expressing such a preference. Preferences for risky investments, such as stocks and options, were almost the same as preferences for average-risk investments, with 33 percent of baby boomers and 15 percent of their parents, respectively, indicating ownership or preference for such investments. The risky investment preferences among baby boomers do not come as a surprise, since younger people have more time to recover from any adverse investment effects, while the older generation must rely on its investments for regular income after retirement. Interestingly, we found that the older generation has the same tolerance for both average and high-risk investments, although the propensity to take risks declines with age.

Why do some older people show the same tolerance for very risky investments as they do for average-risk investments? First of all, many older people who are financially well off can afford to risk a small portion of their discretionary assets to hedge against inflation. Second, increasing life expectancy has given the older person more time to think in terms of risk. A person in his or her late 50s can live another 20 to 30 years, making it easier for someone at this age to invest for the long haul in higher-risk ventures.

Financial security is a strong motive for asset accumulation. Those with less than adequate financial resources in late life know that they will have to work to make ends meet. For example, in one of our national studies of 318 adults, we found a smaller percentage (35 percent) of those who had assets in excess of $75,000 were concerned with finding employment after retirement, compared with their less affluent counterparts (59 percent).

People in the younger generation, especially the younger baby boomers, are faced with more challenges, such as accumulating adequate savings for retirement, and experience several life changes that require financial attention, such as saving for their children's college education. They are more likely to change their financial goals or set new ones to fit their new life circumstances. In a survey of 866 adults, we found a larger share of baby boomers (38 percent) than their parents (24 percent) had set new investment goals in the previous 12 months. Similarly, in another study of 666 adults over a five-year period, we found baby boomers to be more likely to change their investment plans than their parents. More than half (55 percent) of the younger group, compared with less than a third (31 percent) of the older group, had set new investment goals in the previous three years. In another national study of 866 adults, we found that 44 percent of older baby boomers, compared with 22 percent of younger baby boomers, had created new investment plans in the previous 12 months.

Although a person may have a steady income, changing life circumstances may adversely affect one's financial well-being. Baby boomers, especially older ones, are more likely to experience worsening financial status as a result of life changes. In the study we conducted of 866 adults, 31 percent of the older baby boomers, compared with 22 percent of younger baby boomers, reported a worsening financial situation in the previous 12 months.

One of the reasons older people save is because they are concerned about their future financial well-being. Parents of baby boomers tend to be more pessimistic about the financial future than their children. In our study of 666 adults, we found that the older generation was more likely than their baby boomer children to expect a deterioration of their financial status, with 23 percent and 13 percent of them, respectively, indicating the likelihood of this happening in "the next few years." The older generation continues to have this pessimistic perception of the future, despite improvements in their financial status compared with their baby boomer children. In our study of 866 adults, twice as many parents as their baby boomer children reported a major improvement in their financial status in the previous 12 months, 16 percent and 8 percent, respectively. A larger percentage of the baby boomers, in comparison with the older adults, had experienced financial circumstances that were "a lot worse than usual," with 26 percent versus 17 percent reporting such losses, respectively. Among those who had experienced a worse than usual financial status, 30 percent reported an increased responsibility for an aged relative in the previous 12 months, compared with 21 percent of those adults who had not experienced such a responsibility. Thus, we can see that unexpected caregiving responsibilities appear to hit the pockets of baby boomer caregivers quite heavily.

People in both generations have the main portion of their assets in the form of home equity. We were interested in investigating how they feel about this type of asset, and how they would use it if they had to, and how they feel about the options available to tap into home equity. In one study, we asked adults of different ages how they would use home equity they had built up. Baby boomers expressed preferences for cash, with 43 percent of them (compared with just 28 percent of their parents) saying that they would like to get all the cash up front and make monthly payments to the lender. On the other hand, the older generation expressed a preference for a variety of other uses of home equity. Compared with their children, parents of baby boomers would prefer to:

- sell their home but continue to live there and receive a small monthly payment from the lender;
- sell, rent another home, and keep the cash from the profit;
- sell and buy a less expensive home; or
- receive cash either as a lump sum or as monthly payments and let the lender have their home when they move or after they die.

Home improvements are necessary for people who live in their homes for a lengthy period of time, and baby boomers would rather use home equity for these investments than any other source of financing. More than three in five baby boomers (or 62 percent), compared with 27 percent of their parents, prefer to use home equity to pay for home improvement expenses. Conversely, 57 percent of parents of baby boomers expressed a preference for using other investments, compared with 49 percent of their children.

Financing Retirement

Retirees must pay for a wide variety of expenses related to activities of daily living, leisure, and other necessary and discretionary expenses. In one of our studies, we asked people how they plan to pay for such expenses during their retirement years. We found that the plans of baby boomers differ from those of their parents. Half of baby boomers, compared with one-third of their parents, plan to use tax-sheltered investments such as an IRA or Keogh to pay for vacation or travel expenses after retirement. Also, more baby boomers than older adults expect to use home equity (9 percent vs. 3 percent) and other investments (76 percent vs. 67 percent) to pay for vacation or travel.

Half of baby boomers plan to use IRAs or Keoghs to pay for vacation or travel after retirement.

Nursing home and long-term care are major expenses later in

life. Baby boomers and their parents also differ in how they expect to finance these expenses, as the younger generation plans to use a wider variety of resources. Specifically, one-third of baby boomers, compared with a little over one-fourth of their parents, plan to pay for nursing home expenses using IRA or Keogh investments, as well as other taxable investments (35 percent vs. 29 percent). Only three percent of the older generation, compared with 11 percent of the younger generation, believes they can count on their children to help with these types of expenses.

Moreover, baby boomers are counting on a wide variety of other investments to finance major purchases in post-retirement years. Half of baby boomers, compared with one-third of their parents, plan to use IRA or Keogh investments toward major purchases, while 18 percent of the younger group, compared with 6 percent of the older generation, plans to use home-equity funds for major purchases.

In comparison with their parents, baby boomers are less likely to own a long-term care insurance policy. About one-third of the older generation, compared with one-fourth of baby boomers, have a long-term care (LTC) insurance policy. Although fewer baby boomers own a LTC insurance policy, a larger percentage of them count on LTC insurance to pay for a wide variety of post-retirement expenses. More baby boomers than their parents count on LTC insurance to pay for unexpected medical bills (83 percent vs. 66 percent) and nursing home expenses (81 percent vs. 61 percent), suggesting that a little more than half of baby boomers who have yet to purchase LTC insurance plan to do so in the future.

Life does not end after retirement. Many retirees pursue new business ventures and set new personal investment goals. We asked adults in one of our large-scale surveys to tell us how they plan to finance such ventures. Once again, a larger percentage of baby boomers, in comparison with their parents, prefer to use IRA or Keogh investments to finance new business ventures, with 43 percent and 29 percent expressing such a preference, respectively. Similarly, a larger percentage of the baby boomers (70 percent), compared with the older group (55 percent), plan to use other taxable investments for business and personal purposes in their post-retirement years.

Baby boomers also count on their investments as a source of gifts to relatives and charities. Compared with their parents, baby boomers are more likely to plan on using IRA or Keogh investments (34 percent vs. 23 percent) as well as other taxable investments (76 percent vs. 56 percent) for gifts to relatives and charitable organizations.

The Affluent

We wanted to take a closer look at the financial lifestyles and habits of affluent people in the two generations. We consider "affluent" to be those with greater-than-average annual household incomes. Baby boomers and their parents are wealthier than prior generations. The average age for millionaires in this country is approximately 57. As a result, there are large numbers of people in both generations with substantial assets. For this reason, we were also interested in looking at the differences between millionaires and non-millionaires among the upscale households. Finally, we wanted to learn how the self-made millionaires compare with those who have inherited their fortunes.

Differences between the two generations

The average affluent individual is most likely to be an older person, retired, living in a large city with his or her spouse (but not with children) and, as expected, with a higher level of education and income. In order to find out how affluent baby boomers differ from their affluent parents when it comes to financial matters, we compared the financial behavior of the two generations and found some interesting differences.

First we examined the asset composition of both affluent baby boomers and their parents. The two affluent groups hold roughly the same percentages of their assets in cash, closely held business partnerships, and real estate. However, the older group has twice as much in securities as the younger group. Nearly half (44 percent) of the older group has at least 20 percent of their assets in securities, compared with 24 percent of the younger generation. On the other hand, the younger generation has more in tangibles and collectibles than their parents do (76 percent vs. 64 percent).

We investigated sources of income for affluent baby boomers and their parents and found that baby boomers, in comparison with their older counterparts, get most of their monthly income from salary and bonuses. Eighty-eight percent of affluent baby boomers, compared with two-thirds of their parents, said they get 20 percent or more of their income from salary. Twenty-three percent of the younger group, compared with 17 percent of the older group, derives 20 percent or more of their monthly income from commissions, bonuses, or profit sharing. Both groups derive equal percentages of their monthly income from professional fees and business profits.

Affluent baby boomers and their parents do not have similar preferences when it comes to ownership or use of financial products. Affluent older adults have or use a wider variety of financial instruments. Baby boomers, by comparison, own or use more stock options or commodity contracts more than their parents do (20 percent vs. 16 percent).

However, the older generation, compared with their baby boomer children, own or use more:

CDs of $10,000 or more:	48 percent	vs.	27 percent
Savings account:	34 percent	vs.	14 percent
Real estate (personal use):	93 percent	vs.	87 percent
Undeveloped property:	28 percent	vs.	19 percent
Stocks and corporate bonds:	80 percent	vs.	61 percent
Tax-free municipal bonds:	34 percent	vs.	21 percent
U.S. Treasury bills: ($10,000 and over)	21 percent	vs.	11 percent
IRA/Keogh:	39 percent	vs.	30 percent
Life insurance:	82 percent	vs.	65 percent

Thus, affluent people in the older generation appear to be a far more sophisticated group when it comes to investing because they use a wide variety of financial instruments.

Affluent people in the older generation appear to be a far more sophisticated group when it comes to investing.

We examined the lifestyles and financial practices of affluent baby boomers and their parents and we found several differences between these two groups. The differences in the financial lifestyles of the two generations are shown in Table 5-1. The younger group spends more time thinking about money, takes more risks when investing, and looks for loopholes in the tax laws. However, a smaller percentage of baby boomers can say that they personally earned their family's wealth in comparison to their parents (64 percent vs. 80 percent).

TABLE 5-1

Financial Practices: Affluent Baby Boomers vs. Their Parents

in percent

	Baby Boomers	Parents
Spend a lot of time planning their financial future	54.8	47.8
Need very little advice when making major financial decisions	32.6	36.8
Usually have sufficient time to handle their investments properly	53.1	59.6
Will take substantial risks when investing	28.1	20.3
Always looking for loopholes in the tax laws	54.9	40.8
Have personally earned most of the wealth their family possesses	64.6	80.4

With respect to their financial practices, baby boomers are more likely than the older generation to:

- borrow more money
- show interest in on-line banking
- have as a major financial goal the increase of their assets over protection of their assets
- be opinion leaders for financial services

The affluent parents are more likely than their affluent baby boomer children to:

- view bank employees as cold and impersonal
- consider themselves to be financially well-off

- have a will
- have an estate plan
- have a net worth of $1 million or more

The two affluent groups seem to carry the same types of credit cards. A slightly greater percentage of baby boomers (76 percent) than their parents (63 percent) carry MasterCard, and a larger percentage of the older group carries a Neiman Marcus card (24 percent), compared with the younger group (14 percent).

Next, we looked at the financial goals of affluent people in the two generations and we found significant differences in the financial goals of the two groups. These are shown in Table 5-2. In general, affluent baby boomers have a wider variety of financial goals than their parents do. They want to make a lot of money fast, retire early, enjoy life, and pass some of their wealth on to their children. On the other hand, their affluent parents' main preoccupation is with preservation of their wealth.

TABLE 5-2

Financial Goals: Affluent Baby Boomers vs. Affluent Parents

percent in each affluent group that considers each goal "very important"

	Baby Boomers	Parents
Assure the best college education for their children	74.3	67.0
A guaranteed rate of return on their investment	43.4	47.9
Develop and follow a financial plan	52.6	56.4
Eliminate financial risks	34.9	43.1
Investment diversification	61.7	66.2
Use much of the money they have/earn for personal enjoyment	30.9	16.9
Put a major portion of their wealth in liquid or near liquid assets	22.3	29.5
Achieve maximum wealth by retirement	58.3	51.1
Make significant contributions to tax-exempt organizations	19.4	14.3
Protect their family financially in case of their premature death	82.4	82.1
Retire earlier than most people	45.1	25.6
Finance new business ventures	38.9	12.6
Minimize taxes	85.1	74.8
Not fall below their current standard of living	91.4	82.4
At least double their wealth during the next 5 years	72.6	33.4
Retire in comfort	86.3	83.2
Leave an estate for their children	58.9	47.9

The perceived importance of financial services among affluent baby boomers and their parents was also examined. We found that in comparison with their affluent parents, affluent baby boomers are more likely to value:

use of ATMs:	53 percent vs. 19 percent
seminars on financial planning:	35 percent vs. 23 percent
overdraft privileges:	35 percent vs. 21 percent
advice on tax shelters:	62 percent vs. 50 percent
premium entertainment and travel cards:	43 percent vs. 31 percent
loan requests or approvals by phone:	49 percent vs. 25 percent
real estate investment advice:	50 percent vs. 35 percent
loans for purchases of securities:	21 percent vs. 14 percent
financial advice in their home by appointment:	20 percent vs. 13 percent
preferred loan rates:	77 percent vs. 52 percent

On the other hand, a larger percentage of elderly parents, compared with their baby boomer children:

prefers a personal line of credit:	68 percent vs. 54 percent
needs financial advice on retirement:	44 percent vs. 33 percent
needs to prepare a will:	75 percent vs. 51 percent

Finally, we examined the sources of information used by affluent people in the two generations when making financial decisions. We found a larger percentage of affluent baby boomers (44 percent), in comparison with affluent older adults (28 percent), would seek financial information from a life insurance agent. In contrast, a larger percentage of older adults (30 percent) prefer to consult with a bank trust officer for financial matters, compared with a smaller percentage of baby boomers (22 percent).

Millionaires vs. non-millionaires

How do people become millionaires? The average millionaire is a salaried employee. Although a substantial portion of those who have become wealthy are self-employed, working for someone else does not limit your ability to become wealthy. During one of our surveys of affluent Americans, we found that while most millionaires (61 percent) get a regular paycheck, a significant percentage of them also receive their income from business profits (34 percent) and fees for their professional services (18 percent). On the other hand, a larger percentage of non-millionaire affluent people (74 percent) are salaried employees, and a smaller percentage of them receive income from business profits (12 percent) and professional fees (14 percent).

Obviously, the amount of money a person earns is likely to determine the size of one's net worth in the long run. We found that 40 percent of those with an annual household income greater than $100,000 were millionaires—having a net worth of $1 million or more—compared with only 4 percent of those with an annual household income of less than $100,000.

We also uncovered significant differences between millionaires and non-millionaires in the way they spend or use their monthly income. Both millionaires and their less affluent counterparts spend roughly equal portions of their monthly paychecks on healthcare services and education for their children. A larger percentage of millionaires compared with non-millionaires contribute five percent or more of their money to charitable organizations, 40 percent versus 28 percent, respectively. More than half (52 percent) of the former group, compared with 44 percent of non-millionaires, spend five percent or more of their income on travel, and they give more gifts of cash and securities to their relatives (73 percent vs. 52 percent). Investing habits are another major difference between the two different groups. Two-thirds

> Both millionaires and their less affluent counterparts spend roughly equal portions of their monthly paychecks on healthcare services and education for their children.

of the millionaires, compared with two-fifths of their less affluent counterparts, invest more than 10 percent of their annual incomes.

Among people who are affluent, millionaires differ from the less wealthy in several other ways. First, they tend to be older. More than half of millionaires (54 percent) are older than 55 years. Parents of baby boomers are twice more likely than their children to be millionaires. Second, although the majority of millionaires are salaried employees, the largest percentage of millionaires (58 percent) also tends to be self-employed, compared with 31 percent of non-millionaires who are self-employed. Compared with the less wealthy group, millionaires have more of their assets invested in closely held business partnerships and securities. They have less invested in liquid instruments, real estate, and tangibles or collections. More millionaires tend to have a will (93 percent), compared with 86 percent of the less wealthy, and two-thirds of them have an estate plan, compared with two-fifths of their less wealthy counterparts. Both affluent groups are equally likely to have a Master-Card and VISA in their wallets, but a higher percentage of the wealthier group carries American Express as well as upscale department store cards such as Neiman Marcus, Saks Fifth Avenue, and Lord & Taylor, while the less affluent group is more likely to carry Sears and JCPenney's cards.

We also found differences in asset ownership and use of financial services between millionaires and non-millionaires, which are shown in Table 5-3. As expected, millionaires have more diverse assets than non-millionaires. The percentage differences in asset ownership are the greatest for commercial and rental real estate (64 percent vs. 31 percent), tax-free municipal bonds (53 percent vs. 27 percent), a variety of tax shelters (50 percent vs. 26 percent), proprietorships (39 percent vs. 18 percent), and closely held stocks or partnership interest (68 percent vs. 32 percent).

TABLE 5-3

Asset Ownership and Use of Financial Services of the Affluent
by percent, millionaires vs. non-millionaires

	Millionaires	Non-millionaires
Regular savings account	80.6	90.1
Liquid asset/money market funds	78.2	64.6
All-savers certificate	37.5	29.9
Commercial/rental real estate	64.0	30.9
Undeveloped property	43.6	23.7
Listed common/preferred stocks/corporate bonds	86.1	75.9
Tax-free municipal bonds	53.3	27.3
Stock options/commodity contracts	19.2	14.0
U.S. treasury bills (e.g., $10,000 minimum)	26.2	16.7
Corporate retirement plan	53.0	61.1
Tax shelters (ventures in oil, gas, mineral, etc.)	42.8	18.9
Proprietorship	39.1	17.9
Closely held stocks or partnership interest	68.0	32.4
Yacht	9.4	4.6
Trust account	40.2	20.8
Precious gems	43.8	30.3
Stamp/painting/coin/art/antique collection	40.9	34.8

Both millionaires and non-millionaires have fairly similar financial goals. We investigated 20 different financial goals and found significant differences between the two groups for only five of the 20 goals. These differences are shown in Table 5-4. Specifically, millionaires are more motivated to achieve financial success for building an estate for their children, financing new business ventures, and making significant contributions to charities. On the other hand, upscale adults with assets under $1 million are far more averse to risk than millionaires.

TABLE 5-4

Financial Goals of the Affluent
by percent, millionaires vs. non-millionaires

	Millionaires	Non-millionaires
Leave an estate for their children	64.0	47.8
Finance new business ventures	28.9	14.7
Make significant contributions to tax-exempt organizations	19.2	13.1
Eliminate financial risks	33.1	41.7
Guarantee return on their investments	35.7	47.6

We also examined the financial lifestyles and habits of the affluent, and significant differences were discovered between millionaires and non-millionaires. These differences are shown in Table 5-5. Generally, millionaires are more involved with managing their financial affairs, borrow more money, and are more charitable and helpful to others, while the affluent who do not have as much are less interested in leaving a legacy when they pass away. Clearly, millionaires are driven by the desire to make or leave a legacy for their children and to help others.

TABLE 5-5

Financial Lifestyles and Habits of the Affluent
by percent, millionaires vs. non-millionaires

	Millionaires	Non-millionaires
Spend a lot of time planning their financial future	62.7	45.3
Have sufficient time to handle their investments properly	63.3	55.6
Take substantial risks when investing	31.0	20.6
Read as much financial news as they can get their hands on	65.9	54.3
Much of their income comes from sources other than salary	63.0	33.6
Are not interested in leaving an estate when they pass away	8.7	15.9
Borrow more money than most people	35.4	15.4
Have given substantial amounts of their wealth to charitable organizations	20.2	8.6
Give more advice to others about investments-related decisions than they receive	49.9	34.7

How do the affluent perceive the various services available from financial institutions? Table 5-6 shows how millionaires and other affluent people with assets less than $1 million view various financial services. Compared with non-millionaires, the more affluent group places a premium on overdraft privileges, personal line of credit, advice on tax shelters, investment-management services, premium travel and entertainment cards, and loan requests or approvals by phone. The more affluent group finds additional services more attractive, including real estate investment advice, safe deposits, estate planning, term investments (such as CDs over $100,000), loans for purchase of securities, asset appraisal services, preparation of complete consolidated financial statements, and preferred loan rates. The less wealthy group, on the other hand, places greater value on seminars about financial planning, financial advice for retirement, and the availability of ATMs.

TABLE 5-6

Importance of Financial Services Among the Affluent
by percent, millionaires vs. non-millionaires

	Millionaires	Non-millionaires
Seminars on financial planning	18.9	25.7
Overdraft privileges of $5,000 or more	29.7	23.9
Personal line of credit of $20,000 or more	55.1	32.8
Advice on tax shelters	57.7	52.2
Investment management services (actual investment decisions made for you)	35.2	28.8
Premium travel and entertainment cards (e.g., American Express Gold Card)	43.8	31.9
Financial advice for retirement	32.5	43.9
Loan requests/approvals by phone	40.9	27.4
Real estate investment advice	45.1	36.9
Safe deposit/vault for large objects (e.g., paintings, antiques, silver service, etc.)	33.9	25.4
Estate planning	60.1	48.0
Term investments (e.g., $100,000 CDs)	43.8	14.1
Loans for the purchase of securities	24.1	16.0
Asset appraisal service	27.3	22.1
Preparation of complete consolidated financial position statement	43.8	31.8
Preferred loan rates	66.9	56.7
Automated teller machines	15.7	25.4

Self-made vs. old money

How do those who made their millions differ from those who inherited their wealth? What characteristics distinguish the two groups? What are the financial habits and lifestyles of the millionaires in these two groups? In order to answer these questions, we analyzed responses from a large national survey of affluent Americans that included several hundred millionaires. Those who indicated that they had earned most of their wealth were labeled as "self-made." The rest of the millionaires were classified as "old money," assuming that they inherited their wealth from other sources.

First, the vast majority of individuals in the self-made group are self-employed, compared with their old money counterparts, 86 percent versus 37 percent, respectively. Second, they tend to be somewhat older, suggesting that they had to work longer to make their fortunes. Self-made millionaires keep a larger percentage of their wealth liquid, with one in five of them having 20 percent or more of their wealth in cash, compared with just 8 percent of their counterparts who inherited their fortune. In comparison with "old-money" millionaires, those who earned their wealth are more likely to own real estate (68 percent vs. 49 percent) and a proprietorship (43 percent vs. 25 percent). Many self-made millionaires run their own businesses, and a significant percentage of them (43 percent) invest a portion of their monthly paycheck into that business. On the other hand, among business owners who inherited their fortunes, just 28 percent of them invest in their own company; they prefer to invest in the stock market. The self-made group is more likely to carry American Express and Lord & Taylor credit cards and is less likely to have an estate plan than their counterparts who did not have to work as hard. Finally, the self-made millionaires are more likely to have more prestigious job titles than those who inherited their wealth.

> Self-made millionaires keep a larger percentage of their wealth in cash and give less to charity than those who inherited wealth.

Self-made millionaires are more likely to get their monthly income from business profits, with 37 percent of them, compared to 25 percent of those who inherited their wealth, indicating that at least one-fifth of their income comes from business profits.

Regardless of income level, about four in five affluent people claim that they have personally earned most of their family's wealth. However, among millionaires, eight in ten of those who have annual household incomes in excess of $100,000 state that they have earned most of their family's wealth compared with seven in ten self-made millionaires with annual incomes less than $100,000.

Both groups spend their money in a similar way, with one exception Self-made millionaires give less to charities. Thirty-seven percent of them, compared with half of those who inherited their wealth, give about five percent of their annual income to charities.

When it comes to their financial goals, self-made millionaires are more likely to be motivated to make a lot of money before retirement, compared with millionaires who acquired their wealth through other means, with 53 percent versus 38 percent of them reporting this goal, respectively. A greater percentage of them than old-money millionaires tend to retire early (37 percent vs. 25 percent) and finance new business ventures (32 percent vs. 17 percent). However, self-made millionaires are less motivated to leave a legacy than old-money millionaires, with 60 percent versus 79 percent of these rich individuals indicating this motive, respectively.

With respect to financial habits and lifestyles of the two groups, self-made millionaires differ from those who inherited their wealth in a number of ways. First, a larger percentage of them do not seek or use advice when making financial decisions. Second, they are willing to take substantial risks when investing. Third, they are always looking for loopholes in the tax laws. Fourth, they are not interested in leaving an estate when they pass away. And finally, nearly half of the income they receive comes from their salaries, compared with 80 percent of millionaires who inherited their wealth and derive much of their income from sources other than salary.

When we looked at the perceptions of financial services and the financial-service providers, we found few significant differences between self-made millionaires and those who acquired their wealth via other means. A greater percentage of the former group (58 percent), compared with the latter group (45 percent), values a personal line of credit. The "old money" group is more likely to value investment management services than the self-made group, with 46 percent versus 32 percent indicating this preference, respectively.

CHAPTER SIX

What They Have, What They Use

THE CONSUMPTION PATTERNS of baby boomers and their parents show some interesting and surprising differences. Whether one looks at their possessions, preferences for products, or buying habits, several differences are worth mentioning. In this chapter, we will discuss some of these differences in possessions and use of select products and services by people in the two generations. Specifically, we will look at the value and composition of assets and ownership of products that people in the two generations value and use on a day-to-day basis. Also, we will look at the mindsets of those whose lives revolve around their possessions, especially those that are socially visible—their homes, cars, jewelry, and clothes. And we will look at some of the most widely used types of services baby boomers and their parents use.

What They Own

Based on the results of our surveys, the total value of the possessions of the average person born before 1965 is estimated at a little over $100,000. About four in five adults surveyed nationally reported possessions valued at more than $75,000. While these are not surprising findings, it is interesting to note the differences in the value of possessions between the two generations.

A person's sense of well-being is closely tied to his or her financial assets. In our study of 318 adults, we found a larger percentage of those with assets in excess of $75,000 (92 percent), compared to those with fewer assets (88 percent), had a better sense of well-being. A larger percentage of those with assets in excess of $75,000 were older adults (92 percent), compared with baby boomers (70 percent).

The older folks have more

Baby boomers are not as well off financially as their parents. Our analysis of government data shows that the net worth of the average older adult is ten times higher than the net worth of the average baby boomer, six times higher if one excludes real estate equity. One of our national studies found that, counting all their assets, two in three baby boomers (or 61 percent) have more than $75,000 in assets, compared with a larger percentage of their parents (86 percent) who reported values of assets in excess of the same amount. In another national study of 704 adults, 36 percent of baby boomers, compared with 54 percent of their parents, reported assets greater than $75,000.

The net worth of the average older adult is ten times higher than the net worth of the average baby boomer, six times higher if one excludes real estate equity.

Compared with their children, parents of baby boomers have more assets in cash, with half of them reporting liquid assets in excess of $25,000. In comparison, just one in five baby boomers report the same amount. By the same token, parents of baby boomers have three times as much in securities. In one of our studies we found that nearly half (43 percent) of the older generation had more than $25,000 invested in stocks, compared with just 14 percent of their children.

Both generations have the largest chunk of their assets in real estate. Roughly two-thirds of the older generation has home equity in excess of $50,000, compared with a little over two in five baby boomers. The younger generation, however, has invested substantially more in tangible assets such as cars and home furnishings, with 43 percent of them reporting assets in excess of $25,000 in this category, compared with 28 percent of the older generation.

Who is the typical affluent older adult? The typical older person with sizeable assets tends to have higher income and a better education, lives in a large city with a spouse but not with children, and is retired.

The older the person, the more assets he or she is likely to have. In one of our national studies, we found that 46 percent of younger baby boomers have total assets in excess of $75,000. Six in ten of those aged 55 to 64 have assets exceeding $75,000. While the vast majority (86 percent) of those aged 65 and over has assets in excess of $75,000, 9 in 10 of those aged 75 and over have assets totaling more than this amount. Men have substantially more than women. Those with the most assets tend to have higher income and education levels, live with others in urban areas, and are not likely to have a working family member in their household.

In the same study, we found that real estate is the most valuable asset, with about two-thirds of the average American family placing a value of $50,000 or more on the equity of the real estate property they own. People who have the most real estate assets tend to be the oldest and the most educated, with much higher income than the average person. Most real estate owners are men. Urban dwellers report more real estate assets than people living in rural areas. Those living with others, especially those who are married, also report greater real estate assets.

Another interesting finding of this same study was the amount of investments owned by the average American family, and the differences in investments owned by people of different backgrounds. Sixty percent of all American families reported investments of all kinds valued at $30,000 or more. People who have $30,000 or more in investments differ from those with fewer investment assets in several ways. First, they tend to be older. Three-fourths of those aged 75 and older have investments worth more than $30,000, as do 65 percent of those aged 65 to 74, 50 percent of those aged 55 to 64, 34 percent of older baby boomers, and only 18 percent of younger baby boomers. Men have more invested than women, as do those with higher incomes and education levels, retirees, and those living with others in urban areas.

Sixty percent of all American families reported investments of all kinds valued at $30,000 or more.

In another study, we found the percentage of baby boomers that own more than $50,000 in liquid assets to be four times lower than that of their senior counterparts—or 10 percent versus 39 percent. Baby boomers also own fewer securities valued at $5,000 or more than their parents, with 34 percent versus 48 percent, as well as real estate valued at $50,000 or more, with 44 percent versus 60 percent, respectively. On the other hand, the younger generation has more money than the older generation invested in tangibles and collections, with 70 percent and 65 percent, respectively, indicating amounts in excess of $5,000. They also have more in "other assets," with 49 percent and 38 percent reporting more than $5,000 in such investments, respectively.

The American Dream

Ownership of a single-family house is fairly similar among people of the two generations, with a little over four in five baby boomers and their parents presently living in a house that they own. Of interest, however, are the gender differences in single-family home ownership. Older men are more likely to live in a single-family house than older women. Men, in general, are somewhat more likely than women to live in a single-family home. People who live in rural areas are more likely to reside in single-family houses, compared with those who live in large cities. Nearly nine in ten adults who live with others or their spouse reside in single-family homes.

Why is the incidence of living in a single-family house higher among men than among women in both generations? We think it is a combination of three main factors. First, a greater percentage of men tend to be married and live with one or more persons up to the time of their death because their life expectancy is about six years shorter than women's; they may have younger spouses; and they prefer to remarry if they experience divorce or death of a spouse. These living conditions create a greater need for a single-family house, in comparison with older women who are more likely to live alone and therefore do not have the same housing needs. Second, divorce or death of a spouse is likely to result in economic hardship, making it more difficult for women to own or keep a single-family house. Third, we believe that men, especially older men, consider ownership of a single-family house to be a sign of independence, a symbol of status and success for their accomplishments. In one of our studies, for example, the vast majority (81 percent) of men aged 65 and over, compared with 69 percent of women of that age, agreed with the statement: "I think that people look up to persons who own their homes."

For older men, owning a single-family house is a sign of independence, a symbol of status and success.

The perception of home ownership as a symbol of success and well-being develops at an early stage in life and persists till death. By the time a person reaches adolescence he or she has developed views about the meaning of special possessions and money as symbols of social progress. When a sample of today's young baby boomers were questioned and compared with their parents' responses 25 years ago (when most of the younger group were adolescents), we found that their views about money and possessions were remarkably similar. For example, about one-third of each group agreed with the statement "People judge others by the things they own," and approximately seven in ten agreed with the statement "It is true that money can buy happiness." When they were teenagers, 82 percent of today's young baby boomer women, compared with 63 percent of baby boomer men, believed that money could buy happiness. However, a larger percentage of their middle-aged parents (71 percent) than their children (51 percent) admitted that their dream in life is to be able to own expensive things; 76 percent versus 50 percent thought that others judge a person by the kinds of products and brands they use; 60 percent versus 37 percent said that they were buying some things secretly hoping to impress others; and 73 percent versus 52 percent viewed money as the most important factor to consider in choosing a job. While many of today's baby boomers may have changed their views about possessions since their adolescent years, the study suggests the possible influence of their parents' values on their beliefs about the importance of possessions at a relatively young age.

Having a home is of utmost importance to the poorest people. A significantly greater percentage of the group with an income under $20,000 a year, compared with people whose income exceeds $50,000 a year, would like their relatives to live in their home after they die, with 80 percent versus 62 percent reporting such a preference, respectively. A fairly similar percentage in both groups believes that owning a home is better than renting. As expected, home ownership is higher among older men, those who have a higher income and greater assets, as well as among those who live with their spouses (96 percent), compared with those who live alone (76 percent).

When people stay put, they are forced to repair and remodel their houses. But these activities are not equally common among all homeowners. Middle-aged people are more likely to remodel or refurnish their home. In one of our studies, we found that half of older baby boomers and 45 percent of those aged 55 to 64 had done some remodeling or refurnishing in the previous 12 months. Forty-one percent of younger boomers reported such activities, and among those aged 65 and older only 34 percent had done work on their homes. People who live with others, as well as those still working, do most of the remodeling or refurnishing.

Appliances, electronics, and home furnishings

Besides the purchase of a home and home-related products and services, the purchase of an *automobile* is often the second most important buying decision. Many people prefer to buy new cars frequently, while others tend to hold on to their automobiles for a long time. Those who buy most of the new cars tend to be between ages 55 and 74. They are more likely to be men than women, are better educated and have higher incomes, and are more likely to live with others in working families. Finally, those living in the western part of the country buy more new cars on average than those living in the East.

Those who buy most of the new cars tend to be between ages 55 and 74.

The older a person is, the less likely he or she is to move, according to surveys conducted by the AARP over the past 25 years. The average parent of a baby boomer (over the age of 60) has had the same address for 21 years, according to these surveys. As people stay put or "age in place" later in life, their needs change, as do their preferences for several types of amenities and appliances. We found some interesting differences, for example, in ownership or installation of energy-saving devices and home-security systems. *Home-security systems* are most likely to be found in the homes of the older generation than in the homes of their baby boomer children, despite the fact that both groups are equally likely to live in a single-family home. The typical person who has a home-security system tends to be older, better educated, and of higher socioeconomic status. Twice as many homes in western states than homes in north-central states have home-security systems. People in the two generations who have *energy-saving appliances* or installed devices tend to be better educated, have a higher income, and most likely live with others.

> Home-security systems are most likely to be found in the homes of the older generation than in the homes of their baby boomer children.

Several other differences were found between baby boomers and their parents with respect to ownership and use of a variety of household appliances, such as microwave ovens and PCs, as well as home-related services such as cable and telecommunications services. Based on several studies, we can briefly summarize some of the major findings:

- Older baby boomers appear to be the group of consumers who most value convenience in their homes. Nine in ten older boomers, compared with 76 percent of younger baby boomers and 80 percent of older adults, use a *microwave oven*. Ownership of this appliance is the highest among those with the highest incomes who live alone and are employed.
- People who own or use devices such as *DVDs* or *VCRs* and *PCs* have the following characteristics: they are younger, have higher incomes, live with others or with their spouses, and are still working. Those living with others are twice as likely as those living alone to have the need to control their time for television entertainment by using products such as DVDs

Three in four boomers own a PC or laptop, compared with nearly half of their parents.

or VCRs. Based on our studies in the two years prior to the completion of this book, we estimate that three in four baby boomers own a PC or laptop, compared with nearly half of their parents.

- Baby boomers are three times as likely as their elderly counterparts to own or use *telephone answering machines*, with 47 percent and 17 percent of them, respectively, indicating ownership and use. These small appliances are gradually being replaced with more recent devices such as cell phones or voice mail services, but many consumers still own both. At the time of publication, we estimated that approximately two-thirds of baby boomers and nearly half of their parents leave their homes with a *cell phone* in their pockets or purses.

- People who have or use a *telephone answering machine* or a *cell phone* tend to be younger and better-educated with higher incomes. They are twice as likely to live in a western state than in a north-central state and to have a working family member. Owners and users of telephone answering machines and cell phones are more likely to live in urban than in rural areas of the country.

- People in the older generation are twice as likely to have a *home-security system*, whereas about half of both groups have energy-saving products and appliances.

- Users of *cordless phones* tend to be younger, live with others, have higher incomes, and have working household members.

- Users of *premium* or *custom calling telephone services* (such as call-forwarding) tend to be younger, better educated, and have higher incomes. They are twice as likely to live in urban than rural areas, and are more likely to be found in north-central states than in southern states.

- Subscribers to *cable television* tend to be younger, with higher incomes and education levels, and live with others. They are more likely to be found in northern states than in southern states.

Other possessions

Baby boomers buy as many new *clothes* as their parents, but fashion consciousness becomes less important with age. Those most likely to buy the latest style of clothes are women in the highest income brackets. The biggest spenders on clothes are the young baby boomers. People spend less on clothes as they get older. A larger percentage of women (27 percent) than men (17 percent) are likely to have spent more money than usual on clothes in the previous 12 months. A larger percentage of upper social class individuals, as well as those who work, are likely to report spending more than usual on clothes in the previous 12 months than those in lower social classes who are unemployed.

Because many older baby boomers and their parents have more money and are also likely to be grandparents, we reasoned that they would be buying many products as *gifts* for younger members of their extended family. To our surprise, this did not turn out to be the case. People who buy the most gifts for others tend to be younger women who are less educated, employed, and have lower levels of self-esteem.

Besides owning objects, people in both generations have *companion animals* of different varieties. Pet owners and lovers tend to be younger adults. Sixty-five percent of people under the age of 55 own a cat or a dog, compared with four in ten older adults. Pet ownership declines with age and increases with levels of education and income. A little over half (52 percent) of people living in western states, compared with about four in ten adults residing in other parts of the country, are animal lovers. People in rural parts of the country are more likely to have a pet, as are those who live with others or their spouse. New research has documented the benefits of interaction with companion animals on the person's health, especially for older people of poor mental and physical health. Increasing evidence shows that pet owners live longer, feel less lonely, and recover faster from surgery. Interaction with animals appears to lower blood pressure and reduces levels of aversive emotions, such as stress and depression, that threaten our health.

Who Is More Materialistic?

We expected baby boomers to be more materialistic than their parents for two reasons: first, in comparison with their parents, baby boomers were brought up during more prosperous times and have become accustomed to the comfort material possessions can provide. Second, they are at the middle stage in life, when people are most likely to define themselves and find meaning in life with the things they own, in comparison with their parents who define themselves and life in general with the things they have accomplished and their life experience.

In one of our recent studies we asked several hundred people in a mail survey, where they could remain anonymous when giving their responses, to indicate their levels of agreement or disagreement with a list of statements that were developed by other researchers and were considered accurate tools in assessing people's materialistic values. We grouped affirmative responses ("somewhat agree" and "strongly agree"), and tallied them separately for the participants who were classified into the two groups based on their age. Table 6-1 shows the results of our tally by generation.

TABLE 6-1

Attitudes Toward Material Possessions: Baby Boomers vs. Their Parents

percent who "somewhat or strongly agree"

	Baby Boomers	Parents
The things I own say a lot about how well I'm doing in life.	34.1	29.3
The things I own say a lot about what I value in my life.	43.0	39.7
My life would be better if I owned certain things I don't have.	36.6	20.9
Buying things gives me a lot of pleasure.	41.2	27.4
I'd be happier if I could afford to buy more things.	30.2	24.2
I admire people who own expensive houses, cars, and clothes.	8.1	8.4
Some of the most important achievements in life include acquiring material possessions.	14.0	6.7
I like to own things that impress people.	4.7	4.4
I like a lot of luxury in my life.	23.3	12.2

Overall, a greater percentage of baby boomers than their parents agreed with the nine statements. Specifically, adults in both generations appear equally indifferent with regard to the impact their possessions have on others or others' possessions have on them. However, when it comes to owning expensive things for their own satisfaction, baby boomers out-score their parents across the remaining seven statements.

Marketers and advertisers interested in developing messages that appeal to these groups should be aware of the differences across cohorts in regards to the value placed on material possessions, and then tailor their messages accordingly. For the baby boomer market, luxury products should be positioned as objects that make life more comfortable and enjoyable, and relate to "the good life." For the older generation, luxury products should be positioned as rewards for one's life accomplishments and relate to one's "achievements" in life.

Will baby boomers "age-out" of their materialistic orientations? We believe that there will be aging effects that might weaken the strength of these orientations, but we also can expect some cohort trends to endure. Thus, while we expect the baby boomers' materialistic orientations to become weaker later in life, they most likely will be stronger than those held by their parents today.

While we expect the baby boomers' materialistic orientations to become weaker later in life, they most likely will be stronger than those held by their parents today.

The Kinds of Services They Prefer

When it comes to the use of services available on the market, the minds of most people in the two generations are likely to be preoccupied with those services that are of central importance to their present and future well-being. They include primarily services related to the accumulation and use of wealth, their physical and mental well-being, safety and security, and having fun.

Financial services

Baby boomers prefer a larger number of financial services than their parents. When it comes to *investing*, risk tolerance decreases with age. Two-thirds of the older generation and four in ten baby boomers prefer safe investments. However, twice as many baby boomers as their parents prefer average-risk investments, with 35 percent of boomers and 16 percent of their parents expressing such a preference. Risky investments are preferred by three in ten baby boomers but only by half as many of the older generation. In both generations, those who have more assets and higher income also have stronger preferences for various types of investments.

Forty-five percent of baby boomers prefer *overdraft privilege or personal line of credit,* compared with 36 percent of their parents who prefer this service. Only *electronic funds transfer (EFT)* services are preferred less by baby boomers than by senior citizens, with 32 percent and 58 percent, respectively, indicating a preference for having their checks deposited directly at the bank. This may reflect older adults' preference to have their Social Security checks directly deposited because it is a more convenient and safer way to do so.

Baby boomers *borrow* more. They appear to use a larger number of credit cards than seniors. While the number of credit cards reportedly used is higher for baby boomers, the data should not be interpreted as frequency of credit used by the two groups. Baby boomers use department store cards less frequently, with two-thirds of them reporting use in the previous six months, compared with nearly three in four of their parents. Both groups collectively use department store cards more than other cards. Visa is also popular among baby boomers, with 74 percent of them reporting use (compared with 68 percent of seniors), while MasterCard is used by about half of the people in both groups. Baby boomers are more likely than their parents to report use of American Express, with 21 percent versus 16 percent, respectively, and both groups are equally likely to use Discover, with nearly one in four reporting usage. Finally, use of gasoline cards is reported by nearly half of people in the two generations. Use of other premium cards (Diners and Carte Blanche) is negligible. Generally speaking, those who use credit cards the most tend to have more assets, higher levels of income and education, live with one or more family members in large cities, and are employed.

Baby boomers borrow more. They appear to use a larger number of credit cards than seniors.

What motivates baby boomers and their elders to invest for the long haul? We asked Americans in both generations to indicate how they would use several *long-term investments* by giving us their preference for ways or places they would spend their IRA/Keogh and other investments in post-retirement years, and took a close look at their responses.

As reported in chapter 5, half of baby boomers would use *IRA/Keogh investments* to travel and buy major durable items such as cars and furniture, compared with one-third of their parents who would do the same. Baby boomers are also more likely than older adults to use these funds for personal and business investments, with 43 percent and 29 percent, respectively, reporting such intentions. Nearly one-third (or 33 percent) of baby boomers intend to use these IRA and Keogh investments to pay for nursing home or long-term care (LTC) or to buy gifts for relatives (34 percent), compared with 22 percent and 23 percent of seniors, respectively. About one in five baby boomers and seniors would use IRA/Keogh investments to pay for home improvements, and the same proportion of the two groups would set these funds aside to pay for any large unexpected medical bills.

Half of baby boomers would use IRA/Keogh investments to travel and buy major durable items such as cars and furniture, compared with one-third of their parents.

Both age groups would more freely spend funds from *"other" investments*—except IRA/Keogh, home equity, and supplement long-term care insurance. Baby boomers prefer to spend such "discretionary" long-term investments on gifts (76 percent), vacations (76 percent), major purchases (74 percent), and for personal reasons or business ventures (70 percent). A substantially smaller percentage of them would pay for large, unexpected medical bills (32 percent), home improvements (48 percent), and nursing home or LTC (31 percent). These figures are generally higher than those of seniors with the exception of two expense items: unexpected medical bills and home improvements. A larger percentage of seniors would use "other" investments to pay for these expenses, with 38 percent and 56 percent reporting this preference, respectively.

Travel and leisure

While both the young and the old like to travel, they differ when it comes to things they prefer to do and pay for. Generally speaking, the younger generation has a greater interest in a variety of travel and leisure services. In one of our studies, we found significant differences in preferences for selected travel and leisure services. More than half of baby boomers (54 percent) use or would like to use airfare packages (unlimited trips for one price), compared with 41 percent of older adults. About one in five baby boomers (or 22 percent) are, or would like to be, members of a travel club or program where one must pay $50 to $100 to join in order to get discounted rates and rebates, compared with about one in six of the older generation. Finally, about twice as many baby boomers as older adults are members of one or more restaurant club programs where they must pay to join in order to get discounts at member restaurants.

> *More than half of baby boomers (54 percent) use or would like to use airfare packages (unlimited trips for one price), compared with 41 percent of older adults.*

Insurance services

In two of our national studies, we examined generational differences in preferences for four insurance services: long-term care (LTC), "Medigap," car insurance, and home health-care insurance. While nearly all baby boomers (98 percent) have or would like to have car insurance, 88 percent of the elderly expressed such preferences. Nearly as many baby boomers as seniors have or would like to have LTC insurance, with 75 percent and 70 percent, respectively, expressing such a preference. Almost 59 percent of baby boomers and 61 percent of seniors have or would like to have home healthcare insurance, while 43 percent of the younger group, compared with 88 percent of seniors, prefer "Medigap" insurance.

The perceptions of the importance of LTC for baby boomers and older adults also differ. While some coverage areas are more important to older Americans, several areas are of greater importance to baby boomers. In one of our surveys, 49 percent of baby boomers and 43 percent of seniors said that they would pay now to cover nutrition and preventive healthcare programs they might need in the future. The other LTC benefit which is of greater importance to baby boomers is money management and bill payment services. Almost a third of baby boomers (or 31 percent), compared with one in four seniors (or 24 percent), would pay now to cover future benefits.

Turning to LTC benefits that are considered less important to baby boomers than to seniors, we can see significant differences in perceptions with respect to six of the nine areas we looked at in the same study. Freedom to choose place and type of care is most important overall, with 84 percent of baby boomers and 89 percent of seniors indicating a willingness to pay for this benefit. Access to health care and personal care services is also an important benefit, with 63 percent of baby boomers, compared with nearly three-fourths (or 72 percent) of older adults indicating a willingness to pay for this type of coverage.

The percentage of baby boomers who would pay to have access to tax and legal advice later in life is smaller than that of seniors, with 42 percent versus 49 percent, respectively, indicating that preference. Paying for housekeeping and chores is important to a little over one-third (or 35 percent) of baby boomers, whereas 46 percent of seniors feel this benefit is important. The two groups also perceive companion and monitoring services differently, with 27 percent of boomers and 36 percent of seniors expressing a willingness to pay for these services. There are differences in perceptions of the importance of transportation or escort services, with 24 percent of boomers and 36 percent of seniors indicating such a preference. Finally, a smaller percentage of baby boomers than seniors (22 percent vs. 33 percent) would pay for access to adult day-care services that they might need in the future.

Health care

There are marked differences between the two generations in preferences and use of healthcare products and services. In one of our studies, we asked people in both generations to tell us whether they presently own or use, or would like to own or use, two healthcare-related products (at home): self-diagnostic medical equipment and exercise equipment. A smaller percentage of baby boomers (9 percent), compared with older adults (15 percent), reported ownership or use of self-diagnostic medical equipment, but 44 percent of baby boomers and 37 percent of seniors reported ownership or use of exercise equipment. The same people were also asked to tell us whether they presently use or would like to use four selected health-care-related services: health club membership, paid at-home assistance with personal needs and chores, health-membership program (for routine medical check-ups), and medical-care services at their home.

About half of baby boomers (52 percent), compared with 19 percent of seniors, use or would like to use a health club membership, while about three in ten of the people in both generations prefer to receive assistance with personal needs and chores. Two-thirds (or 68 percent) of baby boomers, compared with 43 percent of seniors, prefer health-membership programs. However, a smaller percentage of baby boomers than older adults prefer to have medical services provided at their home, with 32 percent and 43 percent expressing that preference, respectively.

About half of baby boomers (52 percent), compared with 19 percent of seniors, use or would like to use a health club membership.

CHAPTER SEVEN

Buying Habits

PEOPLE IN THE TWO GENERATIONS differ in many ways when it comes to looking at their buying habits, whether one looks at their selection of retail outlets, use of information sources, choice of specific products and services, preferences for methods of payment, overall satisfaction with the marketplace, or patterns of product consumption.

Before presenting detailed information, it is worth noting some general findings on the habits of shoppers in the two generations. *Locational convenience* is highly valued among shoppers in both generations, and it is a major reason for patronizing specific stores, especially among the older generation. Many seniors would pay a higher price to shop at a conveniently located store rather than go out of their way to save money. In one of our national studies, we found that more than four in ten shoppers are willing to pay a higher price for location convenience. Those who are willing to pay higher prices for convenience tend to be older, have higher incomes, have had a better education, live alone, and are not married. The importance of convenience is also shown in shoppers' preference for one-stop shopping. Again, the older generation prefers one-stop shopping more than their baby boomer children. One of our studies found about six in ten people prefer one-stop shopping. Those most likely to appreciate this type of convenience not only tend to be older, but also have less education and income, and are most likely to live in north-central and southern states than in other parts of the country.

> Many seniors would pay a higher price to shop at a conveniently located store rather than go out of their way to save money.

There are *other types of convenience* valued more by the older generation, including valet parking, easy check-out, and payment for purchases made. People who appreciate the convenience of having their cars parked when they go shopping also tend to have less education and income, and are more likely to live in northern states than in western states.

Once people choose a product, they do not like to spend time in *check-out lines*. Many would rather pay cash and get out of the store quickly. Who wants to see more "cash only" registers in the stores? Logically, those who prefer to pay with cash do not want to wait in lines. These individuals are primarily older, with lower income and education levels. They are also more likely to be male shoppers. The same type of shoppers are of the opinion that stores should charge less when a person pays "cash" for purchases, an opinion that married shoppers are more likely to have than those who are not married.

Once people choose a product, they do not like to spend time in check-out lines.

Reasons for Patronage

Reasons for patronage tend to differ according to the type of establishment patronized, as well as by generation. In one of our large-scale national studies, we examined patronage reasons for various types of establishments. The following are some of our findings categorized by type of establishment.

Restaurants

When it comes to deciding where to eat out, people in the two generations are looking for different things. However, there are three factors that stand out. First, seven in ten baby boomers consider the restaurant's comfort for socializing, compared with half of the older Americans. Seven in ten baby boomers also consider the restaurant's location in relation to their place of residence or work, compared with nearly half of the elderly. Finally, six in ten baby boomers and four in ten older Americans value a recommendation from a same-age patron.

When baby boomers go out, they do more than just eat. They also run errands, shop, go to a movie, or visit other retail establishments. As a result, they value convenient locations more than their parents. Half of baby boomers consider a restaurant's location in relation to other types of patronized retail outlets, compared with just one-third of their elderly counterparts. Similarly, restaurant service is important to one-third of baby boomers but only to one-fourth of their parents (or 34 percent vs. 25 percent). As expected, senior discounts are more attractive to older adults because senior discounts are available only to the aged.

Drug stores & pharmacies

When patronizing drug stores and pharmacies, location is of the utmost importance to baby boomers, but this factor is not as important to the older generation. Eight in ten baby boomers, compared with nearly two-thirds of the latter group, consider location of a drug store in their patronage decision. Location near other establishments one patronizes is slightly more important to a larger percentage of baby boomers than to their parents, with 57 percent and 53 percent, respectively, mentioning this factor. The last factor important to baby boomers, but of lesser importance to the elderly, is ease of locating merchandise, with three in ten and two in ten, respectively, mentioning this as a motivation. On the other hand, several factors important to baby boomers are of even greater importance to their parents, such as availability of products suitable to their health needs (51 percent vs. 64 percent), availability of familiar brands (55 percent vs. 59 percent), and helpful personnel (41 percent vs. 50 percent).

Food/grocery stores

Although a significant number of people in the two generations mention the same reasons for patronizing specific grocery stores, the two generations differ with regard to the emphasis they put on those specific reasons. We found a larger percentage of baby boomers than older people patronize food stores as a result of location convenience, with 91 percent and 83 percent, respectively. However, a smaller percentage of baby boomers than their parents consider items on sale (67 percent vs. 77 percent), personal assistance (27 percent vs. 41 percent), special-assistance services (23 percent vs. 41 percent), recommendation of same-age peer groups (13 percent vs. 19 percent), and as expected, special discounts to customers over a certain age (7 percent vs. 31 percent). In comparison with baby boomers, members of the older generation prefer grocery stores that tout low prices, though they tend to be less concerned with prices when choosing a department store.

Department stores
Less than two-thirds (or 64 percent) of people in the older generation told us that they patronize specific department stores because of sales or specials, while 79 percent of their baby boomer children said they shop specific department stores for sales and specials. But price is not the main reason boomers shop at a department store. Ease of returning products or getting refunds is considered important by the largest majority (86 percent) of baby boomers, compared with two-thirds of their parents. Two-thirds of baby boomers patronize department stores because items can be located with considerable ease, familiar brands are readily available, the personnel are helpful, and the store location is convenient. All these factors are of lesser importance to their older counterparts. In fact, the elderly value nearly all these factors less than baby boomers. Both groups value the availability of products suitable to specific physical/health needs equally, and age-based discounts are considered more by the elderly due to their availability.

Lodging
When it comes to traveling and choosing a place to stay, once again baby boomers care more about price. About three-fourths (or 77 percent) of baby boomers consider room rates, compared with six out of ten older travelers. Discounts to certain age groups, such as children or seniors, are of importance to nearly half of baby boomers

(46 percent) and six in ten senior travelers. The following set of factors is considered by approximately one-third of baby boomers, while the same factors are less important to the older generation: convenience in doing business by phone (36 percent vs. 21 percent), accessibility of the hotel or motel (36 percent vs. 19 percent), and group or membership programs available (33 percent vs. 18 percent). The remaining factors are less important to both groups, especially to older travelers.

Airlines/cruise lines
When people in both generations think about traveling and destinations, their main preoccupation is not convenience or services; it is price. We found economic factors motivate the patronage decisions of both age groups when choosing airlines or cruise lines. The economic motive is stronger among baby boomers than among older adults, with 66 percent of boomers and 46 percent of seniors indicating a price preference. Baby boomers look for special deals through group or membership programs more than the elderly, with 44 percent compared to 29 percent, respectively. Discounts for different age groups appeal equally to younger and older travelers, with 41 percent of boomers versus 43 percent of their parents looking for such offerings. Ease of doing business by phone or by mail is important to nearly four in ten baby boomers, while this factor is important to only one in four older travelers.

We also looked at some additional factors that make people choose certain travel-service providers, and we found them to be of lesser importance to both groups. However, explanation of various services by staff is nearly twice as important to baby boomers as it is to the older generation (24 percent vs. 14 percent). Similarly, advice of same-age peers is more important to the younger than the older group, with 33 percent and 18 percent expressing this preference, respectively. The way people of various ages are portrayed in advertisements of airlines and cruise lines is neither a very important reason (mentioned by only one-fifth of the respondents) nor is it perceived differently by the two age groups.

Financial institutions

There are two main reasons people in the two generations choose to do business with a specific financial institution: convenience in reaching the service provider, and the staff's ability or willingness to explain various services. Nearly half of baby boomers, compared with one-third of seniors, mentioned both these reasons in one of our studies. About four in ten of the younger generation say they decide to patronize certain financial institutions because of their fees, the ease of having related services at the same place, and the ease of doing business by phone or by mail. A somewhat smaller percentage (about one-third) of seniors considers these factors important. Also of importance to about one-third of the younger group is staff assistance in filling out forms, referrals or endorsements, and the advice of same-age peers. A smaller percentage of seniors also indicated the importance of these factors.

In general, people prefer to receive different services from different financial service providers, although we see generational differences in such preferences. For example, commercial banks are the most preferred financial-service providers for savings and checking accounts. Seven in ten baby boomers and nearly eight in ten seniors prefer commercial banks. Nearly four in ten of the younger generation prefers to have savings and checking accounts at credit unions, compared with only half of their parents. Both groups equally prefer receiving such services from savings and loans (S&Ls) institutions, with about three in ten expressing this preference.

Insurance companies

When deciding to buy an insurance policy, baby boomers do more shopping than their parents and deliberate longer before buying. In one of our surveys, we mentioned 13 reasons people decide to do business with an insurance company. We asked the people surveyed to tell us if these reasons were important to them. We found nearly every reason to be more important to the younger generation than to the older group. Price leads the list, with seven in ten baby boomers, compared with half of their parents, indicating its importance. Assistance with filling out forms is not very important to seniors, but it is apparently a critical factor for younger people choosing between insurance-service providers, with 57 percent of baby boomers and nearly one-third of seniors expressing a preference for this type of assistance. Apparently, the convenience of not having to deal with those forms, which might be time consuming, is of greater importance to baby boomers, although their response may also reflect a large number of these individuals who might be responsible for assisting their older relatives and need such help. Nearly as many baby boomers (56 percent) as seniors (42 percent) indicated that the convenience of doing business by phone or by mail is also important in their patronage decision.

When deciding to buy an insurance policy, baby boomers do more shopping than their parents and deliberate longer before buying.

Preference for payment methods is important to nearly half of baby boomers, but this attribute is not nearly as important in the patronage decision of their parents, with just 28 percent of the latter group expressing this preference. Nearly four in ten baby boomers are influenced by the convenience of reaching the service provider, compared with 23 percent of the older generation. Nearly 37 percent of baby boomers patronize certain insurance companies because of the referrals they receive from various professionals, compared with just 13 percent of seniors.

Approximately one-third of baby boomers are influenced by the advice of same-age peers, compared with just 14 percent of seniors, and convenience is twice as important to the former than to the latter group (32 percent vs. 17 percent). The advice of children or close relatives is twice as important to baby boomers as it is to older adults, with 28 percent and 13 percent valuing this advice, respectively. Age-based discounts are of equal importance to both age groups, while age-stereotyping in ads is less important to baby boomers than to seniors, with 12 percent and 19 percent, respectively, indicating the importance of this factor. Special deals through group or membership programs are not important in the patronage decision of either age group.

The importance of different reasons for patronage also varies according to the type of insurance policy under consideration. For example, when buying LTC insurance, those with less education and income tend to be influenced by the sales agent.

Reasons for choosing an insurance company when buying an LTC policy vary according to certain demographic factors: Among baby boomers, three-fourths of younger baby boomers, compared with only half of older baby boomers, rely more on the amount of coverage for home health care.

- A larger percentage of the older generation, compared with baby boomers, rely more on coverage of home health care (86 percent vs. 65 percent), and on the name and reputation of the insurance company (87 percent vs. 61 percent).
- Those in the two generations with the least education choose an insurance company based on the recommendation of friends and relatives, a sales agent's explanation of insurance policy features, and direct mail brochures explaining policy features.
- Regardless of age, those with the least income choose an insurance company on the basis of home healthcare coverage and a sales agent's explanation of LTC policy features.
- Baby boomers and their parents from eastern states are at least twice as likely as those from other parts of the country to choose an insurance company based on direct mail brochures they received.

Hospitals

When they are free to choose, how do people decide the hospital from which they will receive healthcare services? Baby boomers consider many more factors than their parents, but convenient location is of utmost importance to both generations. Personnel-related reasons also appear to be important to both age groups, with 45 percent of baby boomers and 36 percent of seniors indicating that assistance with filling out forms is an important factor in their patronage decisions. Another 41 percent of boomers, compared with

31 percent of seniors, report that a staff's willingness to explain various services is another important factor.

Twice as many baby boomers as seniors (35 percent vs. 17 percent) rely on referrals by firms or professionals, and 38 percent of boomers versus 21 percent of seniors patronize a specific hospital because of reasons related to billing/payment policies. Nearly three in ten baby boomers, compared with a little over one in ten seniors, consider the advice of children or close relatives, whereas the importance of the advice of same-age peers is more important to baby boomers than to seniors (25 percent vs. 19 percent).

Physicians and surgeons
Convenience appears to be of importance to the majority of people in both generations in deciding where they are going to look for a doctor. Baby boomers consider a large number of factors when choosing a doctor, and certain reasons for that choice are more important to them than to people in the older generation. About half of baby boomers, compared with about three in ten older adults, visit a specific physician due to a referral or endorsement from firms or other doctors. Nearly as many of the younger group (47 percent), compared with 36 percent of their parents, choose a physician or surgeon because these professionals take time to explain their services, or because of the advice of children or close relatives (45 percent vs. 32 percent). Four in ten baby boomers, compared with about one in three seniors, visit specific healthcare professionals because their offices assist them with filling out insurance forms. The doctor's billing or payment policies are important to 35 percent of baby boomers and 27 percent of seniors. The advice of close relatives seems to be important to 36 percent of boomers and 23 percent of the elderly.

In contrast, several factors are more important to older Americans than to those in the younger generation when selecting a specific physician or surgeon. These factors include: price, ease of doing business by phone or by mail, discounts to age groups, and proper age stereotyping in ads of physicians.

Buying Products

Many people are cautious when buying products, but people become increasingly risk-averse with age. In one of our studies, we found that 48 percent of baby boomers and six in ten of their parents would not buy a product unless they knew it would be easy to return. The younger baby boomers are the least cautious, with only 42 percent of them, compared with 54 percent of older baby boomers, expressing interest in the store's return policy. Those with lower-income and education are the most cautious, and married shoppers are more concerned than single shoppers about easy returns.

One way consumers demonstrate caution when shopping is through their unwillingness to buy a product without trying it first. Free samples are usually a good way of ensuring the product will be satisfactory. People in the older generation are more hesitant than baby boomers to buy a new product unless they have had a free sample, and they become more reliant on free samples as they age. The lower the person's income and education levels, the greater his or her reliance on free samples. We found women rely on free samples more than men. While a free sample may help a person reduce purchase uncertainty, free samples are also used in evaluating the benefits of new products. Many women may use free samples because they wish to judge the desirability of new products.

People in the older generation are more hesitant than boomers to buy a new product unless they have had a free sample, and they become more reliant on free samples as they age.

We found that those living in eastern states tend to be the most venturesome shoppers in both generations. Two in ten report that they like trying something new every time they are in the store, compared with one in ten of those people living in the western part of the country. Also, women are more adventurous than men when trying new products.

Easterners tend to be the most venturesome shoppers in both generations.

More than seven in ten people spend a great deal of time examining products before buying them. Older people and those living with others spend the greatest amount of time examining products prior to purchase. A major reason older shoppers spend more time examining products is because they have difficulty reading information on packages and labels. While only 12 percent of younger baby boomers often find the type on packages or labels too small to read, one-fourth of older baby boomers report frequent frustration with the size of lettering. Fifty-eight percent of the older generation reports the same problems; 55 percent of those in the 55-to-74 age bracket and 63 percent of those in the 75-and-over bracket report reading problems.

However, poor vision is not the only cause of a consumer's frustration. Another factor is the inability to understand what one reads. We found that people with less education and income also report frequent difficulty in understanding information on packages and labels.

While obtaining information from packages presents a problem to many people in both generations, the availability of overwhelming amounts of information can be equally frustrating. We asked people in both generations what they think about the ease of understanding the information on products, and found that about one-third of shoppers experience difficulty handling large amounts of product information. Approximately the same percentage of people admits that they often do not know how to tell which brand is best for them to buy.

People unable to determine which products are best for them often ask store personnel for help. Those most likely to ask sales clerks for assistance are older men with lower incomes. However, only one in seven admits to getting assistance from salespeople when they go shopping. Again, those who are most likely to value personal assistance tend to be older with less income and education. More than half of people living in eastern states, compared with just over a third of people living in the West (or 36 percent), would be interested in having a personal advisor to assist them.

Shoppers who find it too difficult to discern which product is best, based on information gathered about specific products, will often use practical "rules of thumb" to decide if a product is worth buying. About 45 percent of people admit to judging some products by the name of the store that sells them. And because older people report greater difficulty in judging products based on their merits, they are more inclined than their younger counterparts to rely on store reputation, with about half of them forming impressions about products based on store name, compared with 41 percent of baby boomers who do the same. Those who rely most on store reputation tend to be older, with higher incomes and more education. Urban dwellers are more inclined than rural residents to judge products by the name of the store.

Almost half admit to judging some products by the name of the store that sells them.

How do people in the two generations respond to various promotional appeals? The older generation tends to be more responsive to promotions than baby boomers. For example, in one of our national studies, we found that shoppers attracted to special displays in the store are primarily older, with 41 percent of the elderly and 27 percent of baby boomers admitting attraction to in-store displays.

The older generation responds more to promotions than baby boomers.

Who is most likely to respond to special deals when choosing a specific brand? While approximately six in ten admit that a special sale or discount coupon will tempt them to buy a different brand from the one they usually buy, younger people, particularly men from middle-income families who are married or live with others, are most responsive to such offerings.

Who pays attention to warranties and guarantees? We found that people in the younger generation are more attracted to these offerings than their older counterparts, especially those with more education and higher income.

Although about seven in ten people we surveyed admitted that they often watch the ads for sale announcements, those most likely to pay attention to the ads tend to be older, have low levels of income and education, and are likely to be married or live with others. Similarly, older consumers are more likely than baby boomers to buy products because they like their ads. As expected, a larger percentage of the older generation than the baby boom generation prefers ads targeting older audiences. Specifically, 24 percent of seniors compared with just 7 percent of the younger group prefer such ads. A little more than one-third of those aged 75 and over seem to like ads showing products especially for older people. However, this preference is also higher among lower-income and less-educated groups of people.

The same people who like ads marketing to older people also think there should be less advertising showing older people in situations where they are the authority figure. One reason for this may be that ads targeting older people are often of bad taste. And while people pay equal attention to ads featuring spokespersons of different ages, regardless of demographic background, older people are more sensitive to age stereotypes in advertising. Thirty percent of people age 55 and over, compared with 22 percent of younger adults, told us in one national survey that they had avoided buying certain products because their ads improperly stereotyped younger or older people.

Information Sources

We also wanted to know how much people in the two generations rely on various sources of information and the extent to which these sources affect their purchasing decisions for specific types of products. In several of our studies, we asked many different people to tell us how much they use the various sources of consumer information, and we looked at the differences in responses between the two generations. People in the two generations show different inclinations to use a variety of information sources when buying products and services. Reliance on different sources varies not only based on a person's age but also on the basis of the product or service. For example, when it comes to using various types of information sources when buying *appliances,* baby boomers use a large number of information sources. Specifically, a larger percentage of this group, compared with senior citizens, learns about appliances from radio and TV ads; 46 percent versus 33 percent, respectively. Thirty-nine percent of baby boomers and 26 percent of seniors learn about appliances from articles or TV programs, and 69 percent and 61 percent get information through newspaper and magazine ads, respectively. Twenty-two percent of boomers and 10 percent of seniors get appliance information from relatives other than a spouse; 34 percent and 15 percent get that info from friends or acquaintances, respectively. Help from business reps or professionals is preferred by 13 percent of boomers and 6 percent of seniors in making their appliance-purchasing decisions.

The two main sources of information for new *electronic products* are advertisements and direct mail. Television and print ads are preferred by six in ten baby boomers and older adults, while about three in ten of both groups prefer to receive news about such products in the mail. Learning in group meetings or seminars is a preferred alternative among just 3 percent of baby boomers, compared with 7 percent of older adults. For *telecommunication services*, a greater percentage of baby boomers (64 percent) than older adults (57 percent) prefer to receive information from television or print ads. Slightly less than 30 percent of both groups prefer to receive news in the mail, while learning in seminars or group meetings is less important to baby boomers than to elderly consumers, with 4 percent and 9 percent expressing this preference, respectively.

> The two main sources of information for new electronic products are advertisements and direct mail.

In one study, we asked people in both generations how they preferred to gather info about new *vacation or travel packages*. Nearly half of baby boomers (45 percent), compared with 37 percent of older respondents, prefer to be informed through TV or print ads. About four in ten of the younger group prefer to receive information in the mail, compared with 43 percent of the older group. Finally, obtaining information in group meetings or seminars is preferred by 6 percent of the younger generation, while twice as many older adults (13 percent) prefer to be informed about new vacation or travel packages through these meetings.

In the same study, those questioned were presented with a list of five sources of information and were asked to check the one they preferred in the case of new *drug and cosmetic products*. We found that the majority of baby boomers (63 percent) prefer television and print ads, while direct mail is preferred by three in ten boomers. The percentage of baby boomers who prefer the remaining sources—phone contact, agent visit, learning in group meetings or seminars—is negligible, and the responses given by seniors were similar to those given by baby boomers.

Nearly two-thirds of baby boomers prefer to learn about what is new in *fashion* through TV or print ads. This figure is somewhat higher than the 61 percent of the older generation that prefers TV or print ads. Almost one-third of both groups prefer direct mail. Learning in group meetings is not a very popular way to acquire information about fashion, although this method is somewhat more popular among older consumers than among their baby boomer children (4 percent vs. 1 percent, respectively).

Forty-four percent of baby boomers, compared with 36 percent of seniors, prefer to be informed about *financial services* by receiving news in the mail. About one in five of the younger group would like to be informed through ads or visited by an agent, and nearly as many seniors prefer the same. While about one in ten baby boomers prefer to learn about new financial services in group meetings and seminars, almost twice as many seniors favor this source. The younger group is also less likely than the older group to indicate a preference for telephone solicitation, with 4 percent of boomers and 11 percent of seniors expressing this preference.

> More baby boomers than seniors prefer to be informed about financial services by receiving news in the mail.

In the same study that looked into the information preferences regarding the four previously mentioned types of purchasing decisions, we also questioned people in the two generations about new *insurance products*. We found that baby boomers and older adults do not differ with respect to their preferences for TV or print ads and telephone solicitation, and a greater percentage of baby boomers (42 percent) than older adults (34 percent) prefer to receive news in the mail. In contrast, a smaller percentage of baby boomers than seniors prefer to hear about new insurance products from agents on a person-to-person basis, with 27 percent of boomers and 33 percent of the elderly expressing this preference. Baby boomers are less likely than their parents to prefer hearing about such products in group meetings, with 5 percent versus 8 percent, respectively.

Reasons for choosing specific brands

Let's take a closer look at the results of one of our national surveys that asked people of all generations to tell us why they buy specific brands of grocery products, drug products, and apparel.

Food and Alcoholic Beverages. We asked people of both generations why they choose specific brands of food products and alcoholic beverages. Three-fourths (or 76 percent) of the baby boomers indicated they consider price reductions or special sales during their brand selection, compared with 63 percent of those in the older generation. One in four of those in the younger generation consider the ease of using the product, versus 21 percent of the elderly, and 39 percent of boomers consider the advice of same-age peers, compared with 24 percent of their parents. Finally, nearly half of the baby boomers, compared with 29 percent of older adults, take the advice or request of a relative into consideration when choosing specific brands. The seemingly greater influence of informal sources on baby boomers' decisions, compared with senior citizens, might reflect the latter group's increased social isolation. It is interesting to note that while older shoppers pay more attention to the food store's prices when deciding where to buy their groceries, once they are in the store they are not as likely as their baby boomer children to look for special deals.

Older shoppers pay more attention to a store's prices when they decide where to buy groceries, but once in the store they are less likely than boomers to shop for specials.

Drugs and Health Aids. In the drug store, two factors are considered important by the majority of baby boomers: price or special sale, and ease of reading information on labels or brochures, with 54 percent and 58 percent of boomers expressing an inclination toward these factors, respectively. Price is less important to older adults, with 50 percent of the respondents in our study indicating its importance. Ease of reading information on labels is equally important to seniors and baby boomers, with 59 percent of the elderly declaring its importance. Availability of products is important to nearly half of the baby boomers, but 55 percent of their parents find this factor more important. On the other hand, the ease of using the product is important to 45 percent of baby boomers, in comparison with 38 percent of the older generation who consider this factor in their decision concerning pharmaceutical product brands. This finding runs contrary to the conventional belief that the elderly have greater difficulty than younger people in using medications.

Other factors such as availability of coupons and advice or request of a spouse or other relatives are important to four in ten baby boomers; these factors are somewhat less important to the elderly. Surprisingly, compared with older consumers, baby boomers are less self-conscious about the way others see them because of the brand of drugs and health aids they use.

Apparel and Footwear. When choosing clothes and shoes, a greater percentage of baby boomers (94 percent), compared to their older counterparts (76 percent), consider price. As for the advice or request of a spouse or other relatives, 39 percent of baby boomers, compared with 26 percent of seniors, consider such advice when making a purchase. More baby boomers than their parents rely on the advice of same-age peers, with 31 percent and 26 percent indicating this habit, respectively. Baby boomers care more about what others might think of them because of the brand names they wear, with 22 percent of boomers compared with only 10 percent of seniors admitting this self-consciousness. Surprisingly, baby boomers are more affected than their parents by how apparel ads stereotype people their age, with 22 percent versus 15 percent, respectively. And finally, 16 percent of baby boomers factor in the availability of coupons when making decisions, compared with just 10 percent of the elderly. On the other hand, baby boomers are less likely than their parents to rely on the recommendations of salespersons, with 21 percent of boomers compared with 27 percent of seniors depending on this information. Seniors are also more likely to mention that the ease of reading information on apparel products is an important consideration when making a purchase decision, with 12 percent of seniors and 9 percent of their children indicating this preference.

Perhaps the most surprising finding we uncovered from this survey is the greater importance of price and price-related offerings to baby boomers than to their parents. Contrary to conventional belief that older people are more price-conscious, we did not find this to be the case in our survey. We think this may be because today, baby boomers have limited financial resources compared with their parents, and many boomers are aware of needing to make ends meet. It was probably the opposite several years ago, when the seniors were middle-aged, and that contributed to the stereotypical image of a more disadvantaged older population.

At-Home Buying via Phone, Direct Mail, and Door-to-Door. Many people prefer to buy things direct from the source rather than shopping at the mall. But is there a typical person who is the most frequent direct buyer by means of traditional methods (phone, mail, and door-to-door)? We addressed this question in one of our studies, and we found only a few distinguishing factors that describe the frequent at-home buyer.

People from all walks of life buy products and services by phone, regardless of gender, age, or other demographic characteristics. However, the more money people have, the more likely they are to buy products and services by phone. Nearly four in ten adults buy merchandise from catalogs or magazines. People in their retirement years (aged 65 to 74) buy the least, with just 32 percent shopping this way, while women living alone and those residing in urban areas use this shopping method the most. Those people living in the eastern and northern part of the country tend to do the most catalog shopping.

People seem to be more inclined to buy certain products or services directly from the source rather than buying them elsewhere. In one national study, we examined preferences for methods of buying certain products and services, and the reasons for buying or not buying direct. We uncovered some interesting generational differences.

Buying Specific Products and Services. While purchasing *clothes and shoes* at a store is by far the most preferred method for both groups, one-third of baby boomers would also buy such products through the mail, compared with slightly less than one-fifth of the older consumers.

We also investigated preferences for purchasing methods in the case of *prescription drugs, cosmetics, and health aids*. While purchasing such products at the store is the most preferred method for both generations, this preference is stronger among baby boomers than among the elderly, with 95 percent and 90 percent favoring in-store shopping, respectively. Purchasing prescription drugs by phone is preferred only by 7 percent of the baby boomers, versus 10 percent of their parents. Although only 6 percent of baby boomers would purchase drugs through the mail, 14 percent would buy cosmetics and health aids this way, compared with just 9 percent of their parents. While only 9 percent of boomers would buy such products from door-to-door salesmen, an even smaller percentage of seniors (4 percent) would use this method. The most preferred method of purchasing cosmetics and health aids is at retail outlets, with 91 percent of baby boomers and 88 percent of seniors expressing this preference. These findings suggest that more baby boomers than senior citizens would buy prescription drugs, cosmetics, and health aids through multiple channels of distribution.

> Only 6 percent of baby boomers would purchase drugs through the mail, but 14 percent would buy cosmetics and health aids this way, compared with just 9 percent of their parents.

How do baby boomers prefer to purchase *vacation packages*? We asked whether they prefer buying such services at vendor facilities, by phone, through the mail, or from door-to-door salesmen at their home or office (those surveyed could indicate more than one preference). The vast majority of people in both generations indicated a preference for purchasing vacation packages at vendor facilities, with 66 percent of baby boomers and 55 percent of older people expressing this inclination. The two groups differed with respect to their preference for buying vacation packages over the phone, with 27 percent of boomers and 21 percent of the elderly expressing this preference. About one in five in both groups prefers direct mail, while preference for door-to-door salesmen was the least popular option, with just 5 percent of baby boomers and 3 percent of seniors expressing interest in this method.

Baby boomers and seniors prefer purchasing *financial services* at financial-service providers' facilities equally, with about six in ten of each generation indicating this preference. Both groups also prefer buying financial services by phone equally, with about one-fourth of each group indicating this preference. However, baby boomers are more likely than their parents to express a preference for buying financial products from the salesperson who visits them or through the mail, with 15 percent of the younger consumer group versus 10 percent of the older generation showing interest in buying from door-to-door salesmen, and 8 percent versus 4 percent preferring buying through the mail, respectively.

Baby boomers are more likely than their parents to express a preference for buying financial products from the salesperson who visits them or through the mail.

Insurance policies may be purchased at vendor establishments, door-to-door, by phone, or through the mail. We asked participants in our survey which method they favored. Purchasing insurance at vendor facilities is the most preferred way of acquiring such services, with 45 percent of baby boomers, compared with 35 percent of seniors, indicating this preference. Purchasing insurance policies by phone or door-to-door were equally preferred by the two age groups, with 30 percent of baby boomers and 27 percent of seniors reporting this preference, respectively. Only 7 percent of the younger group indicated a preference for buying through the mail. Boomers' responses for the last three methods were fairly similar to these given by the older group.

Eight Reasons for Buying. There are several reasons people decide to buy direct. We reviewed dozens of published studies on this topic, and we concluded that there are at least eight possible reasons that affect one's decision to buy or not buy directly from the sources, regardless of the product or service they contemplate buying. We presented the people we surveyed with a list of these eight reasons and asked them to tell us whether they considered each an important factor in their decision to buy or not buy the following items or services direct: apparel and footwear, insurance policies, electronic products, and drugs and health aids. We found that all eight factors are more important to baby boomers than to their elders when deciding to buy *clothes and shoes* directly from the manufacturer. The main reason for deciding whether to buy these products direct is the return/cancellation and refund policy, with 78 percent of baby boomers and 63 percent of older adults indicating the importance of this factor, respectively. The second most important reason is price, with three-fourths of baby boomers and two-thirds of their parents mentioning this reason. All of the remaining factors examined are perceived to be important by the majority of baby boomers, but not by the majority of their parents, when contemplating direct purchase of clothes.

Factors Considered When Shopping

- Price (including shipping charges)
- Type of credit card accepted
- Return/cancellation and refund policy
- Convenience, in comparison of other ways of buying same product
- Free pick-up service for returns
- Availability of toll-free number
- Selection of products
- Days to wait before receiving

When deciding whether to buy *insurance policies* direct, about half of baby boomers, compared with 36 percent of the older adults, think a toll free number is important. Four in ten baby boomers consider price, compared with one in four older adults. In comparison to other ways of buying the same product/service, convenience is twice as important to baby boomers as it is to seniors, with 32 percent and 16 percent, respectively, indicating the importance of this factor in their decision to purchase insurance policies directly from the service provider. Similarly, twice as many boomers as their parents consider cancellation and refund policies important (or 36 percent vs. 19 percent). Three in ten of the younger generation, compared with only 13 percent of seniors, say they are influenced by the availability of various insurance products. Credit card acceptance and free delivery of, or pick-up service for, required forms are factors that are not as important to seniors as they are to their baby boomer children. One in four baby boomers and nearly half as many seniors (or 14 percent) consider the number of days they must wait before they start receiving insurance coverage a critical factor.

In examining the reasons for buying *electronic products* direct, we again found that baby boomers consider all eight factors more important than their parents do. Price and return/cancellation or refund policy are considered important by nearly three-fourths of the baby boomers, compared with less than half of those in the older generation who consider such factors important. For the remaining factors, baby boomers are twice as likely as older consumers to say that such factors are important in their decision to buy or not buy electronic products by phone or by mail.

For *pharmaceutical products,* price appears to be among the most important considerations for baby boomers, with 45 percent of them mentioning this reason in their decision to buy direct. This factor is even more important to older consumers, with 51 percent of them mentioning this preference. The waiting period prior to receiving the product is of almost equal importance to both groups, with 44 percent of baby boomers and 36 percent of seniors mentioning this reason. The least important factor among those presented to respondents is free pick-up service for returns, a factor that is of even less importance to older consumers than younger ones (19 percent vs. 13 percent, respectively). The remaining factors were important to a little over one-third of the baby boomers, and they were also equally important to their parents.

The Internet as a Source of Information or a Purchasing Channel

We have been researching people's dispositions toward the Internet for 30 years, closely following early trials and field experiments in North America and Europe in the late 1970s and 1980s. Our consulting work with companies that were participating in these trials revealed that at that time, consumers were not likely to accept this new technology very rapidly, and the time needed for a wide acceptance of this innovation would depend on making the service user-friendly, affordable, and valuable to the consumer. But we did not know then just how quickly technology could change to make the use of the Internet attractive to consumers.

Thousands of studies have been done to help understand the kinds of people who are likely to buy new products and services when they first become available in the marketplace; and hundreds have focused on Internet users. What we know and are sure about is that the early adopters of technological innovations have characteristics that make them stand out from the crowd. They are, for example, younger, better educated, earn more money, have a greater exposure to information sources and lead active lifestyles. These observations were also true with respect to the early users of the Internet. Today, however, with the large majority of U.S. households "plugged in," these characteristics do not distinguish Internet users from non-users as well as they used to.

Internet use and growth

Since the early 1990s, we have witnessed rapid growth of Internet use by businesses and households. The first subscribers to this service were individuals who already owned a PC, which they had purchased for reasons other than going online. Recently, people have increasingly been purchasing computers and other high tech devices primarily to have access to Internet services. Today, we estimate that the percentages of people who are PC or laptop owners and Internet users are approximately the same. At the time of publication, we estimated that computer ownership and the use of Internet by U.S. households was approaching 75 percent, based on data from our most recent studies. The percentage of people who use this service in some other developed countries—especially those geographically isolated such as Australia and Iceland—is even higher.

Presently, we estimate that in the U.S. nearly 80 percent of baby boomers and approximately half of their elderly parents have access to Internet services from their homes or work, and frequently go online. These figures will be even higher by the time you are reading this book. *The Digital Future Report* by the University of Southern California, which has been tracking Internet use annually since the beginning of this millennium, shows that use among older adults continues to grow steadily. The percentage of older adults who sign up for these services each year is greater than the percentages of the baby boomers and younger age groups in general, according to the University's recent report. And this trend is not new. Statistics from surveys released by the AARP in its recent publication, *The State of 50+ America,* show growth of Internet use by age from 1998 to 2005. In 1998, 31 percent of those aged 50 to 64, 12 percent of those aged 65 to 74, and only 4 percent of the 75-plus group were going on line. In 2005, these figures were 65 percent, 45 percent, and 24 percent, respectively.

Nearly 80 percent of U.S. baby boomers and approximately half of their parents have access to the Internet at home or work.

Not only do people in the older age groups sign up in greater numbers, but they also make heavier use of the Internet once they log-in. Older Internet users spend roughly twice as much time online than younger users, and the available evidence suggests that they will be spending even more time online in the future. The growing use of the Internet among the older population in relation to younger users is clearly shown in statistics released by Nielsen. For example, the Company's NetRatings, a service provider that tracks Internet use from year to year, showed that within a one year time span, from 2002 to 2003, the percentage of people in the two generations who spent *more* time online were approximately 1 percent for the baby boomers and 20 percent for their parents.

Baby boomers and older adult users

With our estimated figures of three-fourths of baby boomers and half of their parents going online, we were interested in learning more about the users and non-users in the two generations. We therefore looked at our most recent surveys where we had collected information on Internet users and non-users and their characteristics.

In comparison to baby boomers who do not use the Internet, those who go online do the following more frequently:
- Socialize with friends and relatives
- Go shopping
- Eat out
- Do volunteer work
- Take various types of classes/courses
- Attend various events—cultural, sporting, social

And below are the most frequent activities of Internet users in the older generation, in comparison with the ways their non-user counterparts spend their time and money. Older users do the following more frequently:
- Go shopping
- Eat out
- Travel
- Attend various events—cultural, sporting, social

The Internet as a source of information

What do people in the two generations do when they log-in, besides check their email? Both generations surf the web for information on things that affect them and are of a personal nature or do not feel comfortable discussing with others, such as finances and health care. In one of our recent studies we examined preferences for information related to healthcare products and services. We found our respondents in both generations value the information they receive from the web nearly as much as they value the information they get from their doctors, much more than any other source of consumer information about healthcare issues, as the following table shows.

TABLE 7-1

Preferences for Sources of Information for Health-Related Products and Services Among Adults in the Two Generations

in percent

	Baby Boomers	Parents
Doctors	51	49
Internet	44	40
Articles in magazines or newspapers	30	42
Brochures/flyers in the mail	37	29
TV & radio advertisements	16	8
Retailers/salespeople (for health-related products)	13	13
Newspaper & magazine advertisements	11	14
Word-of-mouth (relatives/friends/neighbors)	10	9

What is surprising is not just the high use of the Internet but also the low impact of word-of-mouth. Word-of-mouth is an important source of information when consumer decisions are risky or there is a lot at stake, but it seems that people in both generations consider their health problems more private and do not feel comfortable discussing them with others. It is also possible that informal personal sources are not consulted for information on healthcare-related issues because such sources are not perceived as knowledgeable about these matters. There are only two statistically significant differences in the preferences of the two generations: older people find information they read in articles in magazines and newspapers more helpful than baby boomers do; and baby boomers show a stronger preference for information that is given or mailed to them in brochures and flyers.

Online purchases

What, how often, and how much do people in the two generations shop online? We tried to address these questions in our research and we concluded that the answer depends, in part, on the person's needs and life circumstances. Generally, though, baby boomers buy more. In 2005, we estimated that approximately 43 percent of all baby boomers and about 27 percent of their parents who were "plugged in" had purchased one or more product or service through the Internet, on average. Those with higher incomes purchased more. Travel-related services, such as airline tickets and lodging accommodations, were the most frequently purchased offerings, with about 25 percent of the baby boomers and 22 percent of their parents with Internet access making their travel arrangements online. These figures have led us to conclude that the older generation seems to travel more frequently. Consumer preferences for purchasing travel-related services from the Internet are reflected in statistics released by the Travel Industry Association of America (TIAA) in 2006 based on a survey of 1,300 adults. TIAA estimates that about 79 million U.S. consumers rely on the Internet for travel planning, and more than 65 million of them purchase travel products or services online.

Other products consumers in the two generations are likely to purchase online include clothing and books, with nearly 15 percent of people in both generations with Internet access ordering such products. However, the share of purchases for most products available on the Web is still fairly small when compared with alternate options, even with other forms of at-home channels such as direct mail and phone. A main reason for this is concern with security of the private information that users are asked to provide. A 2005 survey of 1,380 adults ages 18 to 54, conducted by Frank N. Magid Associates, found that 44 percent of the respondents agreed with the statement, "I do not feel comfortable giving my credit card number online," compared with 29 percent of those who disagreed. A recent increase in the number of identity thefts have not helped consumers feel more secure doing business over the Internet.

Despite security concerns, the future of the Internet as a source of information and as a purchasing channel is bright, judging from recent trends in the industry. Savvy consumers go online in increasing numbers to order products, which is affecting the sales of brick and mortar retailers. A recent trend that gives headaches to both retailers and manufacturers is the increasing numbers of consumers who shop for products such as electronics and appliances at retail stores, and once they decide what to buy, order the product directly from the manufacturer over the Internet. Retailers have been suffering due to their salespeople's ineffective use of their time, while manufacturers have been receiving an increasing number of complaints from their distributors. Quite likely, many retailers are going to alter their mix of products and services to keep shoppers from leaving their premises empty-handed by offering additional benefits, such as after-sales services and better credit terms than consumers can get in buying direct via the Internet.

The influence of relatives

Consumers in the two generations do not always make purchasing decisions independently or in a social vacuum. Their decisions are often made jointly with other relatives or are influenced a great deal by them, including their spouse. We looked into joint decision-making with relatives (we excluded those who were not married) for a variety of products and services among consumers in the two generations and found variability in such influence by type of product or service. We present these results in Table 7-2.

TABLE 7-2

The Influence of Relatives on Select Purchasing Decisions of Consumers in the Two Generations

Purchasing Decision	BABY BOOMERS percent who decide: alone	BABY BOOMERS percent who decide: with others	PARENTS percent who decide: alone	PARENTS percent who decide: with others
Travel/vacation package to get	6	85	9	84
Types of housing to move into	4	87	4	85
Cable channels to subscribe to	8	80	13	72
Medical services to receive	34	61	22	70
Appliance and furniture to buy	18	73	16	66
Car to buy	20	63	16	54
Investments to hold	19	64	24	51
Types of insurance to have	22	57	16	54
Non-prescription drugs to buy	54	35	41	49
Meals to fix or order	52	27	41	30

Companies often assume that their consumers are individuals acting to satisfy their own needs in isolation from others in their social environment. The figures presented above for a wide variety of consumption situations suggest that such an assumption is more likely to be the exception rather than the rule. The reality is that most consumer decisions are made jointly or with the help and influence of significant others, especially for products and services that are likely to be consumed by more than one person in the household, such as travel and housing. But even products and services likely to be consumed by only one person in the household, such as healthcare services, are subject to the influence of the consumer's significant others.

What these findings and numbers mean is that marketers who target select individuals within the household may not get the best results because their efforts ignore other players who are likely to have a say in the final purchase decision. They underscore the importance of understanding the social context in which decisions for their products are made. While information about products and services may be sought independently by the consumer—as we have mentioned earlier in the case of Internet use for getting health-related information—we have a different story when it comes to making a decision where there are several individuals who are likely to participate in or influence the buying decision. The marketer's task becomes even more challenging and more expensive in trying to satisfy the information needs of all key players. In many occasions, participants in such decisions are anything but homogeneous and require different marketing strategies—such as advertising messages and types of media to effectively reach them and satisfy their information needs. The task of reaching the target audience becomes easier when the decision maker is likely to be a specific individual in the household acting independently. The information presented in Table 7-2 shows that relatives are most influential on decisions involving products and services such as travel and housing; they are least influential on choices of meals. Therefore, the marketer's task is more challenging in the former situations than in the latter case. But we are not finished yet.

Besides generational factors in some cases, such as the decision on what non-prescription drugs to buy, where the task appears easier when marketing to the younger than to the older generation, there are other factors that need to be entered into the marketing equation. For example, we also found in the same study that the relatives' influence on a person's purchasing decision varies by several other demographic factors. Specifically, we found that:

- Among older adults, one in ten of those aged 75 and older admit that their relatives have the most say in deciding what type of *housing* to move into.

- With respect to decisions concerning the types of *cable channels* one subscribes to, the influence of relatives is greater on baby boomers than on their parents, more on men than women, and more on those with higher levels of income.

- Men are influenced by relatives to a greater extent than women on decisions concerning the types of *medical services* they should receive. Those men with higher levels of income are the most receptive to the advice of relatives.

- The older a person gets, the greater the chances that his or her relatives have the most say in decisions on the type of *appliances and furniture* to buy. Those individuals with the highest levels of education are influenced the most.

- The influence of relatives such as a spouse on a person's decision concerning the purchase of a *car* increases with age through the middle-years and declines later in life. Women and middle-income buyers of cars are influenced by their relatives the most, as are those with less education.

- The influence of relatives on a person's *investment decisions* declines with age later in life, but it increases with income. Women are more influenced by their relatives than men.

- The influence of relatives on a person's decisions concerning *travel* decreases with age. Relatives have greater influence on men than on women and on those with higher income levels.

- The influence of relatives on a person's purchasing decisions concerning *insurance* products decreases with age in later life, but it increases with income. Women are influenced more by their relatives than men are when buying insurance policies.

- On decisions concerning what *non-prescription drugs* to buy, men, as well as those with higher incomes, are influenced the most by relatives.

- The influence of a person's relatives on one's decision to fix or order certain *meals* declines with age in later life, but it increases with income and education. Men are more receptive than women to the suggestions of relatives concerning meals.

While these findings might appear to be too specific for decision makers to be bothered with, they could make a difference in how well companies satisfy their customers' needs. The more you know about the person you market your products to, the greater the effectiveness of your marketing efforts will be; and the better you will be able to satisfy your customers' needs.

Loyal Customers

Who is loyal to brands and retail establishments? In our studies, we found that loyalty to brands is a buying habit common among the majority of all American shoppers, with six in ten of them indicating that they stick to well-known brands. Loyalty to familiar brands increases with age and decreases with level of education. People in urban areas are more brand loyal than their rural counterparts.

Shoppers who would rather switch brands frequently than stay loyal to one brand have the following characteristics:

- are more likely to be female than male
- tend to have less education and lower income
- are more likely to live in rural than urban areas
- are more likely to be older baby boomers
- tend to have low self-esteem

In our studies, we found that older folks are generally those most loyal to products and services. For example, they are twice as likely to stick to the same brand of perfume or cologne, blue jeans or slacks, and credit card companies. But both groups also report equally strong preferences for a particular brand of most of the products they buy, specifically preferences for makes of automobiles, financial institutions and telephone-service providers. Women are somewhat more loyal than men, and so are those with higher incomes. We also learned that older consumers have a set of preferred (usually well-established) brands, and often switch from one brand to another within that set, but they are not as likely to switch to brands outside that set as their younger counterparts.

Loyalty to retail establishments, products, and brands is not uniform across settings or across generations. Rather, it differs from product to product and from one type of retail establishment to another. In one of our studies, we looked into these differences in store loyalty between the two generations. Based on this study, we concluded that baby boomers and older adults appear to be equally loyal to financial institutions and travel vendors, while the older group is more loyal to various other types of retail vendors—department stores, hospitals/clinics, pharmacies/drug stores, insurance companies, food/grocery stores, and fast-food restaurants. People most likely to switch stores frequently tend to have the following characteristics:

- are more likely to be in the 55 to 64 age bracket
- tend to have higher income
- tend to be more educated
- tend to be employed

What we have learned from many of our studies is that a person may be loyal to a brand of a particular product like cereal but show very little loyalty for brands of other types of products, such as soft drinks. By the same token, the reasons people in the two generations choose specific products and services differ according to the type of product or service.

Preferences for methods of payment

In several of our studies, we tried to find the preferences for payment methods across the two generations. In one such study, we found that nearly three-fourths of people like to pay *cash* for most things they buy. Very old people are more likely to prefer paying cash, with 81 percent of those aged 75 and older preferring this method of payment for purchasing products and services. People who have lower income and less education are more likely to prefer cash to other methods of payment, as are those living in rural areas compared to those living in urban areas.

Approximately four in ten people admit to making frequent use of a *credit card or charge card*. However, contrary to conventional belief that older adults do not make frequent use of credit, one of our national surveys found a significantly larger percentage of people aged 55 and over, compared to their younger counterparts, use credit cards for payment of goods and services. People who have more income and education charge the most, and a significantly higher percentage of people who live in urban areas (44 percent) compared to those who live in the country (33 percent) frequently use credit. People living in eastern states are heavy users of credit, with 52 percent reporting frequent use of credit cards or charge cards, compared with 35 percent of people living in southern states. Fifteen percent of people expressed a sense of immediate gratification via the use of credit. People who earn less and have less education are more likely to believe that as long as one can buy things on credit, there is no point in trying to save for them.

If you belong to one of the two generations and only pay the

People living in eastern states are heavy users of credit, with 52 percent reporting frequent use of credit cards or charge cards, compared with 35 percent of people living in southern states.

minimum amount owed on your credit card or charge accounts, you are probably among the minority. Approximately one in five people in the two generations don't pay off the entire balances on their monthly statements of their charge accounts. Those who use revolving credit tend to be younger and have less education.

Preferences for payment methods differ between baby boomers and their parents, but these differences are unique to purchases of specific products and services. In one of our national studies, we examined such preferences between the two generations for payment of a wide variety of products and services. We asked Americans in these two generations whether they would use cash, check, credit card, coupon, or senior/member discount (they could indicate more than one method).

For *grocery/food products,* cash is the most popular method of payment, equally preferred by baby boomers and their parents, with about four in five people expressing this preference. Credit is preferred by 29 percent of baby boomers, in comparison with 23 percent of the elderly, while checks are preferred three times more by the younger than the older group. Baby boomers are also more likely than their elderly counterparts to use coupons, with 11 percent and 7 percent, respectively, expressing this preference. Senior discounts are relevant only to the older generation.

When buying *apparel,* on the other hand, cash is by far the payment method preferred by baby boomers, with nearly two-thirds of them, in comparison with 47 percent of their parents, expressing such a preference. Check payments are the second most preferred method, with 56 percent of boomers and 45 percent of seniors preferring to use checks, while credit cards are equally preferred by the two groups. Although the incidence of coupon use was relatively small, this method had greater appeal to baby boomers than to elderly consumers, with 7 percent versus 3 percent, respectively. Finally, senior/member discount differences tend to reflect the availability of such offerings only to the older generation.

Of the three major methods of payment for *lodging* services, cash and credit are more popular among baby boomers than among older adults. Thirty-one percent of boomers, compared to 21 percent of the elderly, prefer paying cash, while the majority of both groups prefer using credit, with 74 percent versus 58 percent, respectively. Payment by check is preferred equally by about a third of the two groups, while coupons are four times more likely to be used by baby boomers than the elderly (or 13 percent vs. 3 percent). Sixty-two percent of the older generation prefers senior/member discounts. Thus, the younger generation prefers to use multiple methods of payment for hotel accommodations.

Cash and credit are more popular methods of payment for lodging services among baby boomers than among older adults.

Preferences for methods of payment for *meals at restaurants* show a slightly different pattern. About four-fifths of both groups prefer paying for meals using cash. Paying by check is not a common method of payment, with only 18 percent and 7 percent of the two groups expressing this preference, respectively. Payment by credit card is more popular among baby boomers than among elderly consumers, with 11 percent and 7 percent, respectively, indicating such a preference. Four in ten (or 42 percent) of older Americans use senior/member discounts at restaurants.

A similar pattern exists for *airline tickets*. Credit is the most popular method of payment for both groups, with 71 percent of boomers and 55 percent of seniors preferring this method, respectively. Cash is preferred by baby boomers more than their parents, with 27 percent and 16 percent, respectively, expressing such a preference. Payment by check is equally preferred by both groups (40 percent and 44 percent), and coupons are preferred almost three times more by baby boomers than their parents (16 percent vs. 6 percent). Once again, senior/member discounts are preferred by a little over six in ten seniors, but this is not surprising, given the fact that nearly all major carriers offer senior discounts.

We also examined preferences for payment methods for *healthcare services*. Nearly three-fourths of baby boomers and seniors prefer to pay by check, while twice as many seniors as baby boomers (29 percent vs. 15 percent) prefer to use cash. Sixteen percent of baby boomers prefer to use credit, compared with 10 percent of seniors, while member/senior discounts are mostly preferred by the latter group, with just 6 percent of boomers versus 41 percent of seniors. Coupons are not very popular, with only 5 percent of boomers and 2 percent of seniors, respectively, expressing this preference.

Preferences for payment methods were also examined in two other situations: *burglar or fire alarm system* and *home-appliance repair services*. Six in ten baby boomers prefer using checks to pay for burglar alarm systems, compared with slightly less than half of older adults. One-third of boomers would rather use a credit card, compared with only 17 percent of older consumers. Nearly three in ten baby boomers, compared with 18 percent of older adults, prefer to pay cash. Four times as many baby boomers as their parents (8 percent vs. 2 percent) would use coupons. A rather similar pattern of payment-method preference was observed for home-appliance repairs. Baby boomers are just as likely as their parents to write a check for such repairs. Nearly three-fourths of people in the two groups expressed this preference. One-third of baby boomers, compared with 23 percent of seniors, prefer to use cash.

Debit cards are becoming increasingly popular as a method of payment. Annual debit card transactions at the point of purchase have been growing at the rate of about 20 percent since 1996, and presently exceed credit card transactions, according to 2006 reports released by Federal Reserve Board researchers. In contrast, use of checks has been decreasing since the mid-1990s and is currently falling at the rate of 3 percent to 5 percent per year, according to the same source. In 2006, an estimated 52 percent of all U.S. households had debit cards (60 percent of those that had a checking account) and 45 percent of them (85 percent of those with a checking account) used them at least once in the previous 12 months.

While debit cards are growing more popular, ownership and use of debit cards declines with age.

Ownership and use of debit cards declines with age. Among all people who have a checking account, it is estimated that about half of baby boomers and one-third of those aged 60 and over use a debit card at least "occasionally." Among people in the two generations,

82 percent of the younger generation and 71 percent of the older folks use this method of payment occasionally, according to the most recent data reported by the Federal Reserve Board in 2006. Frequency of use varies by age, too. While the average debit card holders use this card three times per week, those in the older generations use their card less frequently, with oldest shoppers reporting the least frequent use. However, age differences are not so great if one takes into account consumer frequency of shopping and income, factors that have to do with the person's lifestyle or *opportunity* to use this form of payment; older people do not go shopping as frequently as younger adults. When we analyzed survey data collected by the AARP on credit card use, we found there are hardly any age differences in using "plastic" among people who shop with the same frequency or have similar income levels. It is also possible that some older shoppers carry a card without knowing it is a debit card, thinking that it is a credit card or an ATM card. In the latter case, there would be an opportunity to increase debit card use among the older population with marketing and educational campaigns, because this card serves as substitutes for cash and checks—the most preferred methods of payment by older adults—according to conclusions researched by Federal Reserve Board researchers.

What is the future of debit cards as a method of payment? Because their usage has been propelled primarily by younger consumers, researchers have tried to determine whether use will "age-out" as younger people move to older age brackets or whether there will be a cohort effect, that is, younger people will not kick the habit of using them later in life. Research that has attempted to determine the future use of various payment systems shows that debit cards will continue to grow in popularity during the next ten years, with the highest increase in the *share* of payment methods expected to be among those age 60 and over, but they will not make major inroads due to the aging of the population; debit card share will increase only slightly, and "cash" will still be the king as the most preferred method of payment, at least through 2016, the Federal Reserve Board reports.

Dis/Satisfaction and Complaints

The post-purchase mindsets and behaviors of the two generations are also interesting. In several of our studies, we examined how people feel about retail establishments they had patronized and about products they have bought. In one specific study, we asked Americans from all 50 states to express their level of satisfaction or dissatisfaction with 11 types of product or service providers. Their level of satisfaction varied from 83 percent for grocery stores to a surprising 27 percent for healthcare providers, as Table 7-3 shows.

People in the older generation are more satisfied than younger adults with a large number of retail vendors including house-repair service providers, financial institutions, insurance companies, utility companies, physicians and dentists, and appliance-repair stores. Younger baby boomers are more satisfied than older baby boomers with appliance makers, utility companies, and cleaners. Women are more satisfied than men with home-repair service providers, department stores, financial institutions, mail-order companies, and appliance repair stores. Adults who have higher incomes tend to be more satisfied with cleaners and less satisfied with insurance companies. Those with the most education are also the least satisfied with insurance companies.

TABLE 7-3

Satisfaction with Different Types of Businesses
percent who are "very" or "somewhat satisfied"

Grocery stores	83
Financial institutions (banks, stock brokers, etc.)	73
Department stores	69
Appliance-repair stores	62
House-repair service providers (i.e., plumbers, painters, electricians)	55
Mail-order companies	54
Insurance companies	49
Dry cleaners	45
Utility companies	41
Appliance manufacturers	40
Physicians and dentists	27

In another study, we tried to assess consumers' satisfaction with product and service providers by asking more than 1,000 adults whether selected types of providers rip-off consumers. The percentages of affirmative responses to this question are shown below.

TABLE 7-4

Types of Businesses That Rip-off Consumers

percent who agree

Insurance companies	49
Hospitals & clinics	45
Financial institutions	28
Pharmacies/drug stores	23
Travel packages vendors	22
Department stores	15
Food/grocery stores	13
Fast-food restaurants	8

As our survey showed, insurance companies and healthcare providers are by far those thought to be taking advantage of their customers. Furthermore, in analyzing how baby boomers and their parents responded to this question, we discovered that baby boomers and seniors do not feel the same about the way different types of establishments treat consumers. Baby boomers are more likely than older people to think that department stores, insurance companies, and fast-food restaurants take advantage of consumers. They are equally as likely as their parents to think that financial institutions, hospitals/clinics, food/grocery stores, and travel-package vendors rip-off consumers. However, seniors are more likely than younger people to think that pharmacies/drug stores take advantage of consumers.

Insurance companies and healthcare providers are by far those thought to be taking advantage of their customers.in southern states.

The highest level of satisfaction with retail vendors is generally found among the oldest consumers, those aged 75 and older. This group is the most satisfied with financial institutions and insurance companies. There are no differences in the level of satisfaction with grocery stores. It seems that regardless of demographic factors, all consumers are equally satisfied with these types of stores. In the same study, we asked baby boomers and their parents how well the eight types of businesses (shown in Table 7-4) respond to their needs as customers. We found a greater percentage of seniors than baby boomers indicated that the eight different types of establishments are responsive to their needs.

In the study where we examined the levels of satisfaction with eight types of businesses, we found baby boomers complain more than older people. A greater percentage of them had complained to six of the eight types of retail establishments. Complaining was equal among the two generations only for pharmacies and travel-packages vendors, although the lower level of exposure to such vendors might have been an influence. When we examined the complaining behavior of those who were dissatisfied, we found that eight in ten people make it a point to let others know of products and services that displease them. People living in the eastern part of the country are more likely to express their dissatisfaction to others than southerners, as are those who live in urban areas and those living with others.

Finally, we looked at people's satisfaction or lack of it with products in the marketplace. We found twice as many seniors as baby boomers (64 percent vs. 35 percent) often find packages and containers very difficult to open. People with the lowest levels of education and income have the greatest difficulty with packages and containers, and women have more difficulty than men.

Excessive Buying

Who is likely to over-consume? We tried to answer this question in a couple of our studies by analyzing behaviors that are compulsive, impulsive, and excessive when it comes to buying and using products. We found that the typical compulsive buyer is male with lower household income. However, we also found intergenerational differences in excessive consumption habits. Specifically, we found that within a certain time span, such as one year, a much larger percentage of baby boomers showed signs of compulsive, impulsive, or excessive buying and consumption. In comparison with older adults, within a 12-month time frame:

Twice as many baby boomers as their parents went
shopping to "take their minds off things." (22 percent vs. 10 percent)

Three times as many baby boomers took on major
credit card debt. (37 percent vs. 12 percent)

Four times as many boomers made only the
minimum payment on credit cards. (31 percent vs. 7 percent)

Two and one-half times as many baby boomers bought
something even though they knew they couldn't afford it.
(20 percent vs. 8 percent)

Twice as many went on a shopping spree.
(16 percent vs. 7 percent)

Three times as many boomers as their parents used
products to "take their minds off things."
(16 percent vs. 5 percent)

A significantly larger percentage of baby boomers went
into a store and bought things they had not planned to buy.
(59 percent vs. 39 percent)

Specifically, we found that baby boomers tend to be more compulsive shoppers than their parents, as attested to by the following activities that characterize a person as a compulsive shopper:

Three times as many sometimes want to buy things
and don't care what they buy. (14 percent vs. 5 percent)

Twice as many feel guilty or shameful about the
money they spend on some things. (29 percent vs. 16 percent)

Twice as many often feel depressed after shopping.
(16 percent vs. 8 percent)

A person's excessive and compulsive consumption habits can have adverse effects on one's quality of life. These habits can affect relationships with others and increase the risk of experiencing other undesirable physical and emotional problems that can have negative effects on a person's well-being.

CHAPTER EIGHT

Planning for Longevity

THE GENERAL THEME that emerges from the findings of the studies presented in the previous chapters is that people can be more in control of their well-being and life in general than they think they can. In this chapter, we highlight some important ingredients for longevity and quality of life and the opportunities they present to businesses for the development of new products, services, and marketing communications to help people live happier lives.

The basic premise for developing guidelines for longevity and well-being later in life is that people are interested and willing to *act now, regardless of age*. They are willing to take steps to build the resources that promote longevity and enhance their quality of life. By "resources," we mean the factors that deter aging, stave off disease and premature death, as well as the factors that contribute to a person's overall satisfaction later in life. These resources can be in the form of attitudes, emotions, physical conditions, social relationships, and financial assets.

Determinants of Longevity and Life Satisfaction

Longevity and life satisfaction are among the most researched areas of social science. With respect to longevity, researchers have cataloged more than 800 factors that affect longevity. Topping the list is the importance of having a purpose in life or (even better) zest for life—passion for something you enjoy doing and look forward to doing daily; and the person's ability to handle difficult (stressful) times that are likely to lead to the development of adverse emotions, stress and depression in particular. With respect to life satisfaction, studies also identify determinants of happiness in late life. However, most previous studies provide less than adequate explanations for the observed differences in life satisfaction. For example, we know that people are most satisfied with life in their sixties, but we do not know the reasons for satisfaction with life at this particular stage.

Topping the list of more than 800 factors that affect longevity is the importance of having a purpose in life or (even better) zest for life.

In this chapter, we are going to present some of the important factors that affect our lives and determine how long we live and the quality of life as well. But rather than discussing the factors that are responsible for our well-being, we will present information useful in developing the tools and resources that would enable one to live a longer and happier life. In concert with this presentation, we will discuss how businesses can help enhance people's well-being and profit in the process.

Parents are happier than their boomer children

Before discussing the factors that make a person live a longer and happier life, we thought it would be interesting to look into people's satisfaction with their life, and specifically whether people of one generation are more or less satisfied with their lives. While we knew from previous studies that people are most happy during their sixth decade of life, we were not sure how happy people in the two generations are, since the older generation includes people of advanced age. In one of our recent studies, we asked our participants to express their levels of agreement or disagreement with five statements which have been widely used to assess life satisfaction. We have combined affirmative responses, which we are presenting in Table 8-1.

TABLE 8-1

Life Satisfaction of Baby Boomers and Their Parents
percent who "somewhat agree" or "strongly agree"

	Baby Boomers	Parents
In most ways my life is close to my ideal.	56.8	66.5
The conditions of my life are excellent.	47.8	62.2
I am satisfied with my life.	60.7	73.2
So far I have gotten the important things I want in life.	62.7	72.2
If I could live my life over, I would change almost nothing.	38.6	49.0

As the figures in Table 8-1 show, a greater percentage of the parents than those in the younger generation agreed with each of the five statements they were presented. Therefore, collectively, the baby boomers who are in their forties and fifties are not as happy as those aged 60 and older. Why the differences in the levels of satisfaction with life between the two generations? We think that there are several reasons, but we will mention a few of them that are suggested by our research and present knowledge in various scientific disciplines. First, baby boomers are more materialistic than their parents, and we know from dozens of studies that materialistic orientations are sources of unhappiness. People who either surround themselves with material possessions, or have a life goal to get or have more material things are not very happy. We think that there are at least two reasons for this: these people are never satisfied with what they have, and they always want more—even things they can not afford, which becomes a source of their chronic misery. Their strong need to own material things adversely affects their ability to allocate money to areas that are actual sources of happiness, such as saving for retirement, health care and travel.

Another reason for the lower life satisfaction among baby boomers stems from their current life circumstances and ambivalence about the future that keep them awake at night, including lack of adequate retirement assets, job security, and uncertainty about their ability to secure work in retirement years. Simply, they are unsure if they are going to have a comfortable retirement. A third reason is their preoccupation with their aging self—they are

> *People who either surround themselves with material possessions, or have a life goal to get or have more things are not very happy.*

increasingly unhappy with their appearance and have been losing the battle to keep their youthful looks.

The last, and perhaps most important, reason for their unhappiness is the constant stress they have been experiencing in various roles—worker, parent, spouse, caregiver—roles that create multiple responsibilities and place great demands on their time. Stress may also be taking its toll on their health, another source of life satisfaction. Free time for them to relax and rejuvenate is in short supply, and there is little money set aside for leisure to help them get their minds off daily pressures.

Based on our research and information from other sources, we have identified four general factors that affect longevity and well-being in later life: physical and emotional health, positive attitudes, active lifestyles, and adequate financial assets.

Physical and emotional health

Good health is the single most important source of an older person's life satisfaction. The greatest fear of people in the later stages of life is that their health will deteriorate or they will become dependent on others as a result of poor health. Good health promotes happiness and increases life expectancy. The good news is that the future state of our health is controllable to a great extent, and so is the number of years we are going to live within the human life span, even for people of very old age. The choices we make daily affect our present and future state of health, longevity and well-being in general. While many other factors, such as heredity, are likely to determine the health of a person at any given stage in life, our studies suggest that, besides physical health (which we will have to say more later in this chapter), two additional main factors affect our emotional well-being and longevity: stress and depression.

> *Good health is the single most important source of an older person's life satisfaction.*

We have known for a long time that *stress* has adverse effects on our health because it taxes our adaptive resources, causing weakening of our immune system and greater susceptibility to disease. But stress does not affect every person the same way because people differ in their abilities and ways they handle stress. It is better for a person's health to face the problem that causes stress and deal with it directly rather than trying to avoid it. Therefore, it is important for people to become aware of the effectiveness of different stress-handling methods so they can try to incorporate them into their stress-response patterns.

This approach presents opportunities for classes in stress management, websites that help people cope with stress, books on stress management, and positioning products as stress relievers. Although there are pharmaceuticals on the market that are designed to help deal with stress, smart product developers and marketers will also look at positioning products such as lounge chairs, herbal teas, milk and soy products, decaffeinated beverages, and services such as vacations and health clubs as stress relievers.

Recent estimates show that *depressive disorders* cost approximately $50 billion each year, and statistics from the CDC surveys suggest that an increasing number of people, especially women, have a major depressive disorder, with more than one in ten non-institutionalized adults likely to have experienced a major depressive disorder at some point in their lives. Mental illnesses such as depression are most common among older people and often go untreated. Older people are those most likely to kill themselves, and nearly all of those who commit suicide show major depressive symptoms. But depressive disorders that have been creeping into the lives of older people are not a normal part of aging.

Health and wellness professionals have numerous opportunities to be part of the solution by stepping up their efforts to identify the signs and symptoms of depression, and to encourage and support their clients in their efforts to seek help. Recent research by Drs. Blumenthal, Babyak, Moore, and others has shown that exercise can reduce depression and be as effective as antidepressants. Also, an increasing body of research has shown the beneficial effects of one's interaction with companion animals on the person's physical and emotional well-being. Healthcare services that can enhance the older person' emotional well-being, such as psychotherapy, are likely to increase in demand as the population ages and an increasing number of people become aware of their benefits.

Positive attitude

Our research also revealed that people with high self-esteem are healthier than those with low self-esteem. We suspect (but cannot prove with certainty) that those with high self-esteem have a higher opinion of their abilities to deal with problems that could have a potentially adverse effect on their emotional and physical well-being. They feel they have greater control over factors that adversely affect them as well as those that promote life satisfaction in general. Although self-esteem is considered to be a personality factor that is likely to develop early in life, it is important for people to become aware of the importance of thinking positively about themselves, thinking more about their strengths than their weaknesses.

We found optimists to be in better health than pessimists. Having a positive attitude about the future and life in general appears to correlate with one's health. It is not clear why optimism affects a person's health in a positive way, and if so, how and why. It may be that optimism is a trait of people who have a positive attitude about everything else, which manifests itself in behaviors that promote good health. For example, optimists feel they have greater control over their lives and are more likely to take action to change circumstances that have negative effects on their emotional and physical well-being. Optimism also promotes positive responses to circumstances that can tax a person's emotional resources and ultimately affect one's health.

There may be a main message here for marketing communications: rather than poking fun at people in mid- and late life, advertisers may want to promote positive images which leave viewers feeling uplifted. They are more likely to respond to product messages that leave them feeling in control of their lives rather than messages that make them feel like bumbling fools who are the butt of jokes.

Rather than poking fun at people in mid- and late life, advertisers may want to promote positive images which leave viewers feeling uplifted.

Active lifestyle

The third source of life satisfaction is the way a person chooses to live his or her life—one's lifestyle. People appear to be happier when they engage in activities that give them a sense of control over their bodies and their environment. Diet and physical fitness programs allow us to exercise control over our bodies. Similarly, the choice to buy and consume certain products reflects a sense of control over our emotions because such activities help us "medicate" adverse feelings such as depression and boredom. As we found in one of our studies, some people indicated greater life satisfaction as a result of their initiation of diet and exercise programs. A busy lifestyle that includes participation in a wide variety of activities, especially activities that involve social contact, such as attending adult education classes and volunteering, appears to enhance a person's life satisfaction. Engagement in such activities gives a person a sense of accomplishment and control over his environment, both of which are promoted through the enactment of various roles, such as the role of a student, volunteer, or employee.

> A busy lifestyle that includes participation in a wide variety of activities, especially those involving social contact, appears to enhance a person's life satisfaction.

Enactment of various roles not only promotes emotional well-being but also appears to deter aging and have positive effects on physical health. We know, for example, that people who continue to engage in mentally challenging activities, at work or in other settings, are less likely to experience deterioration of their capacities to think, recall, or reason. Also, we know that people who have assumed a larger number of nonobligatory roles are in better health, although we do not know precisely why. We suspect that there are two possible reasons. First, people with a larger number of roles are more likely to be exposed to social contacts that can serve as sources of information for better health. For example, one may become aware of the benefits of preventive health care in staving off disease and premature death. Second, a person with multiple roles may have more social support groups, which promote better health by serving as a "buffer" to physical and emotional assaults.

Professionals working with pre-retirees should promote the

importance of having hobbies during retirement, especially hobbies a person stands a good chance of developing a passion for and that are immune to aging. This helps ensure that the retiree's latter part of life will be filled with joy and purpose. Policy makers and charitable organizations, including religious organizations, can make it clear in their messages that volunteering to help others is also a way of helping yourself. As pleas for money and assistance fill the airwaves, baby boomers may need to be reminded of the health and emotional benefits of staying involved with their respective communities, no matter what those communities may be—a book club, a church group, or a political movement—and of the importance of widening their portfolio of leisure activities and taking on hobbies they are likely to be able to pursue into very old age.

> *Baby boomers and their elders need to be reminded of the health and emotional benefits of staying involved with their respective communities, no matter what those communities may be.*

Financial assets

While good health is a necessary condition for longevity, it is not sufficient for optimum well-being later in life. Financial resources also seem to affect a person's overall life satisfaction. But wealth accumulation as the ultimate goal in your quest for happiness does not make you happier, according to the findings of several dozen studies in western countries; it may even have negative effects on the person's well-being. Psychology professor David Myers, in his book, *The Pursuit of Happiness,* presents compelling evidence based on several scientific studies and explains the reasons why money does not necessarily buy happiness. Simply, happiness is a state of mind, a personality trait that is shaped by the choices people make, especially earlier in life; and getting more money does not change their personality—after a few months they get accustomed to the new standard of living and continue to be miserable because they do not have enough or as much as a neighbor. This is not to say that people who do not have enough to eat are happy, but having more will not make you happier if you do not have the right attitude about money.

However if you have the right attitude about money, and properly manage it to accomplish multiple life goals, wealth can have beneficial effects on one's life satisfaction and well-being. Having adequate financial resources contributes to life satisfaction in four important ways. First, you do not worry about not having enough money later in life and therefore becoming a financial burden on other family members. Both baby boomers and their parents are becoming increasingly aware of the "costs" of increasing longevity. Those who have not saved enough for retirement, especially the baby boomers, are concerned with the quality of life in their retirement years, whereas their parents who have more assets are concerned with outliving their savings and becoming financially dependent on others. Such financial concerns undermine a person's emotional well-being.

A second reason adequate financial resources enhance life satisfaction is because they enable people to do things they enjoy the most, and keep them from having to engage in undesirable activities or lifestyles. We know that everyone wants to have fun later in life, but lack of money and having to work indefinitely because of limited financial resources are constraints to a desirable lifestyle in retirement. Third, adequate financial resources allow a person to gain better control over his or her environment, thus enhancing feelings of self-worth and well-being. For instance, people who make significant contributions to a charity are not only in a better position to control the charity's activities, but also are more respected by others, our research findings suggest. Similarly, people who can afford to help family members financially or buy gifts for them have greater influence over their relatives' present and future actions.

People who make significant contributions to a charity are not only in a better position to control the charity's activities, but also are more respected by others.

Finally, money can buy peace of mind. If well-being is enhanced not only by getting or having things that give us pleasure but also by eliminating or reducing negative feelings, then money can help reduce such feelings and enhance a person's quality of life. Many of the things people worry about are controllable to the extent they have the money to pay for them. For example, people lose sleep over things such as personal and home safety, health, and having to do daily chores. People with adequate resources are less likely to be concerned with such things because they can make changes to reduce these concerns, such as moving to a safer neighborhood, receiving proper healthcare services, and paying for at-home chores and caregiving services (such as cleaning and meal preparation). As our studies reveal, people in lower socioeconomic classes experience greater levels of anxiety about such things.

The implications for all kinds of financial services organizations are clear, but financial services companies need to segment this market to carefully target the right services and messages, depending on the needs and resources of the segment. They should educate those in the two generations who are not proficient in investing by helping them understand the various reasons for saving, assess their late life's goals, and explain the types of financial instruments which are most likely to help them achieve their goals that will contribute to a more comfortable life during retirement years.

Strategies for Longevity and Well-Being

A prerequisite to the development of strategies for longevity and well-being is the understanding of the concepts of "life span," "life expectancy," and "functional age." *Life span* is the maximum age human beings can live, which is approximately 120 years. Every person born today has the potential of reaching this maximum landmark. While heredity is believed to affect the number of years a person is going to live, it plays a surprisingly less important role than lifestyle factors. This means that people have greater control over the number of years they will live on this planet than they think they do.

> *People have greater control over the number of years they will live on this planet than they think they do.*

Life expectancy, on the other hand, is the average age a person born today is expected to live. Today, the average life expectancy (from birth) in the U.S. is about 77 years, about three years more for women and three years less for men. For baby boomers, life expectancy is much greater than it was for previous generations, and for parents of baby boomers, life expectancy is even greater. For example, a healthy 70-year-old is expected to live another 20 years, according to national statistics on mortality rates. The greater control people exercise over the lifestyle factors that deter and promote longevity, the closer they will get to their maximum life span.

These observations have three important implications for planning for later life. First, they make people aware of the number of years after retirement age they can expect to live. Today's average retirement age for both genders is about 60 years old. For the increasing number of people who retire at this age, it is possible they have lived only *half* of their adult lives. Many people are likely to spend more years as retirees than they have as employees. When the mandatory retirement age was set at 65, the average person was not expected to live much beyond that age. But today, people reaching age 65 can live, on average, another 20 years. Therefore, marketers and people in general need to rethink "old age" in the context of life expectancy, rather than accept outdated guideposts (such as average retirement age) that signify its arrival.

> Today's average retirement age for both genders is about 60 years old. For the increasing number of people who retire at this age, it is possible they have lived only half of their adult lives.

If marketers mentally restructure life stages in the context of new statistics, they would be able to extend "youth" and "middle age" years to cover chronologically older age groups. Similarly, people could start thinking of old age, beginning at today's life expectancy, in much the same way that old age, defined as eligibility for Social Security benefits, was considered to start at life expectancy in the mid-1930s. This is already changing the way people think about work, retirement, family, leisure, and life in general. More importantly, the new age-based life stages require planning for longer lives which affect the length of educational preparation, careers, the timing of the purchase of products and services, such as homes and vacations, and long-term investment strategies.

Second, marketers who are trying to meet the needs of the aging population should think about longevity and well-being later in life not just in terms of chronological age, but mainly in terms of functional age. *Functional age* refers to the condition of the bodily systems that enable a person to live a normal life. It is a person's ability to function, without reference to chronological age. Functional age is more relevant than chronological age to a person's longevity and quality of life. An older person who has lived to a certain age without serious health problems has probably enjoyed his or her later years of life more than a person who has lived to the same age with a debilitating disease. Therefore, longevity should not only be an issue of how many years one lives but also an issue of quality of life. For this reason, marketers should underscore the importance of quality of life in their efforts to serve the needs of the older population. New products, services, and messages should be consistent with the person's life strategies that promote a long *and* satisfying life.

The third implication for planning for later life is the recognition that people do have control over how long they live and the quality of their lives. This suggests the need for developing strategies that extend life and increase life satisfaction. It also suggests the need for a life-long commitment to these strategies. Marketers need to adhere to the underlying message that the earlier customers begin implementing strategies for longevity and well-being, the easier it is to stick to them and the greater their effectiveness.

In line with these three notions of longevity, we can identify two general proactive strategies for longevity and well-being that are appropriate for any stage in life. The first strategy involves taking steps that help one live longer by (a) deterring and even reversing aging and (b) reducing the chances of things happening that could lead to a shorter life. The second strategy involves building up resources that enable one to (a) better handle the circumstances that could adversely affect longevity and erode the quality of life and (b) engage in activities that can enhance well-being in later life.

Adding years to life
Research studies, including ours, suggest that good health and longevity are, to a great extent, choices. Individual actions determine how healthy people are and how long they will live. People have full control over the things they do to their bodies, including

what they eat. When the effects of exercising are assessed in the context of functional aging, the available knowledge suggests that moderate and regular exercise deters aging and increases longevity. Bed-ridden nursing home residents (some in their nineties) were able to function independently after researchers at Tuft's University put them through a weight training program. Similarly, we know of cases where people in their early sixties entered a nursing home with heart problems, and by exercising were not only able to overcome their frailties, but ran marathons in their eighties. Exercise promotes hormonal growth, strengthens the immune system, and helps the body function more efficiently. It is perhaps the single most important controllable activity that has the greatest benefits, even more than dieting, according to scientists at the National Institute on Aging who have been studying longevity issues for years.

Unfortunately, most people only get serious about exercising and dieting after they experience a serious health problem. For the healthy, exercise and diet programs tend to be of short duration. According to our research findings, the focus is primarily on promoting one's "looks" or physical appearance rather than good health and longevity. The greatest number of younger people who exercise and diet do so to lose weight rather than to proactively build the foundations for long-lasting good health. Exercise and diet programs that are aimed at improving one's body shape may not necessarily have the most desirable long-term health benefits. For example, one could deprive his body of essential nutrients by reducing food intake in an effort to lose weight. Similarly, over-emphasis on physical activities that burn calories, such as jogging, could distract one from the benefits of resistance exercises.

Unfortunately, most people only get serious about exercising and dieting after they experience a serious health problem.

Once again, the underlying marketing message should be: *exercise moderately, but frequently.* It is imperative for longevity planning that exercise be included in any lifestyle. Messages need to help consumers understand that exercising should be an obligatory activity like eating and working, rather than a discretionary activity such as TV viewing. Unfortunately, people are accustomed to measuring the effectiveness of their efforts. They look for short-term physical results, rather than realizing the long-term benefits that exercise and diet have on their bodily systems. Here is some advice that echoes experts in the fields of aging and health care: exercise moderately, but frequently and holistically, *and stop looking for quick results*. Programs that focus on the long-term benefits of exercise can help consumers make positive changes in their lives. Imagine a program that makes these kinds of suggestions and helps consumers adhere to a plan:

- Start slowly, spending only a few minutes at a time exercising. Gradually increase the time, frequency, and rigor of your exercising activities.
- Make a schedule of times and days of the week that you plan to exercise. Stick to the schedule as best you can. At the end of the week, write down the days you were able to exercise and those that you did not (and why). This could force you to admit the reasons you did not exercise and make you more cognizant of your "excuses" that you need to address.
- Exercise at places that do not allow uncontrollable factors, such as bad weather, to interfere with your schedule.
- If you lack motivation, look for an "exercising buddy," a friend or someone to work out with. It is more difficult to cancel on those days you may not feel like exercising.

Pharmaceutical companies, physicians, and insurance companies should encourage consumers to practice *preventive health care*, in part by pricing preventive measures within reach. This encouragement can include (a) acknowledging patients' health problems and the high probability of experiencing the same ailments in the future that their parents had experienced, (b) understanding the patterns and sequence of their development, and (c) proactively sharing the information with the patient and his family. Again, healthcare providers, including insurance companies, can have a significant impact on their "customers" by encouraging frequent check-ups and engagement in activities or behaviors that are likely to deter or prolong the appearances of these health problems. Our research shows some interesting patterns of disease development to heed, further investigate, and validate using information from other professional healthcare sources.

As a minimum requirement, all mature consumers should have a regular doctor and *frequent physical exams*. We found a large percentage of people, especially baby boomers, do not have regular check-ups. Regular visits to a doctor's facilities often reflect the need for treatment and monitoring after experiencing a serious health problem. Proactive or preventive health care is not very common.

Improving emotional health should also be part of the equation. While developing a healthy body through exercise and diet is important in deterring and reversing aging, perhaps of greater importance in efforts to affect life span is the ability to enhance emotional health. The evidence in support of mind-body effects is overwhelming. For example, stress can be the cause of six fatal health conditions and between 60 percent and 80 percent of the symptoms requiring a visit to the doctor. Yet boomers may spend more time preoccupied with physical fitness than with activities to improve emotional health. Emotional health means (a) the absence of negative feelings that can affect physical health, such as stress, anxiety, self-pity (low self-esteem), and depression, and (b) the presence of positive feelings such as optimism, high self-esteem, vitality, and purpose for living. As our research shows, people whose state of mind is characterized by negative rather than positive feelings also tend to have more health problems that may shorten their lives.

There are numerous meditation and relaxation techniques that, if used effectively, promote emotional health. But these techniques may not be adequate for achieving optimal emotional health because they tend to focus on teaching people to manage their emotions. They do little to help them deal with or remove a problem that affects their state of mind. Psychologists suggest that actions and thoughts that remove or solve problems negatively affecting us are more effective and have more positive consequences for health than actions and thoughts that simply help manage emotions.

Marketing messages can help consumers develop coping strategies that enable them to effectively deal with a stressor, solve the problem that creates negative feelings, and thus put it to rest. The following are coping strategies proven to be effective in deterring the occurrence and impact of stressors, and could be promoted by, for example, health insurance companies:

- Develop the habit of planning your life in such a way as to reduce the probability of the occurrence of stressful events. Some examples of events that result in possible emotional dislocation are: setting or agreeing to tight deadlines and choosing connecting flights that have short layovers.
- Learn to anticipate "worse case" scenarios, and mentally rehearse ways to deal with them if they happen. Anticipated events create less stress than unexpected events.
- Learn to downplay the importance of an unexpected event and its consequences. For example, put it in a context of something worse that could have happened, or something worse you previously experienced.
- Spend time with animal companions. Interacting with animals helps reduce negative and unpleasant feelings and has a positive effect on physical health.

Other positive feelings such as optimism and a favorable opinion of oneself also promote good mental health. Boomers need to learn to keep positive thoughts and to quickly dismiss negative thoughts about themselves, others, work, family, and life in general. Even more important is the ability to hold a positive outlook on negative experiences.

Self-awareness and the acknowledgement of negative thoughts, such as "I am angry about this," are the first steps toward alleviating adverse feelings. Next, replace the negative thought by thinking instead of a positive or pleasant thought. Count the number of episodes you were able to change your thoughts, and monitor your progress over time. You could be pleasantly surprised by your ability to control your emotions.

Furthermore, because self-esteem appears to affect our health and, thus, longevity, individuals must learn to think about themselves and their abilities in the context of the things they can do, the positive results of actions, and other people's favorable reactions toward them. Therefore, it is important to think of strengths, not weaknesses. The following are some suggestions to promote a positive attitude which could be used by health insurance companies and other healthcare providers to encourage a balanced mental state:

- Engage in activities that you have special abilities or aptitude in performing, and avoid those you do not perform as well.
- Interact with people who do not criticize you.
- Avoid comparing yourself with others, or think of ways you are better, not worse, than they are. For example, rather than comparing your possessions (a criterion of success) to another's, think of several other ways of defining success and happiness (such as better health, family life, lifestyle, etc.).
- Remind yourself how fortunate you are to have some things many people in the world do not—education, freedom, and good health.

Such thoughts and actions tend to promote positive self-esteem. Smart marketers can incorporate these ideas into their marketing messages to help consumers associate good feelings about themselves with good feelings about a product.

Smart marketers help consumers associate good feelings about themselves with good feelings about a product.

Improving Quality of Life

We can place the strategies for improving well-being later in life into two broad categories: (a) strategies that promote factors that enhance one's quality of life, and (b) strategies that help one avoid experiences that erode the quality of life. Many of these strategies are not mutually exclusive. For example, good health not only promotes longevity but also contributes to the older person's quality of life, whereas poor health undermines life satisfaction. Some of the factors that enhance the older person's quality of life are:

- Absence of health problems
- Adequate financial resources
- Active lifestyle
- Independent living
- Ability to work for reasons other than monetary needs
- Social interaction and support
- Ability to pursue activities that promote empowerment, such as education, and express altruism, such as volunteering

On the other hand, when the factors that enhance a person's well-being are in short supply, they can erode the quality of life. Strategies that reduce the influence of the following factors identified in our studies could also contribute to greater life satisfaction:

- Assumption of elder caregiving responsibilities
- Concerns with changes in one's physical appearance and aging in general
- Excessive debt
- Having to work

With these factors in mind, a person can perform an objective "personal audit" or check-up, with the assistance of professionals when necessary. Here again, a marketer can help consumers perform these personal audits by including them on websites, in product packaging, and by using print advertising checklists. Here are some items that need to be included in a personal audit:

1. **Health.** List present health problems as well as potential health problems you might "inherit" from your parents. Are you being proactive about your potential ailments? What actions have you taken to minimize the adverse effects of existing health problems

that can affect how long you live and your well-being later in life?

2. **Finances.** Inventory your financial assets. Where do you stand in relation to your stage of life and the desired lifestyle you would like to have later in life? Will you have enough money for a longer life, or should you change your investment strategy now to ensure adequate assets in retirement or later life?

3. **Lifestyle.** Is your lifestyle active? Do you have a rich social network and strong social ties with friends and relatives? If not, what opportunities can you see that will expand and strengthen your social portfolio?

4. **Travel and Leisure.** Are you making provisions for travel in later life? Will you have the resources to travel? Do you see any potential constraints to your abilities to travel, such as having to work and possible elder caregiving responsibilities? If so, what are you doing to reduce the possible impact of these constraints?

5. **Independent Living.** Are your present housing accommodations appropriate and adequate for maintaining independence late in life? If not, can remodeling address potentially different needs, or is it likely that you would have to move to a different home? Can you afford the provision of home-care and healthcare services at your home, should you need them?

6. **Work.** Do you plan to work later in life? If so, do you think your skills would be in demand? Should you upgrade or develop new skills that would make you more competitive in the job market?

7. **Caregiving.** Are you adequately prepared for the role of a caregiver? Have you made provisions to lessen the adverse impact of caregiving responsibilities, should you have to assume such a role?

8. **Aging.** Are you concerned with changes in your physical appearance? Do you think of your age in the context of chronological age or in the context of your potential lifespan? Do you think of functional aging? What steps have you taken to deter aging, given that longevity is mostly a matter of lifestyle choice?

9. Consumption Habits. Are your buying habits the source of significant credit card debt? Are you aware of the adverse consequences your debt can have on you later in life? What are you doing to reduce your debt? Are any of your present consumption habits compulsive or at risk of becoming compulsive? Are you aware of the potentially negative consequences such habits might have on your well-being?

10. Activities and Hobbies. Do you have many hobbies or interest in activities that you do with passion? Are these immune to aging? What hobbies or activities can you take up today that you would be able to engage in regardless of possible aging-related limitations?

If marketers can begin to incorporate more of these messages into their product communications, baby boomers and their elders will have more of an emotional connection to the product and its manufacturer.

CHAPTER NINE

How Businesses Can Profit by Making Their Mature Customers Happier

ORGANIZATIONS that market products and services to older consumers are faced with both opportunities and challenges. On the one hand, the changing age composition of the marketplace creates new opportunities and puts pressure on them to respond to the increasing size and wealth of the "maturing" consumer segments, whose needs are largely unmet because they have been ignored as a market. On the other hand, these organizations find it difficult to effectively respond to these new opportunities due to relatively little (and often contradictory) information available about this rather large and heterogeneous market.

While the effectiveness of specific marketing strategies is likely to depend on the specific segment and product or service being marketed, we can suggest a few guidelines that should be of assistance to those marketing or contemplating marketing to the two generations:

1. Understand the needs of mature consumers.
2. Pursue company objectives via strategies that enhance mature customers' well-being.
3. Test before implementing strategies and seek feedback.

Understanding the Needs of Your Mature Customers

Developing an effective marketing strategy to appeal to the mature market requires knowledge about the needs of this large and diverse segment. Specifically, marketers need to understand the needs of mature consumers, how they differ from those of younger consumers, and most importantly why needs differ among consumers in the older generations.

Our present state of knowledge based on our studies and other information derived from several disciplines, including marketing, gerontology, and several areas of social science, suggests that differences in needs are the result of two types of factors. First, they are due to differences in aging processes, which include biophysical, psychological, and social aging. Second, the mature shopper's needs differ due to life circumstances they have experienced that define their values and lifestyles. We review and summarize these factors in the sections that follow.

Aging and shopping behavior

People age differently physiologically. They experience changes in their bodily systems, such as declines in vision and hearing, and the onset of chronic conditions and disease at different ages and at different rates of physiological declines. Specifically, with age, people increasingly have difficulty reading fine print and distinguishing stimuli presented in certain colors; they become more sensitive to glare, and take more time to adjust to certain light conditions; and they experience declining manual dexterity, which creates difficulty in holding and manipulating objects (i.e., opening cans, bottles, and packages). Further, as people age they experience loss in their ability to taste chemical substances—in part due to loss in taste buds and due to other factors such as an increase in use of medications and a loss of the ability to smell. Also, as people age they experience hearing loss that affects their ability to hear sounds at different frequency levels and to distinguish among certain vowel sounds. Such physiological changes affect the way the mature shopper responds to products and services and create different needs for marketing offerings. Marketers need to understand the needs that develop due to biophysical aging processes in

Marketers need to understand the needs that develop due to biophysical aging processes in order to design and market products and services that would enhance customer satisfaction and well-being in the marketplace.

order to design and market products and services that would enhance customer satisfaction and well-being in the marketplace.

People also age differently socially, as they assume roles associated with old age, such as the role of a retiree or a grandparent. As they experience major life transitions, older people assume new roles and responsibilities and develop new needs for products and brands suitable to these newly acquired roles. In her book, *Targeting Transitions*, Paula Mergenhagen cites several examples and studies that show how the experience or anticipation of life events such as retirement can create a set of new needs because, as she points out, the person at or near retirement must deal not only with financial issues, but with social and emotional topics—marital adjustment during retirement, relationships with adult children and grandchildren, and issues such as relocation and volunteering. Companies that understand the mindset of their customers who have recently experienced or are about to make transitions into new roles or life stages are likely to be in a better position to satisfy their older customers' needs and profit by doing so.

Finally, psychologically aging means, among other things, increasingly thinking of oneself as an "old" person; some people of a certain age are still "young at heart," while others of the same age think of themselves as old and act their age. Whether certain mature consumers think, feel, and act their age affects their responses to products and retail offerings in general. For example, a 62-year-old person who does not think of himself as a "senior" would be offended if a clerk offered him a senior citizen's discount, and would not respond to products exclusively marketed to older consumers. Marketers need to understand that just because a person is of a certain age he or she may not necessarily think like another person of the same age; they need to be sensitive to the differences in their customers' mindsets about their age and aging in general.

Cohort and historical influences

Consumer needs also differ due to life circumstances. Cohort and historical factors are forces (independent of aging processes) that shape shopping habits and are likely to influence the future shopping behavior of those in the older age brackets. They tend to affect the mindsets of these consumers and trigger specific needs. For example, the group of consumers between the ages of 50 and 60 grew up in times when novelty and experimentation were higher on the priority list than during any prior generation. This means that while the older baby boomer might try a product or service, such open-mindedness also makes these consumers highly unpredictable.

Companies have a deep interest in understanding how cohort and historical factors are likely to affect the needs and preferences of their present and future customers. For example, because cars made by Toyota have been in high demand among baby boomers, executives in the California-based U.S. headquarters of the company want to know whether its present customers will continue to prefer its products during their retirement years due to possible changes in needs and preferences for different product features.

The answer given to the company by George Moschis is that while biophysical aging is likely to gradually alter baby boomers' needs and preferences for certain product features of its present models, tomorrow's elderly baby boomers are not likely to have the same preferences as those of their parents; they are likely to maintain some of the preferences they developed in early life, many of which were shaped by cohort and historical factors.

In his 1987 book, *Consumer Socialization: A Life-Cycle Perspective*, (Lexington Books) Moschis presents the results of hundreds of studies that show the effects of early-in-life experiences on continuity and changes in consumer preferences in later life. These studies, as well as several dozen more on the buying habits of people in several different age brackets conducted by the authors during the past 20 years, suggest that while continuity and change is a matter of person-environment interplay, cohort and historical factors make a difference too.

Cohort and historical influences can be seen clearly by comparing studies that report on the lifestyles of today's retirees with those that report on the lifestyles of the previous cohort or generation—those who were retired in the 1970s and early 1980s. For example, in a widely-publicized study conducted in 2006 by AgeWave, Inc., a California-based consulting firm, researchers found that once people retire, they break down into four groups in terms of how they are adjusting to retirement: they range from take-charge people who reinvent themselves (with 19 percent of retirees falling into this group), to carefree retirees content to just slow down (19 percent), to people still trying to figure out what to do (22 percent), to those who are struggling and are likelier to feel unhappy (40 percent).

Next, let's compare the results of this study to those of a similar study conducted in the early 1980s by professors Gail Hornstein and Seymour Wapner. The results of this study, which are reported in a 1985 issue of the *International Journal of Aging and Human Development,* also identify patterns of adjustment to retirement—in much the same way as the AgeWave study. The authors of the earlier study also uncovered four lifestyles of adaptation to retirement, but the four lifestyles of adjustment are quite different from those revealed in the latest study. Specifically, the 1985 study reports that people may experience retirement either as a continuation of the pre-retirement life structure, as a new beginning, as a transition to old age, or as an imposed disruption. While there are similarities in some of the lifestyles of the two generations of retirees reported in the two studies, one sees more differences than similarities in patterns of adaptation to retirement, notwithstanding the presence or absence of certain lifestyles and their prevalence. For example, the first study makes no reference to the largest segment of retirees reported in the latest study (40 percent) who are experiencing difficult times and are unhappy. Interestingly, at about the same time as the early study, another large-scale study by the Center for Social Research and Aging found that an estimated 15 million retirees in the U.S.—about half of all retirees—were "comfortably retired." Assuming that these studies are competently done, what do the significant differences in the lifestyles of those adjusting or adapting to retirement tell us?

Collectively, these findings suggest that tomorrow's retirees in a given cohort or generation are not likely to be a carbon copy of any previous generations; and prognostications about the baby boomers as consumers in the years to come should raise eyebrows. The lifestyles of tomorrow's retirees—specifically those of baby boomers —are not likely to be similar to those of today's retirees. Each generation is different in part due to different circumstances and environments they experienced that have shaped their mindsets and lifestyles during their life course. And future social and commercial environments that cannot be foreseen today are going to have an impact as well. The behavior of people at a given stage in life cannot be understood in isolation from the circumstances they face at that stage and the specific experiences they had earlier in life. The theory that behaviors and thoughts of people at a given stage in life are embedded with life experiences and circumstances in earlier life (and should be studied in that context) is considered by many scholars across disciplines one of the most important scientific developments in the latter part of the twentieth century; it constitutes the foundations of the widely used paradigm—known as the "life course approach"—to the study of human behavior in general and consumer behavior in particular.

The lifestyles of tomorrow's retirees—specifically those of baby boomers —are not likely to be similar to those of today's retirees.

Life-changing events. As people age differently and experience various life circumstances, they often change their outlook on life as they re-evaluate their goals, wants, and roles at both personal and consumption levels. People in their 40s, 50s, and 60s, in particular, experience a host of life-changing events, including the onset of chronic conditions due to biological aging. As a result, many consumers in these groups are likely to change their mindsets and consumption priorities, as in the case of an older woman who becomes a widow and needs help managing her finances (something that her late husband used to do). As they go through these changes, older consumers' needs for products are likely to change, and so do their perceptions of, and responses to, other marketing stimuli. Our national studies conducted at the Center for Mature Consumer

Studies over the previous 20 years consistently show that these life-changing events are better predictors of the person's shopping and consumption patterns than age *per se*.

Life-changing events present marketing opportunities as people buy products and services that ease transition and accommodate change. As consumers are trying to adjust to life changes (e.g., retirement, widowhood), they are likely to re-evaluate their consumption priorities, and needs for specific products and brands may develop or be intensified. Whether changes in consumption activities reflect efforts to cope with stressful changes or stress-free responses to change, marketers who understand the circumstances that make people prone to change might be in a better position to build their customer base and to preserve their existing base. Marketers who wish to attract new customers who have previously been using competing products may want to appeal to those who have experienced or are about to experience major life events, especially stressful events. The idea that life events may provide useful insights for strategy development has been suggested previously by well-known marketing scholars such as Philip Kotler, who indicated the need for a company to consider critical events that can mark life's passage to see whether they are accompanied by certain needs that can be met by product or service bundles. However, the value to marketers is in knowing not only the types of needs for products and services related to specific life-changing events but also the reasons consumer preferences change.

Several studies, which we conducted at the Center for Mature Consumer Studies and published in various academic journals from 1996 to the date of the publication of this book, suggest that stress is one of the mechanisms that link life-changing events to changes in consumption patterns. It is therefore imperative that businesses that market to people who have recently experienced life-changing events understand that they are dealing with consumers under stress. The opportunity lies in alleviating consumers' anxiety, not merely in offering products suitable to their new needs; and the challenge is to do so in a sensitive way. For example, upon the loss of her spouse, a widow might expect her service providers (e.g., doctors, bankers, lawyers) to provide emotional support in addition to basic services. Marketers who understand the emotional consequences of a life-changing event are likely to gain a stronger base of loyal customers.

Values and lifestyles. The values and lifestyles of the older generations of consumers are affecting their present shopping habits, and they are likely to affect their future shopping habits as well. We have already mentioned some lifestyles of retirees most prevalent among the older generation. In this section, we also list values and lifestyles most relevant to the baby boomer generation. The following list of *values* is particularly relevant to the baby boomer generation:

Instant gratification. These consumers seek immediate reward; they are not willing to sacrifice or do without the main pleasures of life.

Self-indulgence. They focus on ""self" and "me." They consider themselves "special" in part because they have been pampered and spoiled.

Ambivalent about the future. Many are in debt, not adequately prepared for retirement financially, running out of time, and realizing that they may never have everything they wanted to have.

Youthfulness. Many of these consumers want to maintain continuity in their lives and to "preserve" their youthful self-concept. They are terrified of growing old, defy aging, and redefine "old age."

Personal fulfillment. Although many are family-oriented, most people in this group tend to define themselves in terms of their work and professional accomplishments.

Nostalgia. Many are nostalgic for the "good old times" and years when they had fewer responsibilities.

The following are some of the *lifestyles* of the baby boomer generation:

Health-conscious and health-driven. This group is the most health conscious age group; they report a larger number of health problems, both physical and emotional, than any prior generation of the same age. The most common lifestyle changes people in this group are likely to make are aimed at improving their health through exercising and dieting.

Pressed for time. The average person in this generation is likely to lead a hectic life, trying to handle multiple responsibilities such as work, family, and caregiving to older relatives. Many still have dependent children due to late marriages.

Coping with stress. This group of people is the most likely to have experienced major stressful events in the recent past, such as death of a parent or the onset of a chronic condition; they are trying to cope with such major stressful life changes and the realities of growing old. Many of their lifestyles, consumption behaviors, and leisure activities are aimed at alleviating stress.

Aging processes, cohort and historical influences that shape lifestyles, and values define consumer needs in the marketplace that serve as "drivers" of their buying and consumption patterns. They affect the types of benefits consumers look for in products, the perception of the importance of product attributes, and their responses to specific marketing stimuli and their shopping habits in general.

Companies that target the mature market need to understand the main drivers of the mature consumers' habits in the marketplace. In addition, those who develop strategies to appeal to the mature segment should be cognizant of changing needs over the course of a person's life. Based on their changing needs, mature consumers are likely to change the criteria they use to evaluate and choose products and vendors, as well as the benefits they are seeking from consuming a product or patronizing a store.

Based on their changing needs, mature consumers are likely to change the criteria they use to evaluate and choose products and vendors.

Understanding generations of consumers in other countries

The globalization of the marketplace has been creating increasing interest among companies that sell to consumers of different nations and cultures. Businesses that contemplate selling products and services to consumers outside their borders must understand not only generational differences but also cultural differences. Knowledge about consumers in a generation in one country might not apply to consumers of the same generation in another country; and marketing strategies that have proved effective in one country might not be as effective in another.

Available cross-cultural research offers little help to international or global consumer marketers. Most commercial and academic research points to the differences in consumption habits between or among countries, but offers few explanations for the observed differences. Furthermore, many cross-cultural differences reflect differences in the ways people in different countries respond to questions or measurement instruments rather than differences in cultural values. Because information on generational differences within countries is all too sparse, we would like to offer some propositions that might be used as preliminary guidelines begging further validation.

The older generation of consumers will show greater differences in their consumption patterns across countries and cultures, compared with younger generations. We feel that the reason for this assumption is the fact that younger people in different parts of the world were born and raised in more homogeneous environments (e.g., mass media, retail, educational opportunities, telecommunications, and technology), and therefore they have had more homogeneous socialization experiences than older adults who were raised in more diverse commercial environments. We also suggest that, in time, consumers will become more homogeneous globally.

Regardless of country or culture, the ratio of differences in the consumption patterns within-generations to between-generations is higher in older than in younger generations. This proposition derives from a fairly well-established fact that people become increasingly heterogeneous with age. The longer they live on this planet, the more likely they are to experience different events and circumstances that shape their behavior and set them apart from other people with different sets of life experiences.

Consumer needs driven by biophysical aging processes are likely to be better predictors of similarities in buying and consumption patterns of people across the globe than needs driven by psychological and social aging. This proposition is based on the premise that biophysical aging is similar in humans—programmed aging takes place in a fairly similar fashion, regardless of one's color, country, or culture. But psychological and social aging are likely to be conditioned by cultural values. For example, older adults command more respect in eastern than in western cultures; or assumed roles in different stages of life might differ, as in the case of adult children who are expected to provide for their aged parents in some cultures.

The greater the sociopolitical stability a country has experienced during the life span of its consumers, the smaller the differences in consumption patterns between generations in that country. Social, political, and economic changes and transitions create different environments to which consumers are exposed at difference stages in their life course. Consumer exposure to diverse environments is likely to create greater diversities in socialization experiences and needs than exposure to stable environments over one's life span. Diversity is likely to result in dissimilarities in lifestyles and behaviors across generations that experience such changes at different stages in their lives, leading to different consumption patterns.

There are greater within-generation differences in consumption patterns of consumers in free, capitalistic countries than in countries that have "closed" political systems. Differences in consumption patterns are not merely a matter of individual differences in needs but also the result of options available to consumers. Consumers in capitalistic countries such as the U.S. and the U.K. are likely to have more options available to them than consumers in countries such as North Korea.

Profitable Business Strategies That Can Enhance Well-Being

Knowledge about consumer needs and research findings are not useful unless they are translated into effective strategy in the key marketing decision areas of market segmentation, positioning, product/service development, promotion, distribution, and pricing. Unfortunately, the effectiveness of a specific strategy is likely to vary according to the specific generation, the sub-segment being targeted, and the specific product or service under consideration. Yet, we think that there is enough information that has been generated in previous studies to suggest the desirability of certain strategies in most situations (products and segments). In this section, we suggest helpful guidelines for developing strategies in main marketing decision areas.

Information about the needs, mindsets, lifestyles, and consumption habits of the two generations can form the basis for strategy, and it is imperative organizations translate such information into effective strategy in the key business decision areas. Specifically, effective business strategy should result in greater customer satisfaction, enhance the well-being of the mature consumers, and generate more profits for those companies capable of serving the needs of these customers. The information that we have presented suggests the desirability of implementing certain strategies. While these strategic recommendations are likely to be effective when trying to reach consumers in both generations, they are likely to be more effective when marketing to the older generation of mature consumers.

Market segmentation

Not all consumers in these large groups or segments have the same needs or want to be treated the same way. Companies serving these consumers must realize the high degree of heterogeneity in these cohorts—that is, one size does not fit all their customers, and that people in these segments differ with respect to their needs for products and services and preferences for methods of delivery. This calls for market segmentation.

While age appears to be the most common and easiest way of segmenting the two generations as a market in most cases, it is probably the least effective. This is because people's behavior does not correlate well with age. Instead, we found that older people's behavior is more sensitive to their needs and lifestyles, which are in turn influenced by life-changing events and circumstances they have experienced. We found that segmentation based on these life events and experiences is more effective than segmentation based on age. Simply put, people who experience similar circumstances in life are likely to exhibit similar patterns of consumer behavior. Their consumer behavior differs from those who experienced different sets of circumstances. This approach, which is based on what we call *gerontographics* in our previously published books and articles, has produced four mature consumer segments whose size (percentage of the U.S. population) has been consistent across studies and over time: the *Healthy Hermits* (38 percent), the *Ailing Outgoers* (34 percent), the *Frail Recluses* (15 percent) and the *Healthy Indulgers* (13 percent)

Healthy Hermits are likely to have experienced life events that have affected their self-concept and self-worth. They react by becoming psychologically withdrawn. Many resent the isolation and the fact that they are expected to behave like old people. *Ailing Outgoers*, on the other hand, maintain positive self-esteem and self-concept, despite life events such as health problems. Unlike the Healthy Hermits, they accept their "old age" status and acknowledge their limitations, but are still interested in getting the most out of life. *Healthy Indulgers* have experienced the fewest life-changing events such as retirement, widowhood, and chronic diseases or conditions. They are the group that differs the least from the younger generation of baby boomers. Finally, the fourth group consists of *Frail Recluses*, who have experienced the largest number of life-changing events that denote physiological, social, and psychological aging.

The four segments respond differently to marketing offerings. They have different needs for products and services and for information sources and content; and they have different preferences in regards to product or service delivery. These differences are substantial enough to justify the development of different marketing strategies to effectively reach each segment and satisfy their consumer needs. We discuss these segments and strategies most suitable to them in greater detail in a book titled, *Gerontographics: Life-Stage Segmentation for Strategy Development* (1996, Quorum), and in several articles published in academic and practitioner journals.

Positioning

Positioning involves the creation of an image for a product or service in the minds of consumers. It refers to what consumers think about your product or facility's characteristics or offerings relative to other similar offerings. Positioning strategy is an important aspect of marketing because it defines the specific actions that must be undertaken in the areas of promotion, product development, pricing, and distribution.

By positioning a product or service as having certain characteristics, it stands a good chance of gaining advantage over competitive offerings when consumers associate it with the specific characteristic(s). Our research suggests that different positioning strategies are effective for different segments of the two generations. Yet, there are certain product and vendor characteristics that these mature consumers generally value regardless of type of offering or segment. Thus, positioning a product, service, or vendor along the following attributes is likely to be effective:

Convenience. With age, people increasingly become very convenience-oriented. Convenience means different things to different people, and could include location (in relation to a person's home, work, or other retail outlets), ease of doing business by phone or mail, and ease of using products and services.

Functionality. Mature consumers are interested in a product's intrinsic benefits, its objective characteristics, rather than subjective benefits such as what the product stands for in the eyes of others. With age, people become more introverted and, therefore, indifferent to the social benefits of the product.

Quality. Mature consumers are very quality-conscious. They are willing to pay a higher price in order to get a better-quality product or service. In our research we found that price becomes an important consideration only when the quality of various product and service offerings is the same.

Dependability. With age, people become risk-averse and prefer hassle-free products and services. One way to ensure that they get such offerings is to buy a familiar or reputable brand or patronize a well-established and well-known retail vendor.

Personalized Service. Personal attention is important to mature consumers who prefer to do business face-to-face. With age, they increasingly value the personal relationship with the service provider, and they want to know that someone within the company cares enough to assist them.

Product development

In developing new products or modifying existing products to better serve the mature market, companies have learned that they should not develop products or attributes of interest exclusively to the older person. Rather, an increasing number of providers develop offerings that have an *intergenerational* or *universal appeal*. This means developing products and attributes that can satisfy the needs of both younger and older consumers, but are most beneficial to the older person, such as developing easy-to-open packages and containers.

When buying products, consumers generally try to either maximize benefits derived from using products (e.g., nutritional value) or minimize problems related to product purchase and its use (e.g., ease of opening containers). The former types of benefits are primary in importance, while the latter are secondary—e.g., consumers will not buy a product they do not need regardless of how easily it can be used. However, for highly undifferentiated products that have a place in the consumer's shopping list, secondary benefits can make a difference which brand they choose. In comparison with younger adults, mature consumers show a stronger preference for products that *minimize problems*, rather than products that maximize benefits. For example, a PC that has the capacity to do wonderful things may not be desirable if after-sales-service or repairing it is rather inconvenient. Ease-of-use is also an important element, especially for older consumers who are more interested in a product's performance than in its social appeal. Another example is Sears and its development of functional (casual) shoes for the mature market. The firm stresses "comfort" as the primary benefit and "style" as secondary. The product was not marketed exclusively for the mature market, but comfort is of greater interest to older adults when buying shoes.

Promotion

We have learned much over the past 20 years about the types of messages that appeal to the mature market. First, with respect to spokespersons, we have learned that older people do not relate to older models. They relate more to those chronologically younger by 10 to 15 years. Therefore, spokespersons should be considerably younger than the average age of the target market. Furthermore, when older people develop an association between the product and the older user, many older people may not buy the advertised product because by purchasing it they would admit to their "old-age" status, and using the product would remind them of their old age.

We also have learned that the aging person wants to maintain or preserve his or her youthful self-concept, so messages that reinforce the perception of being the "same person," the notion that a person of a certain age is like a person of *any* age, can be rather effective. Also, an effective way of reducing the perception that an advertisement targets only the mature segment is to use age-irrelevant or intergenerational appeals. For example, ads for Ensure show a white-haired mother and her daughter using the same product. Finally, nostalgia should be considered as an appeal, since older people enjoy products and services that allow them to re-live their youth.

Some additional recommendations suggested by research:

- TV ads that are informative should focus only on a few, key points.
- TV ads should present information at a slow pace.
- Keep the message short and simple.
- Keep background/environment simple and uncluttered.
- Print media should include newspapers.
- Radio ads should be aired during news programs in early-morning hours.

Distribution

In distributing products to older adults, an organization should attempt to use a variety of distribution methods, since the mature market is diverse and prefers the various distribution methods as much as the general population. Although the older generation does not have as much access to the Internet, it is the fastest growing segment of Internet users; and those who have access to it make heavy use of it. When using a direct marketing channel such as mail order, marketers should emphasize company reputation, adopt policies that reduce risk (such as free pick-up services for merchandise returns), and offer a variety of payment options.

When developing traditional retail distribution outlets, the following are recommended:

- Locate retail establishments near other establishments.
- Provide adequate parking and well-lighted parking lots.
- Provide rest areas, such as small café-style areas, or benches.
- Restrooms should be easy to locate.
- Use adequate lighting.
- Mark stairs with contrasting colors for easy height-change identification.
- Use services such as valet parking, gift-wrapping, and package carry-out.

- Consider innovative ways of using coupons (e.g., coupon dispensers, scanners, magnetic cards).
- Offer programs that reward long-term patrons, since older consumers are loyal customers.

Pricing

Pricing decisions should also take into account the needs and preferences of older consumers. Research suggests four general recommendations for pricing strategy:

- Offer price reductions when products and services are similar or standardized across sellers. Generally, older consumers are not price sensitive and less likely to sacrifice quality for lower prices, but lower prices could entice them when no significant differences in product quality or service are perceived.
- Use premium pricing for drastically different products. Older consumers may pay a higher price for products suitable to their needs.
- Price product/service offerings "a la carte." Although older consumers are willing to pay higher prices for certain products, they are not willing to pay for product benefits and services they do not use or need. They are less likely to pay for "bundles" of benefits, when many of the benefits do not interest them. Therefore, when pricing products and services where a buyer has options, such as automobiles and cable services, marketers should make those options available for a cost rather than marketing all of them as a "package" of offerings.
- Do not over-emphasize senior discounts. Generally, senior discounts do not affect switching behavior. Seniors who use these tools buy more of the same brand or shop on different days of the week. Do not ask people to engage in activities that remind them of their old age, label them as "old," or contribute to the definition of one's self as an old person, because the reality is that nobody wants to be old.

Strategy-Effectiveness Testing, Implementation, and Feedback

It is prudent to test-market a strategy prior to its implementation on a large-scale basis. This can be done in a limited number of environments such as retail outlets and geographic regions. When the strategy involves the targeting of multiple segments of the mature market, it is necessary to develop different marketing programs for different segments. In this case, a strategy developed for a specific segment should not only be tested for its effects on that specific segment but also for any effects on other segments of the population. Its effectiveness should be evaluated based on its overall impact, not just its impact on the specific segment for which the strategy was developed. When a Publix supermarket in Lake County, Florida, decided to appeal to the elderly by making its store more "senior-friendly" (such as making motorized carts available), it drove away the younger patrons. The retail strategy had a positive effect on elderly customers, but the younger people did not like to patronize a "geriatric supermarket," in the words of one younger baby boomer patron.

Feedback on the effectiveness of a marketing strategy may be sought in a number of different ways depending on the product, service, or other offerings marketed. It may be assessed by means of changes in sales volume, store traffic, and attitudes, such as levels of customer satisfaction (assessed via "before-and-after" surveys). Feedback mechanisms should be made available to the mature market on a continuous basis, such as having a suggestion box or a toll-free number for complaint handling, because of the constant need to monitor changes in the marketplace and the business environment such as competitors' actions and reactions. It is through continuous feedback that an organization can accurately assess its performance relative to competition and how well its business activities satisfy the needs of its customers and enhance the quality of their lives.

Index

Because this entire book is about baby boomers and their parents we have not indexed those two terms. In most cases, each index item includes comparative data on the boomers and their parents.

2005 National Health Interview Survey, 50

A

AARP, 3, 29, 82, 85, 90, 91, 94, 116, 134
ABC Morning News, 28
Academy of Lifelong Learning, 91
acting one's age or not, 31
acute stress, 72–73
adult education classes, interest in, 88–92
advertising, 19, 156–157, 191, 221–222
affluent adults, 14–15, 117–128
age bias, 43
age composition
 changes in, 2–4
age discrimination, 43
AgeWave, Inc., 210
aging, 6
 adaptation to, 25, 30
 and appearance, 25–26, 30
 and self-esteem, 26–27
 population, 2
 preparing for, 104–107
 redefinition, 2, 30, 195–196
 retirement, 1, 4
 state of mind, 1, 23–31
 terrified of, 37–38
Ailing Outgoers (segment), 218–219
alcohol consumption, 67
alternative housing arrangements, 106–107
American Demographics magazine, 85, 99
American Dietetic Association (ADA), 49
American Express credit card, 109, 120, 123, 127, 140
American Society for Aesthetic Plastic Surgery, 28
American Society of Plastic Surgeons, 28
apparel, 137, 161, 165, 178
Archives for Internal Medicine, 68
arthritis, 10, 28, 32, 34, 55–57, 59, 62, 64, 72, 79
asset-management services, 88
at-home buying, 163–164
attendance at events, 97
automobiles, 20, 134
awareness of needs of older adults, 105

B

back problems, 10, 55–56
birth rates, 2–3
bladder problems, 36
bodily changes, 25
body image, 28
Botox, 28
British Medical Journal, 67–68
Brokow, Tom, 2
Business Week, 85, 93
businesses that rip-off customers, 183
buying habits, 18–19, 145–185

C

career change, 43–44, 81
career focus, 7, 8, 16, 44
caregiving, 3, 4–5, 7, 16–17, 51–52, 101–104, 110
Centers for Disease Control, (CDC), 67–69, 190
Center for Mature Consumer Studies, 24, 37, 84–85, 97, 212

Center for Social Research and Aging, 210
Chamber, Susan, 99
charitable giving, 15, 50–51, 127
check-out lines, 146
China, 2
chronic conditions, 29, 55, 59–60
chronic stress, 70–74
chronological age
   effect on advertising response, 221
   effect on appearance, 24–25
   vs. "feeling" age, 23–24
Cinemax, 95
cohort effects, 7, 28, 207–208, 210–211
companion animals (pets), 137
complaints, 182–184
concerns, 21–22, 25–26, 32–33 (table), 46, 84–86
Consumer Socialization: A Life-Cycle Perspective (book), 209
consumption patterns, 129–144, 211–212
convenience in shopping, 146, 219
Cornell University, 85
cosmetic surgery, 12, 27–28
credit card use, 13, 18–19, 108–111, 120, 127, 140, 177–181, 185
customer loyalty, 175–177

D
daily chores, 38
debit cards, 181–181
debt, 13, 18, 20, 87, 108–109, 110, 185, 203, 205
Del Webb, 28
demographic change, ix
department store cards, 109, 120, 127, 123, 140
dependence on others, 38
depression, 8, 74–78, 190–191
diabetes, 35, 57
diet, 29, 192, 198–199
direct mail, 163–164, 223
disease development, patterns of, 63–64
door-to-door purchases, 163–164
DVD use, 95–96

E
eating habits, 30–31

eating out, 98
Elder Hostel, 94
electronics, ownership, 136–137
emotional health, 7–10, 70–78, 200–201
Employee Benefit Research Institute, 86
Ensure, 221
entertainment, 47–48, 94–97
Equal Employment Opportunity Commission, 43
Euro RSCG, 44
excessive consumption, 184–185
ExecuNet, 43
exercise equipment, 144
exercise, 29, 64–65, 192, 198–199

F
factors considered when shopping from home, 165, 223
fears, 36–39, 85–87
Fidelity Investments, 85
financial goals, 120–121, 128
financial illiteracy, 86
financial issues, 12–15, 21, 108–128
financial need after retirement, 84–86
Financial security, 113, 120, 193–195
financial services, 139–141
   use of by affluent, 121
fix meals at home, 40
flu shots, 50
forgetfulness, 40
Frail Recluses (segment), 218–219
free samples, 154
Freedman, Marc, 100
functional age, 195–197

G
Gallup poll, 65
gambling, 17, 98
gardening, 17, 98
Gerontographics: Life-Stage Segmentation for Strategy Development, 219
gift buying, 137
Good Deeds in Old Age (book), 99
Grand Travels, 94
Great Depression, 87, 109
growth hormones, 28–29
guarantees, 156

H

happiness, 22, 133, 168
HBO, 95
health care, 143–144
health club membership, 144
Health insurance, 86–87, 142
health, 7–12, 34–36, 53–80, 189–191
  and heredity, 61–62
  and lifestyles, 64–69
  assessment of own, 53–54
  chronic problems, 9–10, 34, 54–58, 60, 62
  effect of optimism on, 10
  linked to education and income, 10, 34–35
  table of chronic conditions, 55
Healthy Hermits (segment), 218
Healthy Indulgers (segment), 218–219
healthy, staying, 48–50, 64–66, 189–191
hearing loss, 35, 57
heart conditions, 34–35, 56
high blood pressure, 34, 56, 60, 64
home equity, 114–115, 133
home improvements, 115, 134
home ownership, 19–20, 21, 81, 132–134
Hornstein, Gail, 210

I

immobility, 38
independence, 19–20, 83, 85, 92, 132–133, 204
influence of relatives on purchases, 172–175
information
  difficulty finding, 39
  for product purchases, 158–159
  internet as source of, 169–170
  lack of, 39, 157
  sources of, 157–160
intergenerational appeal, 220–221
International Health, Racquet, & Sportsclub Assn., 69
International Journal of Aging and Human Development, 210
International Spa Association (ISPA), 50
internet, 95, 167–172
investment risk tolerance, 112–113
investments, 130–131
IRA, 116–117, 141

J-K

job mobility, 44
Johnson & Johnson, 101–102
Journal of Active Aging, 44, 91
judgment of products, 155–156
Kenya, 2
Keogh plans, 116–117, 141
Kessler, Emily, 87
kidney problems, 36, 58
Korn/Ferry International, 43

L

learning new things, 16, 47, 88–92
leisure time, 46–48, 92–99
life expectancy, 3, 30, 195
life insurance, owning, 106, 111, 142
Life Option Center, 100
life satisfaction, 187–189
life span, 195
life-changing events, 211–212
lifelong learning, 16, 88–92
lifestyles, 15–18, 64–70, 81–107
  healthy, 64–67, 191–193, 195–205
  unhealthy, 67–69
living arrangements, 81, 83–84, 132–133
locational convenience, 145–146, 219
longevity, 197–199
  guidelines for, 186–205
Long-term care (LTC) insurance, 115–116, 141, 142–143
loss of loved one, 45, 78

M

magazine reading, 96
Malaysia, 2
market segmentation, 217–219
marketing implications, 206–224
marketplace
  unhappiness with, 18–19
MasterCard, 109, 120, 123, 140
materialistic attitudes, 138–139, 188
mature consumers in other countries, 214–216
mature customers, understanding, 206–213
McKinsey & Company, 42–43
MediaMark Research, 99
medical check-ups, 66–67
medical services at home, 144

Medicare, 29, 85–86
medications, 60–62
mental age, 12
Mergenhagen, Paula, 208
Mernam, Dr. George, 28
methods of payment, 177–181
    airline tickets, 179
    apparel, 178
    grocery/food products, 178
    health care services, 179–180
    home appliance repair, 180
    lodging, 178–179
    restaurant meals, 179
    security systems, 180
Metlife, 3
middle age, 28–30
Millionaires, 14–15, 122–128
    demographics of, 123
    financial goals, 124
    investment preferences, 123–125
    spending habits, 122
    use of financial services, 126
Mitchell, Olivia, 85
money (see also financial issues)
    fear of losing money, 37
    financial independence, 36–37
    problems paying bills, 13, 37, 109
    standard of living, 13, 36, 110
Moore, James, 85

N
National Alliance of Caregivers, 102
National Association for Variable Annuities, 86–87
National Center for Health Statistics, 50, 61
National Council on Aging, 85
National Institute on Aging, 85
necessities
    attitude of boomers toward, 87
net worth, 130–131
newspaper reading, 96
number of health ailments, 59–60
nutrition, 3, 11, 31, 49, 65–66, 145

O-P
old money, 126
obesity, 56, 68–69

Opinion Research Corporation, 101
optimism, 10, 191, 200–201
other's perceptions, 45
outlook on life, 78–80, 190–191
packaging
    difficulties with, 19, 154–155, 207
passports, 93
pastimes, 17
period effects, 7
personal audit, 203–204
personal safety, 21, 46
pessimism, 10, 78–79, 201–202
physical fitness, 38, 192, 200
preventive health care, 199–200
pricing, 223–224
Prime Time: How Baby Boomers Will Revolutionize Retirement and Transform America (book), 100
product development, 220–221
product positioning, 219–220
public library, use of, 89–90
Publix Supermarket, 224

Q-R
quality of life, improving, 202–204
radio listening, 97
RAND Corporation, 68
reading, 17, 96
real estate assets, 131
reasons for buying direct, 164–166
reasons for choosing specific brands
    alcoholic beverages, 160
    apparel and footwear, 161
    drugs and health aids, 160
    food, 160
reasons for moving, 83–84, 134–135
reasons for patronage
    airlines/cruise lines, 149
    department stores, 148
    drug stores and pharmacies, 147
    financial institutions, 150
    food/grocery stores, 147–148
    for visiting spas, 50
    hospitals, 152–153
    insurance companies, 150–152
    lodging, 148–149
    restaurants, 146

relationships, 9, 45–46, 185, 208
religiosity, 100–101
religious services, attendance at, 99
repairmen, reliability, 40
respiratory disorders, 58
retirement communities
  plan to live in, 82–83
retirement housing, 28
retirement, 43–44, 208
  adjustment to, 210
  financing, 115–117
risk-averse, 154
Royal Viking Cruise Line, 94
Russell, Cheryl, ix–x

S
sandwich generation, 17, 93
self-diagnosis medical equipment, 144
self-esteem, 8, 49, 202, 218
self-indulgence, 47
self-made money, 15, 117, 126–128
shopping and running errands, 40
shopping from home, preferred methods
  clothes and footwear, 163
  drugs and cosmetics, 163
  financial services, 164
  insurance policies, 164
  vacation packages, 163
shopping, 98–99
  and aging, 207–208
  importance of "deals", 18, 156
  importance of convenience, 18, 145– 146, 223
  online, 170–172
  spending habits, 18, 20–21, 108–109
short-term thinking, 87–88
smoking, 67
social isolation, 9, 45, 185, 208
Social Security benefits, 85–86
Society of Actuaries, 87
spending vs. saving, 111–114
Stanley, Thomas, 87
stress, 7–9, 70–74, 103, 189–190, 201
Survey of Lifelong Learning, 91
Sweden, 2

T
Targeting Transitions (book), 208
television viewing, 17, 94–95
television, effect of, 7
testing, 224
The Greatest Generation (book), 2
The Millionaire Next Door, 87
time pressure, 7–8, 39
Toyota, 209
Travel Industry Association of America, 171
travel, 15, 92–94, 142

U-V-W
U.S. Administration on Aging, 69
United Kingdom, 2
University of Delaware, 91
University of Michigan, 86–87
University of Washington, Seattle, 28
VCR use, 96
venturesome shoppers, 154
Visa card, 109, 120, 123, 140
vision problems, 25, 37, 155, 207
volunteering, 17, 50–51, 99–100, 193
Wapner, Seymour, 210
warranties, 156
wealth preservation, 120
weight gain, 48, 78
weight loss, 31
Weil, James, 3
well-being
  linked to assets, 129–130
Wharton School, 85, 87
will, owning, 106
work after retirement, 15–16, 41–45, 84–85
work-related ailments, 44–45

About the Authors

George P. Moschis, Ph.D.

George Moschis, Ph.D., is Professor of Marketing, Alfred Bernhardt Research Professor, and the founding director of the Center for Mature Consumer Studies at Georgia State University, where he is also a member of the Gerontology Program Faculty.

Through his Center, which is globally known and has been recognized over the years by *American Demographics* as one of the best sources of marketing information in the United States, Dr. Moschis has conducted dozens of studies and has disseminated his research findings to thousands of organizations interested in serving the aging population. Dr. Moschis is a frequent contributor to various consumer and trade publications in this country and abroad, and has been recognized by educators and practitioners on several occasions for his contributions to marketing knowledge and practice.

Anil Mathur, Ph.D.

Anil Mathur, Ph.D., is Vice Dean and Professor of Marketing and International Business at the Frank G. Zarb School of Business, Hofstra University, New York. Dr. Mathur is the author of numerous research monographs, industry reports and proprietary consulting reports, and is co-author of the book *The Maturing Market Place* (Quorum).

Dr. Mathur's research interests are in the areas of cross cultural consumer behavior, services marketing, marketing research, and research methodology. Dr. Mathur is also actively involved in community and professional service activities.